IN FLIGHT WITH THE EAGLE

A Guide to Napoleon's Elite

'When in flight with the eagle look out for squalls'
Old French proverb.

Raymond Horricks

Costello

British Library Cataloguing in Publication Data

Horricks, Raymond, *1933-*
    In flight with the eagle : a guide to Napoleon's elite.
    1. France. Political events, 1804-1815.
    Biographies. Collections
    I. Title
    944.05'092'2

ISBN 0-7104-3040-X

First published in Great Britain 1988

All Rights Reserved. Enquiries to:
D.J.Costello (Publishers) Ltd
43 High Street
Tunbridge Wells TN1 1XL

Typeset in 10 on 12pt Times Roman
Typesetting processed by Composing Operations Ltd, Tunbridge Wells

Jacket design by Greenway Graphics, Tunbridge Wells

Contents

Acknowledgements

I've been haunting the corridors and galleries of Les Invalides in Paris for years. It is far and away the most useful clearing bank for all matters military; and on every occasion the staff have proved considerate and helpful. I particularly have to thank M. Jean Humbert, the *Conservateur* of the library who kindly answered all my final queries about certain generals' titles and dates.

The information on Honoré Grimaldi was supplied by the Monaco archivist in London. Meanwhile, my late father, a chemist himself, made sure I had the right facts about Berthollet. And I have to thank Doctor Z Jagodzinski, librarian of the Polish Library in London, for information on the officers of that nation who served with Napoleon's army; also Andreé L'Heritier of the Bibliotequè National in Paris.

There was also a great pile of researched material left over from the 'Marshal Ney' book, most of it done 'on the spot' in France and Germany – with the assistance of town clerks, local mayors and at other times the local police.

I have managed to visit a number of the 'key' battlefields and this has been illuminating as well as fascinating. Standing on the ridge at Valmy for instance, unchanged since the famous action of 1792, one can imagine something of what it must have been like for the young Revolutionary army to face (and, to their enemy's surprise, withstand) the Duke of Brunswick's furious cannonade.

Finally, I would like to thank my publisher's editors Anne Cree and Randy Brown, for their patience with me.

Mount Felix, France and Italy, 1980 – 87.

Preface

Following years spent satisfying a personal curiosity concerning the tragedy of Michel Ney, 'Le Brave des Braves', examining his life in its special setting of the Bonaparte era and finally writing a book entitled: *Marshal Ney, The Romance and the Real[1]*, at the end I found myself with an accumulation of notes and details about other members of Napoleon's circle which would have filled a good-sized historical dictionary. Hating to let go of the subject, I have, in the years since then, worked intermittently at 'shaking down' these notes into more manageable proportions. I began as if using a kaleidoscope; but as time has gone on I proceeded to a serious conclusion: *Napoleon's entourage was almost as fascinating as the Emperor himself.*

Naturally this was to vary, and a number of people failed to last the course; nevertheless it involved a portrait gallery of characters I believe unsurpassed in French history. In the main they existed entirely because of the Emperor, and only a select few played parts of any significance in the public life of France after his fall. However this in no way lessens their intrinsic merits, nor their achievements in the span of one generation when their master and benefactor made himself the most famous ruler in the nation's (and perhaps in Europe's) continuing history.

Since the shaking-down process I have condensed even further, picking out different 'key' strands in Napoleonic society and so arriving at, what I trust is, a tightly-woven tapestry of a book involving those who surrounded and were important to this most intriguing of leaders.

The magic inner-circle, one discovers, was not very large. Almost always Napoleon relied upon his own vision and energies, the willing support of the French people (both rich and poor), a good middle-management type of executive at *préfet* level, plus a select band of the most remarkable go-betweens. For much of his period at the top he succeeded in keeping *all* the essential reins of government in his own hands, and while his health and luck lasted it worked very well. The only exception to this was within the army, where, when France became involved in several theatres of operation at the same time, he was forced to delegate responsibility for tactics, if not for strategy. By and large though his senior appointments to this branch of the armed forces were good; and until near the end the general staff did much to illuminate his *régime*. (His attitude towards the navy was altogether more ambiguous, as I will refer to later.)

Napoleon wasn't always so inspired in his choice of friends, and his blood-relations posed even more of a problem. Yet they too had their gifts, and certainly no-one could ever accuse them of being dull!

Overall the immediate entourage enjoyed being at the centre of things, either loving or disliking the Emperor while remaining consistently in awe of

[1]*Marshal Ney, The Romance and the Real, Archway Publications 1988.*

him. Subsequently they have provided us with a rich store of *mémoires* and anecdotes. 'That little fellow came very near to frightening me', Masséna once commented, and carried on serving him. It was the same with the majority of the Empire's highest servants.

I realise in making up my selection there are several quite deliberate omissions of people who were rather noisome at the time but who I don't believe contributed all that much to the Eagle's living legend. Others I will have omitted through ignorance. Nevertheless I will defend the relevance of those who are included. They were often prickly, arrogant and some of them were greedy; but they were also a talented group, and under the Emperor's guidance it showed.

A Note on the Revolutionary Calender

The more fanatical members of France's Convention were determined upon more than just cutting off aristocratic and clerical heads. Their aim was the elimination of anything associated with the previous *Ancien Régime*. They dated their new calender from September 22, 1792 (the year I) and renamed the months: Vendémaire, Brumaire, Frimaire, Nîvose, Pluvôise, Ventôse, Germinal, Floréal, Prairial, Messidor, Thermidor and Fructidor. Each month consisted of 30 days, which left five days over known as *sans-culottides*, scattered throughout the year and devoted to festivals. Every fourth year was called an Olympic Year instead of what we call Leap Year. (Even the revolutionaries couldn't abolish Solar time!) The system was devised by Gilbert Romme (1750 – 1795) and the months named by the poet Fabré d'Eglantine.

Best-known months historically are Brumaire ('the month of mist', October 23 to November 21) on account of Napoleon's *coup*; and Thermidor ('the month of heat', sometimes called Fervidor, July 20 to August 18), the month which included the downfall of Robespierre. Napoleon abolished the Revoulutionary Calender in 1805, returning to the Papacy's Gregorian one.

The Convention also renamed the different areas of France after their rivers (Seine, Loire, Gard, Vienne, Hérault, Var, etc.) and this change has remained through to the present for postal purposes. However, throughout France, but especially in the country districts, one still hears the older names used: Berry, Burgundy, Languedoc, Provençe, and so on.

10

A Chronicle of Events

1769

June – Carlo Buonaparte, father of Napoleon swears fealty to Louis XV and as a result becomes a French subject.

August 15 – Birth of Napoleon at Ajaccio, Corsica.

1770

April – Edict of Louis XV 'whereby all Corsicans who can prove their possession of nobility for two hundred years are admitted into the French nobility with the enjoyment of all its privileges'. Carlo Buonaparte makes his application.

1771

July 21 – Baptism of Napoleon.

September 13 – Declaration issued in Paris establishing the Buonaparte family's nobility.

1774 – 5

Napoleon is sent by his mother, Maria Letizia to a girls' school.

1776

March 28 – Louis XVI offers state-paid education to the children of poor but noble parents. Carlo Buonaparte applies on behalf of his sons Joseph and Napoleon.

1778

December 12 – Carlo Buonaparte leaves Corsica with his two sons *en route* for Autun.

1779

January 1 – Napoleon enters the school at Autun.

April 25 – Napoleon enrols at the Royal Military College, Brienne.

1783

Now aged thirteen he abandons the idea of becoming a naval officer and opts for the artillery.

1784

September 15 – The main examinations at Brienne. Napoleon is one of only five pupils selected to go forward to the Ecole Militaire in Paris.

1785

February 24 – Carlo Buonaparte, aged thirty-nine, dies of stomach cancer in the hospital at Montpellier.

September 16 – Napoleon obtains his commission as Second Lieutenant of Artillery. He is the first Corsican to do this.

November – He joins the regiment of La Fère and is assigned to garrison duties at Valence.

1786

He meets Caroline Colombier, his first love. Otherwise he is bored by garrison duties and devotes himself to writing and the study of warfare.

1787

The Assembly of Notables meets in Paris.

1789

April 2 – Napoleon, back from a long leave in Corsica, proceeds to Seurre to put down a rising there. He calls out to the crowd: 'Let honest men return to their homes. I fire only upon the mob.'

May 5 – Louis XVI officially opens the States General at Versailles (308 men of religion, 285 French nobles and 621 deputies: The Three Estates)

June 17 – The States declare themselves a National Assembly. Three days later, meeting in the tennis court, they announce a new constitution.

July 14 – The Fall of the Bastille. Another three days and Louis XVI is made to wear the revolutionary cockade.

July 19 – In another riot at Auxonne in the Burgundy, after the mob has sacked the local tax-office Napoleon's regiment sides with the rioters. The officers restore discipline, but a month later they too have sworn an oath of allegiance to the revolutionary government in France.

September – Napoleon leaves Auxonne for Corsica, where he remains for fifteen months. By October he is heading the revolutionary party in Ajaccio.

November 30 – Antoine Christophe Saliceti, the Corsican deputy and revolutionary, urges in the National Assembly that Corsica be formally incorporated into France. As a result it is proclaimed French territory. Meanwhile Mirabeau (Honoré Gabriel Riquetti) proposes that all

Corsican patriots in exile be allowed to return.

1790

April 16 – Napoleon writes to his colonel requesting an extension of his leave because he is in poor health.

July 14 – On the first anniversary of the fall of the Bastille France is declared a constitutional monarchy.

July 17 – On the return of the patriot Pasquale Paoli to Corsica, Napoleon and Joseph Buonaparte are attacked in the street and narrowly escape death. Their assailants are monks who cry 'Death to the Jacobins'[1]

1791

January – Napoleon leaves Ajaccio to rejoin his regiment, accompanied by his brother, Louis, aged twelve. He reaches Auxonne on February 12.

April 2 – The death of Mirabeau.

June 16 – Napoleon is transferred to the 4th Regiment, again stationed at Valence.

June 21 – The flight of the King, followed by his arrest at Varennes.

August – Napoleon applies for further leave, but his colonel refuses. The young officer, frustrated, decides to ask the help of his former colonel, Du Teil de Beaumont (Baron Jean Pierre) and walks the whole way to his family château at Pommier in Isère. He stays there for several days, after which his host remarks: 'That is a man of exceptional ability; his name will most certainly be heard of'. Napoleon's leave is granted.

September 22 – He arrives back in Corsica. However, Paoli now master of the island is decidedly cold towards him.

1792

January 1 – There is a review of the regiment of La Fère at Valence. Napoleon is declared 'absent without leave', still presumably in Corsica. However a fortnight later he is appointed adjutant of the Corsican Volunteers by the Minister of War in Paris. What follows is something of a chaos...

January 14 – Despite his new position, against his name on a list of lieutenants there is the following note: 'Has given up his profession and been replaced'.

April 1 – Napoleon is now Lieutenant-Colonel of the Corsican Volunteers and loses his French commission by overstaying his leave. That same Easter he fails in an attempt to seize Ajaccio. But on April 12 the Revolutionary Commissioners arrive and demand that both citizens

1 The most violent revolutionaries within the Convention.

and volunteers lay down their arms. Napoleon visits Paoli at Montecello and has what proves to be an unhappy interview. Nevertheless Paoli tells him: 'You are on the ancient model. You are one of Plutarch's men'.

May 13 – Napoleon, now a confirmed French patriot, decides to return to Paris and arrives there as a private citizen on May 28.

June 20 – He observes the mob's attack on the Tuileries.

July 10 – He is reinstated in his regiment, promoted captain and granted full arrears of pay. Also by this time the First Coalition of European nations against France has been formed, beginning the wars which will last – on and off – until 1815.

August 10 – He witnesses the second attack on the Tuileries and the massacre of Louis XVI's Swiss guard, who die to a man.

August 19 – The Revolutionary Tribunal is set up.

September 1 – Napoleon removes his sister Eliza from her school at St.-Cyr. As a result they are in Paris during the September massacres. Between the 2nd and 5th of the month over 1200 people are killed, including 100 priests.

September 9 – Napoleon and Eliza quit Paris. On September 17 a National Convention is opened and on the 22nd it officially proclaims France a Republic.

October 10 – Napoleon and his sister embark at Toulon for Corsica. Arriving on the 15th at Ajaccio the young captain is immediately appointed Commander of the National Guard.

October 27 – At this vital moment in his career, Napoleon is sorely tempted to take service with the British in India; however, a French plan to invade Sardinia diverts his thinking. The expedition proves abortive.

December – The French fleet drops anchor at Ajaccio. There are ensuing riots because the French sailors are by no means welcome in Corsica. The Commander of the National Guard proves an able mediator.

1793

January 21 – The execution of Louis XVI. That same day the Committee of Public Safety is established.

February 1 – France declares war on Great Britain and Holland.

February 22 – Napoleon takes part in the unsuccessful attack on Madalena. As the perpetrator of some quite revolutionary ideas on warfare he is highly critical of French methods. By March 3 he is back in Ajaccio. Meanwhile, 'Banners for the King', a major royalist insurrection, breaks out in La Vendée.

April 17 – The National Convention orders the arrest of Paoli. Napoleon writes an eloquent defence of Paoli in the style which will one day illuminate his claims to being France's most brilliant administrator.

April–May – Having failed to bring about a *rapprochement* between Paris and the Corsican patriots, he lays siege to the citadel of Ajaccio.

May 3 – Due to lack of support, and as his National Guard melts away, he decides to leave Ajaccio for Bastia, where his brother Joseph has joined the Revolutionary Commissioners. On the way he is captured by Paolists, but escapes into the hills and after a very roundabout route reaches Bastia.

May 11 – Introduced by Joseph to the Commissioners, he submits plans for the capture of Ajaccio; also one to get his mother and younger brothers and sisters away to safety. These plans are adopted.

May 23 – Napoleon's mother and the younger children are rescued from Ajaccio. However, in revenge the Paolists invade and devastate the Casa Buonaparte.

May 31 – Under the direction of the Committee of Public Safety 'The Terror' begins in France as an instrument of official policy.

June 11 – Napoleon embarks with his family for France. Arriving at Toulon, he travels on alone to rejoin his regiment at Nice where he receives his commission as *capitaine commandant*.

July 29 – Publication of his controversial pamphlet, *Le Souper de Beaucaire*, which is very strongly in favour of the Jacobins continuing in government. He assists in an attack upon the anti-revolutionaries in Avignon.

August 28 – The British and Spanish fleets are welcomed at Toulon by a royalist junta, who have taken control of the port. Napoleon hurries to join General Carteaux in besieging it.

September 7 – Once more, briefly, in Paris, he is appointed *chef de bataillon* in the second regiment of artillery.

October 9 – The fall of Lyon to the republicans, which allows a much larger investing force to proceed towards Toulon.

October 11 – The execution of Queen Marie-Antoinette.

December 19 – The fall of Toulon: hastened by Napoleon's brilliant opportunism. (This was also the occasion when he received as *aide-de-camp* and formed a friendship with Junot.) However the behaviour of the French in taking reprisals against the inhabitants of Toulon disgusted him and strongly influenced his attitude towards the defeated in all his future wars.

1794

February 6 – Napoleon assigned to the Army of Italy. He is 24 years of age.

February 21 – For his remarkable performance at Toulon Napoleon is created *géneral de brigade*. On the same day Great Britain succeeds in persuading Russia to join the alliance against France.

April 1 – Hostilities begin against Austria, the dominant power in Italy and Sardinia.

April 2 – The National Convention approves Napoleon's plan of campaign but already he has begun to put it into operation and on April 5 the French advance is under way, Masséna leading the van.

April 27 – The Sardinians serving as mainland troops are driven back by the French.

June 27 – 'Insult of insults', the Corsican patriots accept George III of England as their King. Three days later the Augustin, Robespierre, sets off for Paris carrying Napoleon's plans of campaign for both the Army of Italy and the Army of the Alps.

July – Napoleon is sent on a secret mission to meet with wealthy and anti-Austrian Councillors in Genoa, but by July 19 the Committee of Public Safety has approved his plans and the invasion of Piedmont is decided on.

July 21 – Leaving Genoa firmly on France's side, the young general returns to his troops. Two days after this occurs the 'new' Revolution of Thermidor and the fall of Maximillien Robespierre.

July 27 – Napoleon rejoins his old regiment in Nice. As an active servant of the Committee of Public Safety he is automatically under suspicion.

July 28 – The execution of Robespierre.

August 9 – Napoleon is suspended from duty and placed under arrest. Already Carnot, the Minister for War, is sending out orders to France's armies to cease all offensive operations.

August 14 – Napoleon pens and sends off his defence to the Representatives.

August 19 – He declines the offer of rescue by his fellow-officers, and writes to Junot: 'My conscience is easy, therefore please do nothing. Your actions would only compromise me'.

August 20 – There is an obvious lack of evidence: Napoleon is released and reinstated. Also, Carnot's directives are overruled. The campaign against the Allies is continued.

August 23 – Carnot orders a general retreat upon France with the idea of invading Corsica. Napoleon agrees with him: 'Our next move must be to deliver the island of Corsica from the tyranny of the English'.

1795

September–February – Napoleon, in Toulon, helps to prepare for the expedition.

March 4 – The expedition sets sail, but is dispersed in by the hovering English fleet. Both the *Ça Ira* and *Censeur* are captured. Napoleon, although he escapes, is now without a job.

March–April – He receives orders to take command of the artillery in *La Vendée*. However the war of attrition against the royalist guerillas holds little appeal for him. He requests permission to rejoin the Army of Italy.

April 5 – In Paris, a Jacobin-inspired mob attempts to overthrow the National Convention. The National Guard commanded by General

Pichegru and under the orders of the wily politician Paul Barras puts down the resulting riots.

May 2 – Napoleon sets off for Paris accompanied by his brother Louis, Junot and another acquaintance from the Siege of Toulon, Captain Marmont.

May 7 – Fouquier-Tinville, former Public Prosecutor and fifteen others associated with The Terror and the Committee of Public Safety are guillotined.

May 10 – Napoleon arrives in Paris. Takes lodgings at the Hôtel Liberté.

June 12 – He is ordered to join the Army of the West. He excuses himself on the grounds of ill-health. Does temporary work for the War Office. Meets Josephine.

September 15 – There is a proposal that Napoleon should set off at once for Constantinople and help train the army of the Grand Turk. Appalled, he appeals to Barras, who appoints him second-in-command of the Army of the Interior.

October 3 – 2nd Vendémiaire. 'Paris is ablaze since morning', Napoleon writes, 'I must be careful and cautious, having little or no influence here'.

October 4 – He is summoned to an emergency meeting with Carnot, Barras and other revolutionary leaders, and as a result entrusted with the defence of Paris.

October 5 – The National Guard, urged on and supported by a pro-royalist mob, rebel against the Convention. Napoleon disperses them with the celebrated 'whiff of grape-shot' in the Rue St.-Honoré. From this moment he is widely regarded as 'a coming man'.

October 11 – He is restored to the army as a general of division.

October 25 – He takes over command of the Army of the Interior.

November 1 – The French Directory is chosen, with Barras as its grand manipulator. Napoleon will spend the winter in Paris, devoting much of his time to the developing love-affair with Josephine.

1796

February 9 – The banns of marriage are proclaimed between Napoleon and Josephine.

February 23 – Napoleon is appointed by Barras to command the Army of Italy.

March 9 – He is married to Josephine. He signs the register as 'Bonaparte', dropping the original Italianate spelling of his surname.

March 12 – Despite Josephine's tears he leaves to take up his new command in Italy. Upon arrival at the border on March 27 he finds the troops in a deplorable condition.

April 4 – After several Herculean days devoted to reorganisation he lifts morale by the most stirring proclamation and on April 10 the campaign

17

against the occupying Austrian army in Italy begins.

April 12 – Napoleon defeats the Austrians at Montenotte, ably supported by Masséna.

April 14 – Napoleon defeats the Austrians at Millesimo, this time ably supported by Augereau.

April 15 – Napoleon defeats the Austrians at Dego.

April 22 – Napoleon defeats the Sardinian troops of Piedmont at both Ceva and Mondovi.

April 24 – He writes an angry letter to the Directory complaining about lack of supplies and arrears of pay, uniforms, etc. for his troops.

April 28 – The King of Piedmont and Sardinia signs the Convention of Cherasco: in effect giving up all his mainland fortresses to the French.

May 7 – Napoleon attacks Beaulieu, an *emigré* general, and then crosses the River Po at Piacenza.

May 10 – He forces the passage of the bridge at Lodi, with Masséna the first officer across. It was here that French soldiers began to refer to Napoleon affectionately as 'The Little Corporal'.

May 14 – He writes to the Directory refusing to share his command in Italy with General Kellermann, the hero of Valmy.

May 15 – Napoleon enters Milan, very much the conqueror of northern Italy.

May 21 – Carnot, still at the War Ministry, writes to say that the Directory agrees to Napoleon retaining sole command in Italy.

May 25 – Lombardy rises against the French. Napoleon orders Pavia, the main city, to be pillaged for twenty-four hours. However – and this is a crisis point in his life – he cannot bear the sight of useless destruction and stops the French troops after only three hours.

May 30–31 – He defeats Beaulieu and smashes through the entire Austrian centre at Borghetto, driving their troops back into the Tirol.

June–July – Napoleon lays siege to Mantua.

June 18 – He enters Modena.

June 19 – He enters Bologna and expels the Papal administrators.

June 23 – He signs an armistice at Foligno with Pope Pius VI.

June 24 – In the north the French force the passage of the Rhine.

June 30 – Josephine arrives in Milan, but will not be joined by Napoleon until July 13.

July 5 – General Moreau defeats the Archduke Charles of Austria at Radstadt.

July 30 – Napoleon raises the siege of Mantua.

August 5 – He defeats Würmser at Castiglione and drives him back into the Tirol.

August 8 – Napoleon re-occupies Verona and on the 11th lays siege to Mantua again.

September 3 – General Jourdan defeated by the Archduke Charles at Würtsburg. Only one day later Napoleon defeats the Austrians at

Roveredo.

September 15 – The rout of Würmser at Bassano. He and the remains of the Austrians retire to Mantua.

October 8 – Spain, having signed an alliance with France, declares war on Great Britain.

October 10 – Peace with Naples is signed and on October 22 the British give up their bases in Corsica. The Corsicans themselves opt for an alliance with France.

November 1 – The advance of General Alvinzi.

November 13 – Napoleon writes to the Directory complaining about the non-arrival of reinforcements. The following day, however, he prepares for the inevitable battle.

November 15–17 – He wins a great victory over Alvinzi at Arcola.

November 17 – Death of the Empress Catherine II of Russia. Her successor, Paul I, will become an almost fanatical admirer of Napoleon.

November 18 – The successful French re-enter Verona. Würmser attempts a sortie against them from Mantua, but is beaten back.

December – Napoleon, on France's behalf, agrees to the formation of the Cisalpine Republic, giving the Italians of Lombardy a recognised freedom from Austrian rule.

1797

January 10 – He marches off to face another Austrian advance.

January 14 – Again Alvinzi is defeated, this time at Rivoli. Once more Masséna plays an important tactical role in the battle. He is then detached by Napoleon and on January 26 smashes the Austrian reserve force at Carpenedolo.

February 2 – Würmser, another broken general, surrenders Mantua.

February 19 – Napoleon invades the Papal States and concludes a treaty (of Tolentino) with Pope Pius VI. The latter agrees to give up Avignon, the Venaissin Bologna, Ferrara and the Romagna; also to disband his army of mercenaries, to pay France an indemnity and to give up certain art treasures.

March 16 – Napoleon defeats the Archduke Charles of Austria at Tagliamento. The following month he advances into Carinthia and reaches Leoben (Styria) where the Austrians ask for an armistice.

May 3 – Napoleon declares war upon the Venetians after they had fired on French shipping. In Paris, General Pichegru attempts but fails to overthrow the Directory.

May 16 – The French occupy Venice.

June 28 – Another French force takes Corfu.

July 9 – The Festival of Milan. Inauguration of the Cisalpine Republic.

July 16 – Again in Paris, Citizen-General Hoche is appointed Minister for War. Two days later Talleyrand makes his first appearance as Minister for Foreign Affairs.

August 10 – Napoleon writes to the Directory about the importance of holding Malta if his plans to annex Egypt are to be successful.

September – Royalist risings combined with a constitutional opposition threaten the Directory. Napoleon still supports Barras and General Augereau puts down the revolt (which came to be known as the Revolution of Fructidor).

September 13 – The Directory having been fully occupied with the attempted coup, Napoleon again writes to the members suggesting the seizure of Malta.

October 17 – Treaty of Campo Formio with Austria. Napoleon obtains for France very advantageous terms.

November 26 – He is appointed Minister Plenipotentiary at the subsequent congress at Rastadt.

December 5 – He returns to Paris, and with the government's approval the name of the street where he lives is changed to Rue de la Victoire. His re-entry into the capital is greeted with widespread applause and he is elected to the French Institute, a singular honour.

December 27 – There are riots in Rome. Joseph Bonaparte is publicly insulted.

1798

January–February – Napoleon goes to survey the coast for the first time opposite England.

February 15 – Berthier, Napoleon's future Chief-of-Staff, proclaims the Roman Republic – and there are signs of a growing animosity between he and Masséna.

April – Napoleon is appointed to command the expedition to Egypt.

May 19 – He sets sail from Toulon.

June 12 – The French occupy Malta.

June 26 – Nelson and the English fleet are sighted by the French, but a sea-fog prevents the enemy from giving chase.

June 28 – Nelson reaches Alexandria ahead of the French. Finding no one there he sets sail again.

June 30 – Napoleon himself arrives at Alexandria and disembarks his troops without incident.

July 3 – The French ships then anchor on the far side of Aboukir Bay.

July 21 – The Battle of the Pyramids. Napoleon defeats the Mamelukes under Murad Bey.

July 26 – The French enter Cairo and begin to reorganise Egypt as a French Protectorate. Also, the medical and scientific teams with the expedition begin their work.

August 1 – The Battle of the Nile. Nelson surprises and destroys the French fleet in Aboukir Bay.

September 12 – Turkey joins the alliance against France.
September–October – Napoleon kept busy with risings in Cairo.
October 20 – The Turkish army begins to concentrate at Damascus.

1799

February – Napoleon invades Syria.
February 19 – He takes El-Arish.
February 25 – He takes Gaza.
March 4 – He lays siege to Jaffa.
March 7 – Jaffa is taken by storm. Twelve hundred prisoners, mostly Turks and Arnauts, are executed for having broken their previous capitulation and treaty at El-Arish.
March 15 – Sir Sidney Smith disembarks at Acre.
March 29 – Napoleon lays siege to Acre.
April – New European Coalition against France.
May 20 – Napoleon raises the siege of Acre and begins to retreat towards Egypt. He re-enters Cairo on June 14.
June 22 – Turkey, Portugal and Naples join the Coalition against France.
July 25 – Napoleon defeats the Turkish army at Aboukir.
August 30 – He secretly embarks for France.
October 9 – After eluding the English fleet he lands at Fréjus and is given a tremendous reception by the people.
October 15 – He arrives in Paris, again to a hero's welcome.
October–November – He plots with Talleyrand and others to overthrow the Directory.
November 9–10 – *Coup d'etat* of 18/19 Brumaire. The Directory is abolished and the Legislature dissolved.
December – The Consulate is established. Napoleon is created First Consul for a period of ten years. Constitution of the Year VIII.
December 26 – The new First Consul writes letters of peace to George III of England and the Austrian Emperor.
December 27 – *Le Moniteur* appointed sole official government journal.

1800

January 17 – Napoleon suppresses sixty out of seventy-three political journals and forbids the publication of any new ones.
February 7 – He orders France into mourning following the death of George Washington and despatches a wreath for his tomb.
February 13 – The Bank of France established.
February 19 – Napoleon and Josephine take up residence in the Tuileries.
February 20 – The self-styled Louis XVIII writes inviting Napoleon to 'play the role of General Monk' and restore him to the French throne.
March – Peace negotiations between France and the United States.

March 5 – Meeting between Napoleon and the royalist plotter, Georges Cadoudal. The First Consul refuses to help restore the Bourbons to power. From this moment on Cadoudal is bent upon Napoleon's assassination.

April 5 – Three more journals suppressed. Theatre censorship established.

April 18 – Masséna is besieged in Genoa.

May 6 – Napoleon sets off upon his second Italian campaign.

May 9 – He arrives at Geneva and immediately takes the field against the Austrians.

May 15 – The French cross into Italy by the St.-Bernard Pass. Their guns are transported in hollowed-out tree trunks each one pulled by a hundred men.

June 2 – Napoleon enters Milan.

June 5 – Masséna surrenders Genoa but is allowed to leave 'with the full honours of war'.

June 9 – Battle of Montebello. Lannes and Victor defeat the Austrians. Napoleon departs from Milan.

June 14 – Napoleon defeats the Austrians under Melas at Marengo, but the real hero of the battle is Desaix who in turn is fatally wounded.

June 15 – Convention of Alessandria between Napoleon and Melas ends 'The Campaign of Thirty Days'.

June 16 – Napoleon writes to the Austrian Emperor, offering to renew the Treaty of Campo Formio.

June 17 – Returning to Milan, he is hailed by the populace as 'the Liberator of Italy'.

June 19 – In the north, General Moreau defeats the Austrians at Hochstadt.

June 23 – The French re-occupy Genoa, a symbolic achievement.

June 25 – Napoleon starts back for Paris.

June 29 – At Lyon he writes: 'I intend to arrive in Paris unexpectedly. I want no triumphal arches the only real triumph is the satisfaction of the people.'

July 2 – He enters the capital at midnight.

July–August – Napoleon gives Malta to the Tzar Paul of Russia and recognises him Grand Master of the Knights of Saint John. He also sends home a group of Russian prisoners, 'well-clothed and bearing their own arms'.

September – Following two years' maritime blockade Malta surrenders to Great Britain. The latter refuses to accept the Tzar's claim to it, and Paul I now comes out openly on the side of Napoleon, joining the League of Armed Neutrality against Britain.

September 15 – Austria accepts an armistice with France in Germany.

October 3 – Great Britain's King George III, 'in the interests of peace', gives up his title 'King of France', a claim going back to the Hundred Years' War.

October 7 – By a secret treaty made at St.-Ildefonso France renews her alliance with Spain.

November 12 – Renewal of hostilities both in Germany and Italy.

December 3–4 – The Battle of Hohenlinden. By a combination of Moreau's strategy and General Ney's guts and determination the French shatter the Austrians, who lose eighty cannon and over nineteen thousand men dead, wounded or captured.

December 24 – The British-backed attempt to blow up Napoleon in the Rue St.-Niçaise while on his way to the opera. However, Cesar his coach-driver, said to be drunk, whips up the horses and passes the explosive device before it goes off. The First Consul escapes with a bad shaking; but half the street is demolished and twenty citizens die.

1801

January 29 – The secret Treaty of Madrid.

February – In London, William Pitt resigns.

February 9 – The Peace of Lunéville between France and Austria. It means the end of the Second Coalition.

March 8 – The English land at Aboukir.

March 21 The Battle of Alexandria. General Abercromby defeats the French. On the same day the Treaty of Aranjuez is signed between France and Spain.

March 24 – The assassination of Tzar Paul I of Russia. He is succeeded by Alexander I.

March 28 – Treaty of Florence between France and Naples.

April 2 – Nelson shells Copenhagen and cripples the Danish fleet.

June 7 – The French evacuate Cairo.

July 15 – Napoleon makes his Concordat with Pope Pius VI.

August 4 – Nelson makes his unsuccessful attack on Boulogne.

August 15 – The English admiral again attacks the port, and is repulsed for the second time.

August 31 – The final battle at Alexandria. Menou (Jacques François, Baron de), who had succeeded at Kléber to the command in Egypt, surrenders to Hutchinson and the British occupy Cairo. Menou, cut off from France, is not blamed by Napoleon and afterwards will be appointed Governor of Venice.

October 1 – The beginning of Napoleon's much-hoped-for peace talks between France and Great Britain.

October 8 – Peace signed between France and Russia.

October 9 – Treaty between France and Turkey.

December 13 – The expedition to subdue insurrection in San Domingo sails from Brest, commanded by General Victor-Emmanuel Leclerc, the husband of Napoleon's sister Pauline who accompanies him on the voyage. Meanwhile Napoleon forms a flotilla in the Channel.

1802

January – The reorganisation of the Cisalpine Republic becomes Napoleon's chief preoccupation.

January 4 – Marriage of Louis Bonaparte to the First Consul's step-daughter Hortense de Beauharnais.

January 25 – Napoleon created President of the Italian Republic.

March 25–27 – Peace of Amiens between Great Britain, Spain, Holland and the French Republic.

April – Promulgation of the Concordat with the Vatican. *Les Articles Organiques* passed.

May 7 – In San Domingo, Toussaint L'Ouverture surrenders to the French.

May 19 – Institution of the Legion of Honour.

May 23 – Treaty with Prussia.

May 24 – Treaty with Bavaria.

June 10 – Toussaint L'Ouverture is tricked, seized and despatched to France (where he died, still a prisoner, in 1803).

June 29 – The Ligurian Republic established. Previous excommunication of Talleyrand withdrawn by the Pope.

August 1 – Napoleon proclaimed First Consul for life. Constitution of the Year X. Elba annexed by France.

August 15 – Napoleon's thirty-third birthday. Anniversary of the Concordat with Rome. Festival of the Assumption, with Paris illuminated for the occasion.

September – France occupies Piedmont.

September 15 – Napoleon meets and is extremely flattering towards the English pro-French politician Charles James Fox.

September 30 – The First Consul makes a dramatic intervention in the disturbed affairs of the Swiss Cantons.

October 9 – Death of the Duke of Parma. The Duchy is now annexed by France.

October 11 – Treaty with Russia.

November 2 – Death of General Leclerc at San Domingo.

November 18 – The Tzar refuses to accept the Peace of Amiens' arrangements in connection with Malta.

December 12 – Lord Whitworth, the English ambassador, is presented to Napoleon, who receives him with the utmost cordiality.

1803

February 18 – Napoleon complains to Lord Whitworth about the British delay in evacuating Alexandria and Malta.

February 19 – Act of Mediation. Settlement of Swiss affairs.

February 21 – British troops evacuate the Cape of Good Hope.

February 26 – Napoleon offers a pension of two million francs per annum to the Comte de Provençe (still styling himself Louis XVIII), now resident in Warsaw, if he will renounce on behalf of his family all claims to the French throne.

March 8 – George III and his ministers, under pressure from English merchants, who are losing trade to the French, ask their Parliament to vote money for war supplies.

March 11 – A furious Napoleon begins his own preparations for war, and on March 13 delivers a calculated insult to Lord Whitworth on the subject of Great Britain's 'treachery'.

March 17 – British forces leave Alexandria but not Malta.

April 30 – France agrees to sell Louisiana to the United States for sixty million francs.

May 1 – Diplomatic reception at the Tuileries. Lord Whitworth deliberately absents himself.

May 2 – Lord Whitworth sends for his passports, but is asked to stay to receive Napoleon's reply to Britain's demands.

May 12 – Whitworth quits Paris.

May 17 – The French ambassador leaves England.

May 18 – France declares war.

June 1 – Napoleon seizes Hanover. He also begins his preparations at the Camp of Boulogne for an army of invasion.

June 23 – St.-Lucia in the West Indies captured by the British, followed on June 26 by Tobago.

July 8 – Nelson blockades the port of Toulon.

August 23 – Georges Cadoudal lands in France.

September – Berbice, Demerara and Essequibo seized by the British. Napoleon establishes strict press censorship.

October 1 – Now aged thirty-four, he issues instructions for the erection of the Vendôme column.

October 3 – He orders the expulsion from France of Madame de Staël.

November 30 – The French evacuate San Domingo.

December 5 – The marriage of Jerome Bonaparte to Elizabeth Patterson in Baltimore: guaranteed to anger Napoleon.

1804—5

Preparations for the invasion of England continue.

1804

January – Pichegru and other conspirators enter Paris and attempt to persuade General Moreau to join the royalist cause.

February 14 – Querelle, captured by Napoleon's police, reveals details of the plot.

February 15 – Arrest of Moreau.

February 28 – Capture of Pichegru.

March 1 – Napoleon receives information implicating the Duke of Enghien in the plot.

March 9 – Capture of Georges Cadoudal.

March 20 – The Duke of Enghien is kidnapped from neutral territory in Germany. He is brought to Vincennes at half-past five in the evening, interrogated and found guilty by a group of Bonapartist colonels, then shot at 2.00am the following morning.

March 21 – Napoleon's Civil Code passed by the Legislature.

April 6 – Pichegru found strangled in his cell, it is thought by his own hand – although others will claim differently.

May 10 – In London, Pitt at the head of the pro-war party returns to office.

May 18 – Napoleon created 'Emperor' by decree of the Senate and as a result of popular demand by both the army and the people.

May – Franco-Dutch treaty.

June 24 – Execution of Georges Cadoudal.

June 25 – General Moreau sails for America – his two-year sentence having been set aside on condition he quits France.

July 14 – The Legion of Honour extended.

August 20 – Death of Admiral Latouche Tréville. Eight days later Napoleon appoints Admiral Villeneuve to the command at Toulon.

October 2 – Sir Sidney Smith mounts an unsuccessful attack upon the invasion flotilla at Boulogne.

October 8 – Dessalines crowned 'Emperor Jean Jacques I' of Haiti (San Domingo).

November 2 – Pope Pius VII departs from Rome to be present at Napoleon's coronation.

November 6 – Secret treaty between Austria and Russia.

November 25–28 – Napoleon meets the Pope and they enter Paris together.

December 2 – Napoleon and Josephine crowned in Notre Dame.

December 3 – Treaty between Great Britain and Sweden.

December 12 – Spain declares war against Great Britain.

1805

March 13 – Napoleon is proclaimed 'King of Italy'.

April – Treaty of St.-Petersburg between Great Britain and Russia.

May 26 – Napoleon crowned at Milan.

May 30 – France annexes the Ligurian Republic.

June – The Civil Code extended to cover Italy.

July – Napoleon visits the Camp of Boulogne and is fêted by his marshals there.

July – Austria joins the alliance against France.

July 22 – Battle of Cape Finisterre.

August – Third Coalition against France. The land war with Austria and

26

Russia is about to begin.

August–September – The Grand Army marches from Boulogne to Bavaria.

September 27 – Napoleon joins his army at Strasbourg.

October 17 – Spearheaded by Marshal Ney, who storms the bridge at Elchingen, French forces surround an entire Austrian army at Ülm. The Austrian General Mack has no alternative but to surrender.

October 21 – At Cape Trafalgar Nelson wins a great victory for Britain against the combined fleets of France and Spain. However, the English admiral is mortally wounded in the battle.

November 14 – Napoleon arrives at the Schönbrunn Palace, near Vienna. Convention between Prussia and the Allies.

December 2 – Napoleon and the Grand Army completely overwhelm the Austrian and Russian forces at Austerlitz, and Tzar Alexander leaves the battlefield in tears; the Austrian Emperor is forced to seek terms.

December 26 – Treaty of Schönbrunn with Austria.

December – France annexes Genoa.

1806

January 23 – Death of Pitt. His great rival Fox immediately returns to office and endeavours to negotiate with France: even informing Talleyrand of a new plot to assassinate Napoleon. (Unfortunately, the negotiations prove both difficult and drawn out and when Fox himself dies on September 13, 1806 the pro-war party in London once more gains the initiative.)

February – Napoleon returns to Paris. Within the month he has signed a treaty with Prussia.

March – He creates Joseph Bonaparte 'King of the Two Sicilies'. Formation of the Grand Duchy of Berg.

June – Napoleon formally abolishes the Holy Roman Empire.

June 6 – Louis Bonaparte is created 'King of Holland'.

July – Napoleon forms the Confederation of the Rhine. He also creates the kingdoms of Bavaria and Würtemburg.

September – War with Prussia.

October 14 – The French defeat the Prussians at Jena and Auerstadt.

October 27 – Napoleon enters Berlin as conqueror.

November 21 – He issues his 'Berlin Decree' against Great Britain, aimed at denying her merchants access to Continental markets and thus bringing about the defeat of his enemies by economic means.

December – The French march against the Russians.

December 28 – Battle of Pultusk. War between Russia and Turkey. Napoleon decides to annex Dalmatia and Ragusa; and to add Venice to the Kingdom of Italy.

1807

February 8 – Napoleon only narrowly defeats the Russians and Prussians at the bloody battle near Eylau, mostly fought in a snow-blizzard.

March – In London, a new government is formed by Lord Portland. George Canning becomes Foreign Secretary.

April – Convention of Bartenstein between Russia, Prussia, and Sweden.

May 26 – The capitulation of Danzig to France.

June – Britain joins the Confederation of Bartenstein.

June 14 – The Grand Army, again spearheaded by Marshal Ney, shatters the Russian forces at Friedland.

June 25–26 – Napoleon meets the defeated Tzar Alexander on a tented raft in the middle of the River Niemen.

July – Formation of the Grand Duchy of Warsaw. Extension of the Confederation of the Rhine.

July 8 – Peace of Tilsit between France and Russia; which also imposes ignominious terms upon the Prussians.

August – Napoleon returns to Paris.

August 19 – Suppression of the Tribunate. Jerome Bonaparte becomes 'King of Westphalia'.

September – English seizure of the fleet at Copenhagen.

October – Stein becomes Minister for Home Affairs in what remains of Prussia; Prussian Edict of Emancipation. Scharnhorst begins to reform the Prussian army. Franco-Spanish treaty signed at Fontainebleau.

November – Napoleon invades Portugal. The French led by Junot occupy Lisbon. Flight of the Portugese royal family aboard British ships.

December – Napoleon occupies Tuscany. Completion of the Simplon road between France and Italy.

1808

January – Napoleon returns to Paris.

February – Invasion of Spain.

February 2 – French troops enter Rome.

March – Constitution of the Imperial University of France. Revolt of Aranjuez. A new, Imperial nobility created in France.

March 19 – Abdication of Charles IV of Spain; his son proclaimed king as Ferdinand VII.

March 27 – Pope Pius VII excommunicates Napoleon. Meanwhile, ever opportunist, Russia invades Finland.

May 2 – A great insurrection (the *Dos de Mayo*) in Madrid. Murat puts it down but with much bloodshed. It is the signal for guerilla warfare throughout the Iberian peninsula.

May 6 – Ferdinand abdicates under duress at Bayonne.

June – Further insurrection in Spain, and on June 15 a French squadron surrenders to Spanish forces at Cadiz.

June 6 – Napoleon makes his brother Joseph 'King of Spain'.

July 14 – The Peninsular War proper begins. Great Britain Spain and Portugal in alliance against France.

July 19 – Dupont, tipped as a future marshal, surrenders at Baylen with 20,000 men including marines of the Imperial Guard: almost a third of France's forces are in Spain.

August – Sir Arthur Wellesley arrives in Portugal.

August 21 – The Battle of Vimiera, another French defeat, this time of troops under Junot.

August 30 – Poor negotiating by the British at Cintra allows Junot to remove his remaining units from Portugal more or less intact. Wellesley is incensed.

September 8 – Convention of Paris between France and Prussia.

September 22 – Napoleon leaves St.-Cloud for Erfurt and another meeting with the Tzar.

October 12 – The Treaty of Tilsit renewed. This leaves Napoleon free to intervene personally in Spain.

December 4 – He enters Madrid, accepts the city's surrender and abolishes the Spanish Inquisition. Then he sets out to clear Spain of British units.

1809

January – Treaty of the Dardanelles between Great Britain and Turkey. Napoleon returns to Paris, leaving Soult, Ney and other marshals with the almost impossible task of 'policing' the Iberian Peninsular. But the Emperor is preparing for a new clash with Austria. He writes: 'I am leaving my best troops with Joseph and am starting alone for Vienna with my little conscripts, my name and my long boots!'

January 16 – The Battle of Corunna. Death of Sir John Moore.

April 12 – He hears finally that Austria has declared war and leaves for the front that same night.

April 15 – The French cross the Rhine at Strasbourg.

April 20–22 – The French defeat the Austrians at Abensburg, Landshut and Eckmühl and on the 23rd they drive them out of Ratisbon.

May 12 – Napoleon enters Vienna after first bombarding the capital.

May 21–22 – In attempting to cross the Danube the French suffer near-defeats at Aspern and Essling. The Austrians are again commanded by the Archduke Charles.

June 10 – Napoleon is once more excommunicated by Pope Pius VII.

July – Wellesley pushes Soult out of Portugal; Ney is having difficulty putting down insurrections in Galicia and the Asturias.

July 5–6 – The French cross the Danube at night and on the 6th fight the Battle of Wagram, when the Archduke is defeated.

July 7 – Pope Pius VII is arrested.

July 27–28 – The Battle of Talavera. It is an Allied victory but Wellesley loses 5,000 men and cannot exploit the situation because of Spanish inefficiency.

October 12 – Napoleon, now aged 40, survives an attempt on his life by Staps, son of a Lutheran pastor in Erfurt.

October 14 – Treaty of Schönbrunn with Austria.

October 22 – Napoleon leaves Vienna for Paris.

October 26 – He arrives at Fontainebleau.

December 16 – He divorces Josephine.

1810

January – Treaty of Paris between France and Sweden. French conquest of Andalusia.

February – Rome becomes the 'second city' of the French Empire.

March 11 – Napoleon marries the Archduchess Marie Louise by proxy.

April 1 – The marriage is formalised at St.-Cloud.

July–August – France annexes Holland and Westphalia.

August – Masséna invades Portugal but is in serious conflict with Ney and his other officers.

September – Wellesley, now created Viscount Wellington and Baron Douro, is constructing the Lines of Torres Vedras.

September 6 – Napoleon writes to Charles XIII of Sweden giving his permission for Bernadotte to become Crown Prince of that country.

September 27 – Masséna, against Ney's advice, attacks the British positions at Bussaço and suffers a severe repulse.

October – Fontainebleau Decrees, aimed at smashing London's trade. Also Sweden declares war on the British.

December – France annexes north-west coast of Germany.

December 5 – Russians fortify the banks of the Dvina and Dneister.

1811

February 28 – Napoleon writes to the Tzar, angry and alarmed to discover that the latter has entered into an agreement with London. It threatens to ruin his 'trade' war.

March 20 – Birth of the King of Rome.

March–April – Masséna abandons Portugal to Wellington and retreats into Spain's western provinces.

June 2 – Baptism of the King of Rome in Notre Dame.

December 19 – Napoleon calls for the detailed accounts of the campaign by Charles XII of Sweden in Russia and Poland.

1812

April – France declares war upon Russia. Secret alliance between Sweden and Russia.

May 19 – The French army regroups near Dresden.

May 28 – Peace of Bucharest between Russia and Turkey.

June 24 – Napoleon crosses the River Niemen.

June 28 – He occupies Vilna and sets up a 'provisional' government for the occupied territories of Russia.

July – Peace between Great Britain, Russia and Sweden.

July 22 – Battle of Salamanca, another Wellington victory. Marmont is seriously wounded during the battle.

August 18 – The Russians are driven out of Smolensk.

September 7 – The Battle of Borodino. This most hard-fought and bloody event is finally turned into a French victory, thanks largely to the tenacity of Ney and Murat. However, Napoleon – ill and indecisive – fails to exploit their success. A large part of the Russian Army is allowed to escape.

September 14 – Meeting no further opposition the Grand Army occupies Moscow.

September 15 – Moscow burns. Four hundred incendiaries are shot.

October – The Malet Conspiracy in Paris.

October 20 – Napoleon leaves Moscow. He has failed to bring the Tzar to a discussion of peace-treaty terms. The subsequent retreat, in terrible cold and despite Ney's amazing rearguard action, sees the gradual disintegration of the Grand Army.

November 26–27 – The French effect the difficult crossing of the Beresina.

December 5 – Napoleon leaves the remainder of his army and returns to Paris.

December – War between Great Britain and America.

1813

February–March – Uprisings in Germany. The alliance of Austria, Russia and Prussia against France: their 'War of Liberation' begins.

April 15 – Napoleon travels from St.-Cloud to Mayence (Maintz) where units of his army are regrouping, enlarged by a hurried draft of conscripts. The Emperor covers this distance in forty hours.

May 2 – The Battle of Lützen. The French 'makeshift' army defeats the seasoned troops of Russia and Prussia.

May 20–21 – Napoleon again defeats the Allies at Bautzen.

June – King Joseph, Jourdan and Soult defeated by Wellington in the Battles of Vittoria and the Pyrénées.

August 26 – The Battle of Dresden. The Allies, now joined by Austria, suffer a further defeat.

October 7 – Wellington enters France from Spain.

October 16–18 – Napoleon comes close to winning the Battle of Leipzig, the so-called 'Battle of the Nations'. However by the second day he is running out of ammunition and on the third day he is in retreat. The accidental blowing of a vital bridge leaves a part of his army stranded.

November 2 – Napoleon recrosses the Rhine. On the 9th he arrives in Paris.

December–January – France is invaded by the Allies.

1814

January 18 – Napoleon exclaims in frustration, but perhaps also to stiffen France's defensive resolve: 'If I had had 30,000 rounds at Leipzig – I should today be master of the world!'

January 25 – He takes the field with his remaining units. Ney, MacDonald and other marshals are still with him.

January 29–February 3 – Against all odds the French defeat the Prussians at Brienne.

February 1 – Napoleon is himself defeated at La Rothière. He prepares to fall back upon Paris.

February 10 – He defeats Blücher at Champaubert.

February 11 – He defeats Blücher at Montmirail.

February 12 – He defeats Blücher at Château-Thierry.

February 13 – He defeats Blücher at Vauchamp.

February–March – Futile peace-talks at Chatillon-sur -Seine.

March – Unresolved actions at Laon and Craonne.

March 31 – The Allies enter Paris and set about restoring the Bourbons.

April 11 – Napoleon officially deposed by the Senate. At Fontainebleau, under pressure from the marshals he signs the form of abdication.

May – Louis XVIII (brother of the executed Louis XVI) arrives in Paris.

May 4 – He lands at Elba.

May 29 – Death of Josephine at Malmaison.

September 30 – The Congress of Vienna assembles.

1815

January – Defensive 'triple alliance' of Great Britain with Austria and France. Napoleon organises balls and fêtes on Elba as a cover for his planned return to France.

February 26 – He sails from Elba under cover of darkness.

March – New treaty signed by Great Britain, Russia, Austria and Prussia against Napoleon.

March 1 – Together with his most faithful supporters he lands near Cannes. 'The Hundred Days' begins.

March 20 – After a triumphal progress via Grenoble and Lyon he re-enters Paris to a tumultuous reception. Louis XVIII and his court have fled to Ghent.

March 29 – The Emperor abolishes the slave trade. He is also hastily putting together a revived Imperial army. Most of his veterans are eager to rejoin.

June 1 – The *Acte Additional* sworn to in Paris.

June 12 – Napoleon leaves to join his troops in Belgium. He crosses the border on June 15.

June 16 – While Ney is locked in a deadly struggle with Wellington at Quatre Bras, Napoleon inflicts a sharp defeat upon Blücher at Ligny.

June 18 – The Battle of Waterloo.

June 21 – The Emperor returns to Paris for the last time.

June 22 – His second abdication.

June 29 – He leaves Malmaison for Rochefort on the Atlantic coast, intending to board a ship for the United States.

July 3 – As Napoleon reaches Rochefort, Louis XVIII is about to re-enter Paris.

July 15 – Napoleon surrenders to Captain Maitland on board HMS *Bellerophon.*

July 24 – He is off Torbay and on the 27th in Plymouth Sound.

August 8 – He sets sail to begin his exile on St.-Helena aboard HMS *Northumberland.* The vessel is under the command of Admiral Sir George Cockburn.

October 15 – He arrives off St.-Helena.

November – The Peace of Paris between the Allies and the restored Bourbons.

December 7 – Execution of Marshal Ney.

December 9 – Napoleon having been in temporary quarters, now moves to his final residence at Longwood. Meanwhile Joseph Bonaparte has moved to the United States.

1816

January 12 – All members of Napoleon's family excluded from France for ever under the Bourbon's 'law of amnesty'.

April – Sir Hudson Lowe takes up his command on St.- Helena. Napoleon is dictating his *mémoires* to Gourgaud and Montholon.

1818

July 25 –. The sympathetic Dr O'Meara leaves the island, the British government having signed an order for his removal. Napoleon's health is already in decline.

1820

October 25 – 'Perhaps Death will soon put an end to my suffering,' Napoleon remarks. There is now much conflict and unpleasantness between the ex-Emperor and Sir Hudson Lowe.

1821

April 2 – On the recent sighting of a comet the prisoner comments: 'It was the same omen which foretold the death of Caesar.'

April 16 – 'I wish my ashes to rest by the banks of the Seine in the midst of the people of France whom I loved so dearly.'

April 19 – He suddenly exclaims: 'I feel the end drawing near . . . I shall meet the brave in the Elysian Fields.'

May 5 – Death of Napoleon at approximately 6pm.

1840

May 12 – In Paris the Chambers decree the removal of the ex-Emperor's remains from St.-Helena for transportation back to France.

October 15 – The tomb on St.-Helena is opened up by permission of the British government.

October 16 – The remains embarked on the French frigate *Belle Poule* under the command of the Prince de Joinville, son of King Louis Philippe.

November 30 – The *Belle Poule* anchors at Cherbourg.

December 15 – The remains are taken into the Hôtel des Invalides.

1841

August 15 – (Napoleon's birthday.) A bronze statue of him is placed on the column of the *Grande Armée* at Boulogne.

1852

February 17 – Under the rule of his nephew, Louis Napoleon, his birthday is declared a national holiday.

1861

Napoleon's remains are moved to their final position in the crypt of the Hôtel des Invalides and placed beneath a slab of red porphyry brought – ironically – from Russia.

=1=
Meritocracy: A Self-Made Man

I found a crown in the kennel.
I cleansed it of its filth, and placed it on my head.
– Napoleon Bonaparte

Despite an Italian lineage of nobility dating back to the early Middle Ages Napoleon was far from being born with a silver spoon in his mouth. His father, Carlo Maria Buonaparte contrived to get him a good education at Autun and Brienne (the military school where fifty to sixty boys of the poorer *noblesse* were admitted each year at the King's expense, a sum equal to thirty pounds being handed over for each pupil). But Carlo died in 1785 at the age of thirty-nine and left no family money. Napoleon then, rather than his elder brother Joseph, assumed full responsibility as the head of the family.

Until the mid-1790's and until General Dugommier had praised his conduct of the Siege of Toulon to the Convention in Paris, the young artillery officer remained almost permanently broke. He lived like a church-mouse: on bread and olives and the thinnest of Burgundy. His uniform was coming apart at the seams; his boots were down-at-heel. Every single franc he had to spare was passed on to the other members of the Buonaparte family. It became his accepted way of life.

When eventually he became all-powerful in France – which included overall control of the Treasury – he proved to be an extremely generous friend and master, but he still spent little on himself and was even thriftier if the nation's basic prosperity was involved. He believed in high rewards for work done, but only if the work was done well. Corruption appalled him – and once proven led to instant dismissal.

Another unusual (and scarcely-known) facet of the younger Napoleon is how close he came to joining the British Army. He seriously considered joining the Indian service, where wages were better than in the French forces. This came to light earlier in the present century in a batch of letters discovered by a Mrs A.G.A. Beyts, great-great-granddaughter of the eminent lawyer Sir Fitzroy Kelly, (after 1837 the MP for Ipswich). Kelly's friend, Peter Evan Turnbull of Brighton recalled in one of these letters a conversation he'd had with Napoleon's godfather, the Corsican 'General' Paoli thirty years before: 'He (Napoleon) observed,' he said, 'that for a young man situated as he was, without connections or patronage, there was a very poor prospect of advancement in the service of France, that he was inclined, if he could, to pass into that of England (and) that he hoped I would sanction his doing so.' In fact Paoli's advice, given in the early 1790s, was that he perceived great political changes in France and Napoleon should wait for a year at least. How different the modern history of Europe would be if he had encouraged his godson to make the change!

However, if the young Napoleon was kept exceptionally poor he was at the same time tremendously gifted, very ambitious and above all resourceful. Given the drift and venality of Paul Barras' administration it seemed logical and only a question of forming alliances with Barras' disillusioned colleagues before he became 'the inheritor of the Revolution'. France was then all set to enjoy her finest and most efficient period of government since the early 17th Century.

Nearly everyone within it was promoted on merit. The self-made man at the top had had too much of a struggle himself to believe in sinecures or 'jobs for the boys'. He would promote a friend certainly; and hope that it would result in loyalty. But these so-called 'friends' he had usually observed at close quarters in battle; or come upon them within the former administrations. Robespierre's government, for instance, although bloodthirsty, had been largely free from corruption and remarkably efficient. Carnot and Fréron had both signed the King's death warrant but their departmental abilities were outstanding; likewise Talleyrand's, despite his flaws of character.

Napoleon recruited as and when he needed and from the maximum talent available. He wasn't a social snob. The ritual which surrounded the Imperial Court was more to impress his European allies than because he liked it himself. Once the formalities were over he preferred to relax at the opera; while visiting VIPs complained that his suppers were poor and always hurried. (Not the fault of his chef but because he regarded mealtimes as a bore.) Given this informed but easy style, those who came to belong to the *élite* and to serve him were drawn from a broad spectrum of French life: the old aristocracy, revolutionaries of ability, lawyers, members of the new clergy, army officers from every conceivable background, trained and potential diplomats, prefects, secretaries and clerks. In return for their elevation he demanded honesty, hard-work, due deference to his own orders and a genuinely nationalistic spirit.

As the Emperor he was aware of his great abilities and his destiny, but he never forgot his humble origins.

=2=
The Family

The old adage that one can choose one's friends but not one's relatives is never truer than when applied to Napoleon.

The First Consul and Emperor had a far easier time with the relations he acquired by marriage than with those of the blood. He delighted in playing with Josephine's children and when they grew up they did nothing to disappoint him. In contrast his brothers and sisters grew up to be demanding, often incompetent and sometimes downright disloyal. They could have been of the utmost value to him in running France's affairs, instead of which they let him down at nearly every turn. But Eugène de Beauharnais didn't; nor did Hortense.

BEAUHARNAIS, Eugène de, Grand Duke of Frankfurt, Prince of the Empire and of Venice (1781 – 1824)

If there is a cannon-shot, it is Eugène who goes to see what it is; if I have to cross a trench, it is he who gives me his hand!
– Napoleon

Napoleon's stepson; and like his sister a demonstrably better relative than those of the blood. For unselfish loyalty, obedience and genuine affection it would be hard to find a superior record within the *élite*.

The scion of Josephine's first marriage to Alexandre de Beauharnais, when his father was guillotined under 'the Terror' (and with his mother also in prison) he was apprenticed to a joiner. Being an aristocrat, it was thought this would give him added protection. However, upon Josephine's release and marriage to Napoleon his career advanced rapidly. In 1796 he was placed with the Guides of General Bessières and in the Italian campaign of 1796-7 he became Napoleon's junior ADC. He also accompanied his new stepfather to Egypt where he gained the nickname 'Cherubin' for his boyish looks. But he displayed a natural courage during the Siege of Acre and received his first wound there. (In addition he had the nerve to give Napoleon a ticking off over his liaison with Pauline Fourès!) Under the Consulate, still only nineteen he was entrusted with a brigade of Guards and distinguished himself at Marengo (1800). Then in 1804 he was created Prince of the Empire with an annual allowance of 200,000 francs. Unlike the grasping and back-stabbing Bonapartes, Eugène never asked for a thing – which endeared him to the Emperor all the more. This, plus his very real abilities, undoubtedly led to Eugène's appointment in 1805 as Viceroy of Italy and Napoleon's successor to the Iron Crown of Lombardy. It was a post with wide-reaching powers and would fully occupy him until the Russian campaign of 1812.

Meanwhile, in 1806 his stepfather declared him his adopted son and arranged for him to marry Augusta Amelia, daughter of the King of Bavaria. It had meant the breaking off of her engagement to the Prince of Baden, but the marriage proved an unusually happy one. In the dark days of 1814 he was able to write to her: 'I need only think of you, my dear Augusta, to feel sure Providence watches over me...my destiny is united to that of the loveliest, the best and most vituous of women.' And already she had written to him at the time of Josephine's divorce: 'Blotted out from the list of the great, we shall be inscribed upon that of the happy. Isn't this much better?'

Although generally guided by his stepfather the young man's period as Viceroy of Italy was quite outstanding. His territories stretched from Venice down as far as the Kingdom of Naples and Sicily, and of course there was continuous trouble with the Austrians. But he ruled justly and well, doing his best to root out corruption and adding some splendid buildings to the city of Milan where his government resided.

A renewal of hostilities with the Austrians in 1809 placed Eugène in a precarious position. He had only 16,000 men and was forced to retreat upon Verona. However, with the arrival of fresh troops under General Macdonald he was able to take the offensive again, seizing Trieste and winning a notable victory at Raab in Austria itself; which left the way clear for him to join up with Napoleon at Wagram.

In December 1809, the Prince was summoned to Paris to assist with the thorny problems surrounding the Emperor's impending divorce from Josephine. It was for dynastic reasons basically; and Napoleon had indicated that he would be treating his ex-Empress with the utmost generosity. But it was a sad event nevertheless. On the whole, Eugène told his mother, he believed she would be far happier once the divorce went through, because it would remove her altogether from the insults and intrigues of the other Bonapartes. This in fact proved to be the case: Josephine, among her roses at Malmaison, had lost a husband but gained a vital new tranquillity.

In the Russian campaign of 1812 he commanded 4th Corps of the Grand Army, mostly composed of Italians. He led on the left-wing with both bravery and panache at Borodino, and then covered himself with glory during the horrors of the retreat from Moscow, saving many regiments which would otherwise have perished. At one point, after the defection of Murat, he actually commanded all that was left of the French Army – and took the field again alongside the Emperor at Lützen in 1813. But with the growing menace of the Austrians in Italy, Napoleon then dispatched his trusted Viceroy back there.

Eugène scratched together a Franco-Italian army and issued a proclamation to the people, exhorting them to join him in the struggle against an enemy who had long profited from their disunity. Few responded to his call though. Even his father-in-law, the King of Bavaria had gone over to the Allies. And in 1814, in the south, Murat of Naples at last threw off his cloak of professed neutrality and concluded pacts with England and the Austrians. Eugène, suffering from daily desertions, retreated upon the Mincio and inflicted several defeats upon the Austrian forces there. He was still more or less holding the line when the news came through of Napoleon's abdication.

Refusing the various tempting offers from the Allies to win him over (because of Austrian hostility towards the Bourbons he was even considered as a possible successor to Napoleon) he retired into private life at Munich. He accepted the title Duke of Leuchtenberg and gave his word to the Tzar that if left unmolested he would never draw his sword again.

This solemn oath was the real reason why he took no part in the Hundred Days – although it has been claimed that he warned Napoleon on Elba of the Allies' intention to move him elsewhere, possibly as far away as St.-Helena. During the Hundred Days Napoleon created him a member of the new House of Peers. (And later, in the years following Waterloo, Eugène made many direct appeals to the Tzar to ease his stepfather's sufferings on the Atlantic rock.)

Eugène now sold his big house on the Rue de Lille in Paris and settled in Munich permanently. He had an adequate personal income, plus bequests from Josephine and Augusta's dowry. But his health was noticeably declining. He was suffering from high blood-pressure, also a bad heart: which led on to his death from apoplexy in 1824, only three years after Napoleon's own.

However, his children made some spectacular marriages. Josephine Maximilienne to the Crown Prince of Sweden; Hortense Eugènie Napoléonne to Prince Frederick of Hohenzollern; Charles Eugène Napoleon, the second Duke of Leuchtenberg to the Grand Duchess Maria of Russia; Auguste Emilie Eugènie Napoléonne to Dom Pedro the Emperor of Brazil; Louise Theodeline to the Count of Würtemburg; and finally Maximilien Joseh to Queen Maria II of Portugal.

BEAUHARNAIS, Hortense Eugènie de, Queen of Holland (1783 – 1837)

Daughter of Josephine and stepdaughter of Napoleon, of whom she remained extremely fond and loyal to even after the dynastic divorce proceedings against her mother.

Born in Paris, Josephine was still only nineteen while Hortense's father, Alexandre de Beauharnais and his mistress Laure Longpré were in Martinique, where among other things they tried to buy false evidence that the child wasn't his. However this, and the subsequent separation of her parents was soon to be overtaken by the events of the Revolution.

Although an aristocrat Hortense's father was also a Revolutionary (albeit a moderate one) and for a brief period (1790-1) figured as the most important person in the new National Assembly. It was he who informed the Assembly of the 'flight to Varennes', Louis XVI's bungled attempt to skip the country; and he also signed the warrant for the King's arrest. Later Alexandre served as a general with the Revolutionary armies, but even this did not save him from the Terror. Once Robespierre and the Jacobins ('the Mountain') had triumphed over the moderates ('the Girondins') within the Convention then anyone with an aristocratic name was subject to their violence. De Beauharnais was arrested and executed on July 23 1794, only days before the fall of Robespierre himself. Josephine too had been arrested and only narrowly escaped the guillotine.

Hortense meanwhile had been apprenticed to a dressmaker. This was partly because it was thought a safe refuge, but also the Convention had decreed that the children of nobles ought to be instructed in a trade.

Under the Directory she went to Madame Campan's school in St.-Germain, and it was while there that she first met General Bonaparte. Claire de Rémusat has described her around this time as being 'delicate and wistful', but with her school-work she displayed extreme intelligence. Although not a beauty like her mother, she had superb blue eyes, good skin and fairish hair. Moreover she excelled at theatricals – the best performer in the whole school in fact – which made Caroline Bonaparte furious!

Napoleon was kindness itself to her. At first both she and her brother had disliked the idea of Josephine remarrying, but they were soon won over by the general's behaviour and personality. He was continually giving Hortense small presents, and after the *coup* of 18/19 Brumaire, he indicated that she was to take her place alongside her mother as an important member of the First Consul's family. He always pointed to Hortense as a model of femininity and grace, while she for her part never deserted him.

Unfortunately the marriage he arranged for her to his brother Louis proved to be unhappy. It produced three sons (including the future Napoleon III) and, of course, in the political structure her stepfather imposed across Europe during the Empire it meant that she became Queen of Holland. Whilst there, we learn, she conducted herself with great dignity and calm: revealing nothing in public of her increasing domestic unhappiness. In 1807 though, there occurred the death of her firstborn, Napoleon Charles, a child adored by the Emperor and at one stage even considered as a possible heir to the throne. Hortense's own grief was so great that her health was seriously affected; but this did not lead to more than a temporary reconciliation with Louis.

She returned to Paris for the birth of her third child, where the Bonapartes spread the malicious rumour that its father was the Dutch

Admiral Verhuell: a complete fabrication. However she took the opportunity to beg her stepfather not to be sent back to Louis, and upon the latter's abdication and flight to Westphalia, Napoleon gave in to her wishes. Soon afterwards there began the longstanding love-affair with Charles de Flahaut, one of Napoleon's principal ADCs. Her last child was born of this relationship and grew up to become the Duke of Morny: a prominent politician during the reign of Napoleon III.

Hortense had always expressed mildly royalist sympathies: a fact which amused Napoleon who sometimes addressed her as his 'little Chouanne' or 'the Vendéean'. But it placed her in a strong position upon the first abdication. The Tzar compelled the Bourbons to recognise her title as Duchess of St.-Leu and to leave her monies and property intact. Even the stern Duke of Wellington was noticed to unbend in her presence, while she so delighted King Louis XVIII that he promised to intervene in the wrangling with her exiled husband over the custody of their sons.

Nevertheless she returned to Napoleon's side at the start of the Hundred Days and in the absence of Marie Louise acted as his official hostess at the Tuileries. With him she also paid an emotional visit to Malmaison: and found the place 'utterly desolate' following the death of Josephine.

After Waterloo she settled at Arenenberg and devoted herself to the upbringing and education of her third son Louis Napoleon, he elder boy having been taken away by her husband. Apart from her abilities in theatricals she has been credited with a number of popular songs, including the well-known *Portant pour La Syrie*, translated into English by Sir Walter Scott.

BONAPARTE, Caroline (1782 – 1839)

She had Cromwell's head on the shoulders of a pretty woman
– Talleyrand

In the parlance of today's society hostesses she would be referred to behind her well-dressed back as a prize bitch: spoiled, selfish and disloyal. She was certainly unscrupulous, even in the bestowing of sexual favours. Her brother gave her a fortune in francs and a kingdom in the sun; he received back calculated treachery.

Originally christened 'Maria Annunziata', Napoleon added the more fashionable 'Caroline'. Because she was the youngest of the Bonaparte girls, by the time she came to Paris in 1798 her brother was in a position to improve her education by sending her to the leading school for 'young ladies of good family' run by the celebrated Madame Campan. Caroline was quite clever and would later prove her governmental abilities in Naples. She was the only fair-haired member of the family, small and slender, not as beautiful as Pauline, but with a delightful pink and white complexion and brilliant, large eyes.

However, she could also be extremely venomous; while her greed and ambition were to become a legend. At Madame Campan's she first met Hortense de Beauharnais, then one of the school's outstanding pupils as well as a great favourite with Napoleon. Hortense tried to help Caroline with her drawing lessons, only to be rejected with a double dose of spite: prelude to the many insults and intrigues against Josephine and her daughter which Caroline perpetrated over the years.

The question of a suitable marriage now came up. Jean Lannes had wanted to marry her; likewise Augereau; and even General Moreau had been mentioned as a possible husband. But Caroline had met and fallen for the handsome Joachim Murat on a visit to Rome, and as usual over these years she simply went to her brother and got her own way. She and Murat signed the marriage contract in the Palais du Luxembourg on January 18, 1800. The bride received a dowry of 40,000 francs and 12,000 francs' worth of jewels and furs.

As time went on she bore the marshal four children, but more significantly now devoted herself to obtaining ever-increasing wealth and status. She fully believed the end 'justifies' the means. If she couldn't get what she desired by pushing Murat's career or scheming with Talleyrand and Fouché, then she used floods of tears and bitter reproaches on Napoleon himself. She even slept with Junot when he was the Governor of Paris and therefore had precedence over her husband in the capital. (It got Junot the sack!)

Step-by-step though, Caroline went on to achieve her objectives. She became a princess of the Empire in 1804 (after throwing a terrible tantrum at one of Josephine's dinner-parties); Grand Duchess of Berg and Cleves in 1806; plus the idea of making Murat King of France and herself Queen, if Napoleon died on campaign.

Then on August 1, 1808, she became Queen of Naples and the Two Sicilies.

Both she and her husband were warmly welcomed in their new kingdom. Joseph Bonaparte had done much to improve the lot of the people there who for centuries had suffered from indifferent government, and most recently under the ludicrous Spanish Bourbon, Ferdinand IV – *il Nasone* (Big Nose). Caroline revealed an immediate grasp of what still needed to be done in order to improve trade and agriculture: thus yielding the additional taxes for the royal treasury. And to begin with Murat was happy for her to get on with it. Cabinet meetings bored him: he was anxious to put into operation invasions of Capri and Sicily, much more to his liking.

Napoleon meanwhile was highly satisfied with her efforts. His letters of guidance to her over the next two years make extremely cordial reading. He recalled the Murats to Paris in November 1809 to be present for the celebrations upon his signing the new peace treaty with Austria. Consequently she was on hand to share a sense of triumph with the other Bonapartes over the Emperor's divorce from Josephine; and afterwards was detailed to accompany the Austrian Archduchess Marie Louise into France

Napoleon meanwhile was highly satisfied with her efforts. His letters of guidance to her over the next two years make extremely cordial reading. He recalled the Murats to Paris in November 1809 to be present for the celebrations upon his signing the new peace treaty with Austria. Consequently she was on hand to share a sense of triumph with the other Bonapartes over the Emperor's divorce from Josephine; and afterwards was detailed to accompany the Austrian Archduchess Marie Louise into France and to help with her *trousseau*. But she threw another tantrum when called on to hold the Empress's train at the wedding ceremony. However, on this occasion her mother's insistence prevailed.

Back in Naples something of a rift developed between Caroline and her husband. His love-affairs were now matched by several of her own, but also she tended to show contempt for his lack of intellect and will. Added to which Napoleon almost always agreed with her (sensible) governmental proposals and vetoed the King's.

The 1812 campaign took Murat off to Russia and for the next year the Queen held absolute power...

Upon his return in 1813, having abandoned the remnants of the Grand Army to their fate, Murat once more had common cause with his wife (albeit an uneasy one): *to retain their kingdom no matter what this entailed*. This led to their signing treaties with England and the Austrians against France. (So much for sworn oaths of loyalty!) In the final assessment Napoleon placed more of the blame for their treachery on Caroline than Murat – who he said was a fool except on the battlefield – while Madame Mère could never bring herself to forgive her daughter.

To the Murats, of course, it was not treachery but 'a guarantee of personal survival'. Although, in the event it was remarkably shallow and short-lived. The Allies thought nothing of breaking the treaties once Napoleon had fallen. Murat found himself on the run and eventually in front of a firing squad. Caroline found herself deposed and under house arrest in Hainbourg. Metternich (who, it is claimed, had been her lover in Paris) wrote to her in the politest terms. But eventually all she had left were her jewels, a small estate at Frohsdorf and an empty title: the Duchess of Lipona (an anagram of Naples).

Her closing years were sad indeed. Thought politically too dangerous to be allowed near other Bonapartes, once her children had grown up and left she had as her sole companion General Francesco Macdonald (who perhaps she married secretly). There were continual money problems, while both her sons, Achille and Lucien, got into a series of financial scrapes.

She died at Florence, like Napoleon and her father, of cancer of the stomach.

Macdonald had died nearly two years before, and her final lover was a young man called Charles Cavel, obviously on the make. Having failed to secure the contents of her will, he afterwards sold the family her letters for an alleged 60,000 francs.

BONAPARTE, Jerome, King of Westphalia (1784 – 1860)

Napoleon's wayward and improvident youngest brother.

Although born on Corsica, like the rest he grew up entirely in France and then chose to make his career with the navy. He was warm and affectionate by nature, had Italianate good looks and an abundance of energy. But at the same time he was spoiled, headstrong and impetuous to a fault. He also suffered from extreme consumption of the purse. As King of Westphalia his unnecessary debts were a continuous source of annoyance to his brother the Emperor, who despite his own generosity never did manage to keep up with them...

While on duty in the West Indies Jerome's ship was blockaded there by the English. He promptly left it (which was technically 'desertion') and travelled to the United States. At Baltimore he fell in love with and married a Miss Elizabeth Patterson; despite still being a minor. As a result Napoleon refused to admit Jerome's spouse into France. She went to Camberwell in London where she gave birth to a son, Jerome Napoleon, in 1805. Afterwards she returned to Baltimore; the recipient of a 60,000 francs a year pension from Napoleon.

Meanwhile, Jerome, back with the navy, now set out to regain Napoleon's trust. Posted once more to the West Indies, his squadron was separated from the remainder of the fleet by severe storms, but by the time of its return to France in August 1806, it had inflicted severe damage on the British merchantmen and Jerome was decorated with the Legion of Honour and promoted to rear-admiral. However, his subsequent career was always destined to be on land. In the Jena campaign of late 1806 he commanded a mixed division of West Germans and Bavarians and again pleased his brother by the capture of several Prussian towns. Following the Peace of Tilsit, therefore, the Emperor decided to make Jerome ruler of the new kingdom of Westphalia (Hesse-Cassel, the west of Prussia, Brunswick and the south of Hanover).

He also provided him with a new wife: the modest and delightful Princess Catherine of Württemberg. The Pope refused to sanction a divorce so Napoleon went ahead and annulled Jerome's previous marriage by Imperial decree.

In taking up his royal duties the King of Westphalia was instructed by his brother to give the Germans the immediate benefit of the *Code Civile*: 'Just laws and good administration will do more to consolidate your rule than the greatest victories'. The Emperor went on: 'I want your people to enjoy liberty, equality and above all prosperity!'

At least Jerome began well. With the help of two Frenchmen, Siméon and Beugnot, he applied himself energetically to the sweeping away of centuries of Teutonic feudalism. He provided free vaccination, gave social and political equality to the Jews, liberalised trade by drastically reducing customs tariffs and also gave some encouragement to the arts. (He employed as his librarian Jacob, one of the Brothers Grimm.)

Things started to go badly off course though, as the result of a total failure to control his natural extravagance. He spent almost as much on fancy clothes and uniforms as Murat, kept nearly a hundred carriages, scattered diamonds among his mistresses and paid his generals and ambassadors more than they could ever have earned in Paris. Not surprisingly he gained the nickname of 'the Merry Monarch'. His evenings were a continuous round of expensive parties, receptions and visits to the theatre, where the more lavish the production the better the king enjoyed it. Soon a report reached the Emperor that 'the scanty income of the kingdom...is being wasted on useless favourites, the pay of the troops has fallen into arrears and in this spring of 1809 a serious mutiny has just broken out.' It was no exaggeration. The finances of the kingdom simply could not keep pace with its ruler's pleasures.

In addition to local taxation, Jerome had an income of five million francs from France, three million from Prussia and two and a half million from Austria. Even so, he still failed to balance the budget and after putting down the revolt within the army he next faced disturbances from among the ratepayers of the towns. Angrily, Napoleon wrote to him: 'Your kingdom has no police, little organisation and its financial condition is appalling. It is not with idle display that the foundations of monarchy are laid. What has happened comes as no surprise. I hope it will teach you a lesson. Sell your fine furniture, all your horses. Adopt ways and habits better suited to the country you govern...'

He also failed during the Russian campaign of 1812 and as a result suffered the mortification of the Emperor placing him under the command of 'that mere marshal' the severe Davout.

In the following years, with the Empire contracting, he found himself thrown out of Westphalia, then thrown out of France and finally forced to settle with his wife and children in Switzerland, and later Trieste. However, he proved loyal to, as well as somewhat afraid of, his brother. He quickly rallied to Napoleon's cause during the Hundred Days and at Waterloo fought bravely even if he was unsuccessful in his attempt to storm the château of Hougoumont. The French defeat was then followed by another (longer) period of exile, first at Augsberg and later again in Trieste.

He returned to France eventually during Louis Philippe's reign. But his full rehabilitation and more settled honours came during the rule of his nephew Louis Napoleon. In 1848 he became Governor of Les Invalides, in 1850 a marshal of France and towards the end, under the Second Empire, President of the Senate.

BONAPARTE, Joseph, King of Naples and the Two Sicilies, King of Spain (1768 – 1844)

Napoleon's elder brother.

In modern terms I suppose one could call him a hobbled hack. He would be demolished on TV by many of our political commentators – and absolutely treasured by the leaders of our so-called democratic parties. He was loyal, hard-working, reasonably cultured and very good socially. He was also good with money, but without being overly corrupt: exactly what our political animals at the top will accept. (No great danger, and a suitable fall-guy if the going gets rough.)

Unfortunately for Joseph, in the Napoleonic era it wasn't quite that easy. He was, as the late Iain Macleod once described one of *his* parliamentary opponents, 'accident prone'. He was a useful administrator and in Naples did particularly well, (after the French army had gone in first to 'clean the house'). In Spain, where Wellington was in control, and the French marshals (unsupervised by Napoleon) quarrelled, alas! Joseph hadn't a hope . . .

Educated at Autun, he afterwards aligned himself with the French party, and against the Paolists on Corsica, and therefore had to flee the island. He settled at Marseille and in 1794 married Julie Clary, a daughter of one of the richest merchants in the city; also a sister to Napoleon's early love Désirée.

Joseph worked for France as a diplomat in various ways before becoming a member of the Council of Five Hundred in 1798. He proved a skilled negotiator and his first job for Napoleon as Consul was to conclude the treaty with Austria (the Congress of Lunéville) which followed the French victories at Marengo and Hohenlinden (1801). The next year he led the French team which negotiated the Peace of Amiens with Great Britain.

He was proclaimed King of Naples and the Two Sicilies on March 30, 1806: and inherited a mess. The country was bankrupt; the Bourbons had taken everything and done nothing. Joseph made many changes and within two years balanced the books. He also overhauled the legal code, abolished torture, endowed schools and hospitals and started a new network of roads. 'Justice demands that I should make the people as happy as the scourge of war will permit,' he said. In Naples itself he introduced the first street lighting.

In Spain he faced a hostile nation from the outset. He was proclaimed King (and of the Indies) in 1808. When he arrived in Madrid he was greeted by silent streets. Without the French army he had no power-base anywhere in the country, and how do you govern a nation when it is impossible to collect taxes? Eventually Napoleon was sending him a monthly subsidy of half a million francs and in 1811 the Emperor officially united Catalonia with France.

After Wellington's victory at Salamanca (July 2, 1812) Joseph quit the Spanish capital. He then gave battle to the Duke at Vittoria (June 21, 1813) was completely defeated and France's involvement in Spain was effectively over. Napoleon was furious with him and sent him to his country estate. 'His (Joseph's) behaviour has never ceased to bring misfortune upon my army; and it is time to make an end of it!' In fairness, Joseph had had no training as a soldier. Nor in controlling the frequently arrogant and sometimes corrupt marshals.

In 1814 Joseph was appointed Governor of Paris, but upon Marmont's surrender to the Allies he took a coach to Switzerland. His being chased had become a pattern for life.

Upon Napoleon's escape from Elba he returned to Paris and four days after Waterloo there came the fallen Emperor's request that he should urge the Chamber of Deputies to adopt a scheme of national resistance. But this was not to be. As his brother was being transported to St.-Helena, Joseph embarked for the United States, where he styled himself the Count of Survilliers. He also made a great deal of money there, largely through speculation. Later, he visited England and finally settled and died at Florence.

Napoleon wrote of him in his *Mémoires*: 'In discharge of the higher duties I conferred upon him, he did the best he could. His intentions were good and therefore the fault lay not with him but with me, who raised him above his proper station.'

BONAPARTE, Louis, King of Holland (1778 – 1846)

The brother Napoleon always felt most protective towards – although this did not mean that relations remained good between them.

Born at Ajaccio, his godparents were the Count of Marbeuf and Madame Boucheparu, wife of the Royal Commissioner on Corsica.

In 1791, when Napoleon returned to duty at Auxonne he took Louis with him. His lieutenant's pay was barely the equivalent of four pounds per month, but somehow they managed and the younger boy gained his education while they lived on bread, a few olives and watered-down wine. In 1795 Napoleon obtained a place for him in the military school at Châlons and wrote: 'I am very pleased with Louis; he fulfils my hopes; intelligence, warmth, good health, talent, good address, kindness – he possesses all these qualities.' The brothers were together again during the great Italian campaign of 1796. Louis performed with courage and loyalty, but around the time of the Treaty of Campo Formio he contracted the disease which was to leave him permanently morbid and neurotic. It was an acidic condition of the blood, which also affected his hands. He had to write with the pen strapped to his wrist and just the simple act of unlocking a door became extremely difficult.

The first signs of a rift between the brothers occurred when Louis, visiting his sister Caroline at Madame Campan's met and fell in love with Emilie de Beauharnais, Josephine's niece. This did not suit Napoleon's matrimonial plans at all. So Emilie was married to Lavalette and Louis engaged to Josephine's daughter Hortense: a match destined to be miserable for both parties, although it did result in the birth of the future Emperor Napoleon III (their third son).

Meanwhile the other Bonapartes, in their persistent intriguing against Josephine, did everything possible to forment trouble between the married couple, especially Caroline who on one occasion spitefully said that Hortense's eldest son – who died in 1807 – was not his.

From 1802-4 Louis gained promotion from colonel to general of division, despite his illness. He also became a member of the Council of State. However Napoleon now had far grander ambitions for him. In 1806 he created his brother King of the Dutch, with the clear instructions to 'protect their liberties, their laws, their religion, but never cease to be French!'

Modest and diffident, often rendered unsure of himself due to the nature of his illness, nevertheless Louis did not make a bad king. He overhauled Holland's criminal code, encouraged industry and the arts, balanced the annual budget and took care to be seen as often as possible by the ordinary people. He was soon referred to by the Dutch as 'good King Louis'.

On the other hand his relations with his brother the Emperor continued to deteriorate. He began to see himself as a dynastic figure rather than a mere vassal of France. A demand from Paris for the provinces of Zeeland and Brabant in exchange for the Hanseatic towns caused a major disagreement between the two countries. Napoleon accused Louis of becoming 'more Dutch than the Dutch and a dealer in cheese'; also of turning a blind eye to the importing of British goods and of failing to take sufficiently vigorous action against Britain's Walcheren expedition. Louis for his part had moved his capital from The Hague to Amstrdam and was considering proposals to give the Dutch a new nobility.

The year 1810 marked the brother's final separation. Napoleon had left French troops stationed at Walcheren and in Breda and Bergen, thus reducing Louis to little more than a French governor. The latter retaliated by abdicating in favour of his second son and then fleeing to Westphalia. 'My brothers injure me instead of aiding me', the Emperor complained to Caulaincourt. 'And now this from Louis, who I brought up on my pay as a lieutenant, God knows at the price of what sacrifices. I paid for his schooling. Do you know how I managed it? By never setting foot in a *café* or going into society; by eating dry bread and brushing my own clothes. I lived like a bear in a tiny room with books as my only friends!' On July 9, 1810 Holland was formally incorporated into the French Empire.

Louis never did become reconciled to the Emperor; not even during the Hundred Days when the rest of the Bonapartes at last realised that they must stand or fall with Napoleon. The latter offered Louis two million francs and ·estates in France by way of compensation but these were scornfully refused. Louis had separated from Hortense and managed to obtain custody of their elder remaining son. He brought him up mostly in Rome where the young man died during the insurrection of 1831. Otherwise he devoted himself to writing his *Mémoires*, as well as a novel: *Marie, ou les Hollandaises?*

He lived long enough to see his third son fail in his attempt to seize the crown of Louis Philippe by force; but not to witness his election to the presidency of France after the Revolution of 1848.

BONAPARTE, Lucien (1775 – 1840)

The brightest, most individual, and therefore independent, of Napoleon's brothers, which unfortunately led to periods of estrangement beween them: especially in the 'latter, if not quite the last, years of the Empire when Lucien's abilities were sorely missed.

Baptised Lucciano, he was also the best-looking of the Bonaparte sons, having inherited his mother's dark hair and lean features, instead of their father's baldness and tendency to put on weight.

He was educated at Autun and then Brienne in preparation, like Napoleon, for a military career. However, he suffered from defective eyesight and decided to throw this up and become a priest. Already, according to his later *Mémoires*, he was resenting Napoleon's 'heavy' elder brother attitude.

Nor was the seminary at Aix an answer to his restless temperament. He threw this up as well and in 1790 returned to Corsica where over the next few years he was an active Revolutionary. Meanwhile he wrote to Joseph Bonaparte: 'I have already discerned in our brother Napoleon an ambition not entirely egotistical, but which overcomes his desire for the public good. I am convinced that in a free state he would be a dangerous man. He seems to me to have a strong inclination towards tyranny...' Lucien was only seventeen when he wrote this.

Nevertheless, like Napoleon, he had decided that French rule for Corsica was preferable to Paoli and the English. It was, in fact, Lucien's Jacobinism and inflamatory speeches which contributed to the remainder of the Bonapartes having to flee Corsica and settle in the South of France, where Lucien became a government commissary and began to style himself 'Lucius Brutus'. Others, less charitable, referred to him as 'the little Robespierre'. He persuaded the inhabitants of St.-Maxim (between Toulon and Antibes) to change the name of their town to 'Marathon' and then married the beautiful daughter of the local innkeeper, Christine Boyer. This was in May 1794, when he was nineteen and still legally under-age. He overcame this problem by appropriating Napoleon's birth certificate: a move not designed to improve relations between the brothers!

However, Lucien was destined to be crucial at Napoleon's coming to power in France. In 1798, under the Directory and after many political ups and downs, he was elected member of the Council of Five Hundred for Corsica. He duly took his seat in Paris and became something of a social figure (but with the political interests of the Bonaparte family uppermost in his mind).

A temporary reconciliation with Napoleon meant that in 1799 he kept the latter in Egypt fully informed of the increasing failure of the Barras government. (His letters, it is said, were carried by a Greek called Bambouki.)

Lucien's next moves were very well-planned. He was elected President of the Council in October 1799 – and, against Barras, he plotted not only Napoleon's early return from the Middle Est but also his elevation to the leadership of the nation. He found an eager anti-Barras group in Sièyès, Talleyrand and others, and over the night of 18/19 Brumaire 1799, succeeded in dissolving the Council (with the help of Murat and a contingent of grenadiers). 'How dare you ask me to outlaw my own brother,' he barked at the hostile members. To the soldiers he said, 'I swear to plunge my sword into the heart of my brother, if he interferes with the liberties of France!'

It all worked; and so, more than anyone else (including Talleyrand), Lucien could be said to have stage-managed Napoleon's triumph. But after this nothing seemed to go right between them.

Appointed Minister of the Interior, Lucien immediately showed considerable administrative ability. But he wanted to run France's home affairs very much in his own way; leaving Napoleon to fight the wars and look after the army. Naturally, Napoleon being Napoleon, this was an impossibility. The younger brother was then accused of writing a pamphlet about Caesar, Cromwell and Bonaparte: a bitter attack on military government. (In reality he had merely helped out with its circulation.) Their clash of ideas resulted in his being posted as ambassador to Madrid: where he again incurred Napoleon's displeasure, allegedly for accepting a financial retainer from the Portugese.

However, their final parting (until the Hundred Days), occurred in 1803 following Napoleon's opposition to Lucien's second marriage – Christine having died in 1800. Lucien was back in France, a member of the Tribunate and helping to deal with awards of the newly-instituted Legion of Honour. Napoleon wanted him to marry into a European royal family friendly towards France; instead of which Lucien opted for another love match: to a Madame Jouberthon. After which he left for Rome and several years of anti-Napoleon activities within the Bonaparte family. (He urged both Joseph and Jerome to refuse their allocated kingdoms; and himself refused Napoleon's offer of Portugal, although he accepted the title of Prince of Canino from the Pope.)

In 1809 when Rome was incorporated into France's Empire, Lucien left with his wife and family for the United States, only to be captured on the way by the English. For the next five years he lived on a small estate in Worcestershire. Officially this was an imprisonment, but with only one officer to guard his movements and censor his letters.

Probably during this period he began to re-think his personal relations with his brother. Obviously there had been mistakes and miscalculations by both of them. As a result Lucien returned to Napoleon's side during the Hundred Days, was warmly welcomed by him and made a senator. He stood with the returned Emperor at the army review on the Champ de Mai and even after Waterloo urged him to dismiss the French Assembly and in effect stage another 18/19 Brumaire. However, his views did not prevail. Napoleon abdicated in favour of his son: 'sacrificing myself to the hatred of France's enemies'.

Lucien was refused permission to join him on St.-Helena. France was also denied him. He spent the remainder of his life in Italy, an able and intelligent man, yet again unemployed.

BONAPARTE, Maria Anna Eliza (1777 – 1820)

The eldest of Napoleon's three sisters; also the most intelligent. She was far from being pretty, but she made up for this in her brother's eyes by being loyal, fond of the arts and sharing something of his abilities as an administrator.

Due to the influence of the Count of Marbeuf she was enrolled at St.-Cyr as a 'royal pupil'. Such places were reserved for the children of impoverished aristocrats and included free food and clothing as well as a good education; plus a dowry of three thousand francs and a *trousseau* on leaving. While at the college Eliza received visits from Napoleon, his friend Bourrienne, Madame Permon and her brother the Abbé Demetrius. She should have stayed there until the age of twenty, but when she was fifteen Revolutionary events dictated otherwise. St.-Cyr was suppressed by the Convention and its pupils dispersed with only their linen and travelling expenses at the rate of one franc per mile.

Napoleon now took on the responsibility for his sister's safety. He lodged her, first of all, at the Hôtel des Patriotes Hollandais and introduced her to the delights of the Paris Opera. But this was September 1792 and when the mob broke into the prisons and massacred more than a thousand nobles, bourgeoisie and priests he decided it was time to leave for Ajaccio. Eliza's St.-Cyr accent and clothes were obviously a liability. At Marseille her feathered hat brought cries of 'Death to the aristocrats!' Napoleon flung the hat to the crowd, shouting 'We're no more aristocrats than you!' and the incident passed.

There were plans for Eliza to marry Admiral Truguet, Commander of the Mediterranean Squadron, but these fell through. (Probably because she was determined to make her own choice: Pasquale Bacciochi, a retired army officer who played the violin and accepted without protest her complete domination.)

With Napoleon's coming to power after the *coup* of 18/19 Brumaire the couple moved to Paris and Eliza was able to indulge her growing interest in the Arts. She became the friend of Chateaubriand, La Harpe, Arnault and especially Fontanes, on whose behalf she used her influence with Napoleon to obtain the presidency of the Corps Législatif.

But her real ambition was to play some useful role in public life and this was achieved when the Emperor gave her husband and herself the principality of Piombino and the republic of Lucca in northern Italy. Here, from 1805 onwards, she displayed great ability and strength of will. She conducted all foreign affairs herself, corresponding directly with Talleyrand; and she

51

inaugurated a most ambitious programme of public works. The marshes of Piombino were drained and colonised, while the hill country of Lucca was cleared of brigands and then turned to profit: in olive-growing and silk production. For the latter Eliza brought in experts from Genoa and Lyon. Meanwhile she developed the marble quarries at Carrara into one of the most successful trades of the Empire. Sculptors and architects from all over Europe came to either work or buy the marble, noted for its near-perfect whiteness and orders varied from busts of Napoleon (at 448 francs each) to a complete mosque for Tunis.

Nor were the other arts neglected. Eliza established a library and also a music centre where Paganini was a frequent visitor; likewise the famous harpist Rose de Blair.

The Emperor was so impressed that in 1808 he promoted his sister to be the Grand Duchess of all Tuscany and installed her at the Pitti Palace in Florence. Again her able administration brought many improvements to the area. (Although when she took to signing herself 'E' in imitation of the Emperor's 'N' this brought a sharp rebuke from Paris. She was reminded that she was still subject to the laws of the Empire and her blood-ties didn't entitle her to a royal signature.)

Eliza seems to have lived in considerable style at Florence, with an elaborate *étiquette* and many lavish dinner-parties. Her husband for his part developed an absolute mania for parades and changed his name to Felix (the happy). However, after 1812 it became clear that their hold of this large part of Italy was a precarious one. Eliza has been accused of plotting with both Fouché and Murat against the Emperor; but the evidence for this is more hearsay than factual. Undoubtedly she did try to remain at the head of affairs for Florence, only to be ejected after a bloodless *coup*. Murat, now an ally of Great Britain was pushing up from the south. Eliza and her husband and children fled to Genoa, then to Bologna where they were captured by the Austrians.

For a time she was imprisoned at Brünn and even upon release many cities were forbidden to her. She returned to Bologna and called herself the Countess of Campignano. Eventually though she settled for the Villa Vincentini near Trieste where she died of a fever the year before Napoleon himself. She had tried to join him on St.-Helena. Hearing of her death he forecast that he would be the next one of the family to go...

BONAPARTE, Pauline (1780 – 1825)

Napoleon's best-looking and favourite sister.

He criticised her love-affairs and her extravagance, but otherwise seems to have indulged her every whim. She was talkative, scatter-brained, she laughed a lot and was also something of an exhibitionist who enjoyed showing her beautifully-formed body to the ladies-in-waiting after her morning bath. Although loyal to her brother, and appreciative of him as a benefactor, like the rest of the Bonapartes she was jealous of and could be extremely mean towards Josephine.

She was considered the great beauty of the family while still in her early 'teens, with soft dark ringlets and a long but perfectly straight nose. Junot had hopes of marrying her and there was a passionate exchange of letters with Stanislas Fréron, the government's commissioner at Marseille where the Bonapartes had fled from Corsica. But Napoleon was determined for something better and in 1797, when she was not quite seventeen, a marriage was arranged between Pauline and the handsome General Victoire Emmanuel Leclerc who had fought so bravely beside Napoleon at Toulon. More importantly perhaps, he was the heir to a rich flour merchant. Meanwhile the Bonaparte brothers pooled their resources to make up a dowry of 40,000 francs.

The marriage ceremony took place at Mombello, near Milan and all augured well. However, their son Dermide would die in childhood, and Leclerc himself was to die in 1802: a victim of cholera near the end of the San Domingo expedition. Apparently Pauline nursed him through the final days with exemplary skill and attention. Afterwards she had the body embalmed, then placed in a cedarwood coffin, (having first cut off her hair and laid it beside him).

Leclerc's remains were buried with much ceremony in the Panthéon and his widow, overcoming her initial grief, now embarked upon a life of often scandalous pleasure in the capital. There were a number of quite open liaisons, including one with Lafon, an actor at the Théâtre Française. Consequently Napoleon was more than relieved when a marriage was arranged between Pauline and the immensely wealthy Prince Camillo Borghese (1775 – 1832). He duly gave his sister a dowry of half a million francs, but could not attend the wedding, being occupied by military preparations at Boulogne.

The marriage was not a success. Soon both partners went their separate ways, and in Pauline's case with an ever-increasing dissipation. This time though the scandals occurred either in Rome or at Guastella, the small principality the Emperor had bestowed on her in 1806.

Pauline returned to Paris after Napoleon's divorce from Josephine. But whereas her opposition to the latter had found its outlet in malicious gossip or occasionally sticking out her tongue towards the new Empress, Marie Louise, she displayed every possible rudeness. In the end Napoleon commanded her to stay at Neuilly, well away from the court.

However her genuine fondness for her brother led to a revival of the good feelings between them following his first abdication. Pauline placed all her money and diamonds at Napoleon's disposal as well as accompanying him to Elba, where she occupied the floor above at I Mulini. He appointed her 'Organiser of Theatrical Performances' and gave her an orchestra of twenty guardsmen to play for dances (with the proviso that she didn't spend more than a thousand francs on any single production).

After the escape from Elba and the subsequent French defeat at

Waterloo, Pauline returned to Rome with her mother, where the Pope affected some sort of reconciliation with Prince Borghese. But her health was deteriorating and in any case she was more interested in trying to join her brother on St.-Helena. By 1821, with the report from the Abbé Buonavita that the deposed Emperor was showing signs of failing health Lord Liverpool at last agreed to her pleadings. 'I should reproach myself for all eternity if I did not use every means in my power to soften his last hours and to prove my devotion to him,' she had witten. Unfortunately, just as permission was being granted, the news came through of Napoleon's death.

Pauline never fully recovered from the shock. Nor did she survive him by more than a few years, dying at Florence where Borghese had hoped to nurse her back to health.

BONAPARTE, Maria Letizia (1750 – 1836)

Mother of all the Bonapartes, the formidable 'Madame Mère'.

She loved Napoleon and was devoted to his interests, always accepting that he, rather than Joseph, headed the family. In turn she remained the second most important woman in his life: hence her jealousy of and opposition to Josephine. This aside however, by any standards she has to be judged a truly remarkable woman...

Born at Ajaccio, her father Giovanni Ramolino was an ex-army officer turned farmer and miller. However, he died when she was five, and two years later her mother Angela Maria Pietra Santa married Franz Fesch, a Swiss officer serving with the Genoese navy. This second marriage resulted in the birth of Joseph: the future Cardinal Fesch.

The Ramolinos were originally from Lombardy, descendants of the Counts of Collalto. In contrast, the Pietra Santas were of a much older Corsican stock, coming from a part of the island where the vendetta still flourished and blood relationships counted for everything. Lacking the benefits of formal education, they made up for it with their vigour, speed of judgement and resourcefulness in the face of hardship. They also had a darker side: one of passion and quick tempers. Letizia appears to have inherited all of these characteristics, but with the more passionate side subject to an iron will.

Her mother's domestic regime was almost Spartan. Nevertheless she allowed the girl to marry at fourteen (it was a love-match) to Carlo Buonaparte, a handsome lawyer who spoke fluent French and was an active member of the Paolists – or Corsican Independence Party. He owned a fine house along Ajaccio's Via Malerba, plus two of the best vineyards just to the south of the town.

The wedding ceremony took place on June 2, 1764 and Carlo's uncle the gouty Archdeacon Lucciano of Ajaccio officiated. Everyone present commented on Letizia's natural beauty. She was slender and very small – only five feet one – but she carried this with a dignity which made her seem taller. And the rest of her features were classic. A straight nose, delicate mouth and eyes of such dark brown they were almost black. She had a finely-shaped head of chestnut hair and a dazzlingly white complexion – rare in the south – with rose-tinged cheeks. Add to this portrait her long, white hands, but most of all her expression: serious, even severe, and devout (she attended Mass every day for the remainder of her life).

However, over the coming years she would need every last reserve of her will-power and devotion to combat the vicissitudes of fortune. With Carlo a key-figure in the Corsican struggles first against the Genoese and then against the French, Letizi seldom knew where she would lay her head next. Her first two children, a boy (also christened Napoleon or 'Napoleone') and a daughter, both died in infancy. Joseph, born in 1768, would survive. By the time she was carrying Napoleon though, in the spring of 1769, the French had returned in force. The self-styled General Paoli and his guerillas foolishly committed themselves to a set-piece battle and were completely defeated at Ponte Nuovo. Carlo and his family fled into the *maquis*: the dense aromatic scrubland of Corsica, and over the next few weeks Letizia slept in a cave on Monte Rotondo, the island's highest mountain. Eventually the French offered the remaining guerillas a truce – in return for an oath of allegiance – and they were allowed to go home.

Napoleon's birth on August 15 thus passed off smoothly; with Letizia experiencing her first labour-pains during High Mass and the baby being born immediately upon her return to Via Malerba, upon a downstairs sofa. He was christened the same day, after one of his uncles, recently deceased. Years later she recalled that at first he appeared sickly, so as well as breast-feeding him herself she engaged a sturdy peasant wet-nurse...

With Paoli gone to live in London, Carlo Buonaparte now decided to throw in his lot with the French and he became a close friend of the new Governor, General Marbeuf. This was particularly significant because it led to the boys in the family being educated in France. Meanwhile Carlo himself became one of the island's Twelve Nobles or chief functionaries. However, he was improvident with money and enjoyed drinking and gambling, consequently it took all of Letizia's ingenuity to keep the family fed and respectably dressed. In this task she proved herself patient and uncomplaining, and she continued to bear children: six of the eight after Napoleon surviving. 'Always,' he stressed later, 'my mother managed to keep the children happy. The family was her life.'

But the worst of Madame Mère's problems and hardship followed the death of her husband, at Montpellier, France, in 1785.

To begin with these were problems of finance, which being naturally thrifty she was able to cope with. (There were also peridic handouts from the Archdeacon Lucciano.) But in the Corsican rising of 1793 the Bonapartes, belonging to the French party, were suddenly in great danger. When she received a message that the Paolists were near, with characteristic courage she announced that she would defend her house to the death. Then equally characteristically she thought of her family and left for the hills; a wise decision since that same night their house was first looted and then all but destroyed.

At the time Letizia had with her her half-brother Fesch and her children Louis, Eliza, Pauline, Caroline and Jerome. Finally they escaped to Toulon before settling near Marseille, where as Corsican refugees they received a small pension from France's Revolutionary government. Having nothing left of their own they lived like paupers: half-starved and in the cheapest lodgings. Once again, though, Madame Mère coped.

By 13 Vendemiaire, 1795, her problems over money dramatically ended. Immediately after the celebrated 'whiff of grapeshot' incident in Paris, Napoleon became a man of means and some power. As he wrote triumphantly to Joseph: 'I have sent the family between 50,000 and 60,000 livres in silver, paper money and bills. Therefore, distress yourself no further...'

As First Consul he moved the whole family to Paris and installed his mother in a fine house. Under the Empire he settled an income of a million francs on her, together with a chamberlain (Count Cassé-Bruzac) and her own secretary. He also appointed her Protectrice Générale of all France's charitable institutions.

On the other hand, the old habits died hard. Madame Mère continued to use the Corsican dialect; and she preferred to save her money rather than spend it on clothes and jewels, believing that Napoleon's success was too good to last. Jealous of Josephine's hold over her son, she was openly critical of his wife's worldliness and extravagance; while her daughter Pauline came in for the same criticism.

She refused to attend the coronation ceremony of 1804 because of the Emperor's quarrels with the absent Lucien. When Napoleon accused her of loving Lucien more than the rest of the family, she replied: 'I am always fondest of the child who happens to be the most unfortunate.' She had earlier criticised him over the Duke of Enghien affair and in his treatment of the Pope. However, the Emperor got over her absence from the coronation in truly pragmatic fashion. He had Jacques Louis David paint her into the official picture of the ceremony!

Yet her small kindnesses to those genuinely in trouble continued unceasingly, and when Napoleon himself fell she placed her entire fortune at his disposal and followed him to Elba.

After the final outcome of Waterloo she retired to Rome and the protection of Pope Pius VII. Largely due to his efforts once the Treaty of Paris was ratified she was allowed an annuity of 200,000 francs.

She now lived an almost entirely secluded life, but was well looked after by Cardinal Fesch and others. She suffered a crippling fall in 1829 and later from blindness. Nevertheless when she died at eighty-six she had outlived Napoleon by a full fifteen years. According to Michelet she retained her beauty to the very end: 'Something sublime, tragical, but also mysterious, unfathomable'.

=3=

Wives, Other Loves, Mistresses and the King of Rome

JOSEPHINE, Marie Rose Tascher de la Pagerie, The Consul's Wife and First Empress (1763 – 1814)

The most alluring, the most glamorous creature I have ever seen. A woman in the full sense of the word – volatile, spirited, and with the kindest of hearts. She was the woman I loved above all.
– Napoleon

The more one researches and discovers about Josephine the less surprising it is that the young Bonaparte fell for her – and always afterwards continued to love her. Even writing from a distance of over a century and a half later, it is still possible to be dazzled and fascinated by her qualities. She was beautiful, but she also had beauty of character. She loved loyally and once in love she never allowed her feelings to be interfered with by politics. She was totally feminine: soft, warm, generous and although subject to jealousy completely without malice. (What she had to take from the other Bonapartes would have tested even St.-Thérèse of Lisieux; yet on no occasion did she respond in kind.) Her only real defect was extravagance, but again much of this went upon others – in particular the clothes, jewels, the gardens at Malmaison – or to please the man she eventually came to adore. Finally, and most important of all from Napoleon's point of view, she had the ability to calm him down, to smooth over difficult situations, to renew his friendships when all else had failed.

She was born Marie Rose Josephine Tascher de la Pagerie on June 23, 1763 on the French West Indian island of Martinique. Both her father, Joseph Gaspard Tascher, a plantation-owner, and her mother, Rose Claire Desvergers de Sanois, were of the Orléans *petite noblesse*. (Claims that Josephine was a Creole with some African blood, have no foundation whatsoever. On the other hand an old Negress of Martinique did forecast that one day she would be greater than a queen of France.) The eldest of three daughters, she was well-educated in a convent near Port Royal. She grew up to be worldly, intelligent, without being an intellectual, but above all with a natural elegance and charm to grace her good looks. Her nickname within the family was 'Geyette' although she herself preferred Rose, the name of her favourite flower.

Her first marriage to Alexandre de Beauharnais, was arranged by her aunt, Madame de Rénaudin. It took place in 1779 and was unhappy from the outset, even though it resulted in the births of two children, Eugène and Hortense. It also transported her from Martinique to the highest level of French society. De Beauharnais was both mean and unfaithful, but he was popular at court and Josephine was twice received by Marie Antoinette at the Trianon.

By the time of the Revolution the couple were legally separated, however both were thrown into prison. De Beauharnais was guillotined and Josephine herself only escaped execution by four days: due to the fall of Robespierre. While in prison it is said that she became involved in an affair with General Lazare Hoche (1768-97). If so then it must have been a friendship of kindred spirits. Anything more physical would have been impossible given the lack of privacy at the notorious Carmelites. On the other hand her imprisonment did result in Josephine's other important friendship with Thérèse Cabarrus, the future Madame Tallien. Under the Directory the two were destined to become the unofficial 'queens' of Paris society.

Both became in turn the mistress of Paul Barras and Josephine acted as the hostess at his dinner-parties. She was a less conventional beauty than Madame Tallien, but no less alluring. Tall and slender with wonderful breasts (which the light, filmy neo-Grecian dresses of the day showed off to perfection) she obviously moved with a good sense of her own body. Her silky chestnut hair was regularly washed (setting a new, novel fashion), cut into ringlets and usually piled upwards and tied with a ribbon.

For her other features I can't better the description by Constant, Napoleon's valet.

> Never did a woman better justify the saying that the eyes are the mirror of the soul. Hers, of a dark blue were nearly always half-closed by long, slightly arched eye-lids, fringed by the most beautiful lashes ever seen; and, when she looked thus, one felt oneself drawn to her by an irresistible power. The (Empress) would have found it difficult to impart severity to this bewitching look, but she could and did, when necessary, make it imposing. But what contributed more than all the rest to the charm of her person was the entrancing tone of her voice. With this, also her face, so expressive of feeling and goodness, and the angelic grace which characterised her whole personality, she was the most attractive woman in the world.

Constant doesn't mention her one physical blemish. Beneath the straight nose and behind the pretty mouth she had slightly irregular, but also somewhat discoloured teeth, despite regular brushing. (In fact, she was a fetishist about personal cleanliness and took as many baths as Napoleon did later.) However, she overcame the problem by developing a carefully tight-lipped smile.

Josephine had no great feeling for Barras. He pleased her; nothing more. And she enjoyed the social whirl of the otherwise corrupt and decaying Directory years. Nor did she have much depth of feeling for Napoleon at the beginning. He fell for her immediately. 'The torment, happiness, hope and soul of my life', was how he described her in an early letter. But for Josephine it was more a process of gradual crystallisation, as Stendhal would have put it. Apart from her children she had never truly loved before. And Napoleon, on first sight, was not exactly prepossessing: thin, gawky, spindleshanked and with his hair matted with powder. She confessed to finding his smile agreeable and that was all.

It would also explain why immediately after their marriage she appeared to be flattered by the attentions of young and good-looking men like Hippolyte Charles and the painter Gros. This understandably aroused Napoleon's own jealousy, but once she had fallen in love with her husband there can be little doubt that her feelings for him ran even deeper than his for her. She would put up with anything, including the taunts and vicious-ness of his relatives, to make him happy. Even, after the floods of tears, giving him a divorce...

Napoleon said that their first meeting came about due to his helping the young Eugène recover his dead father's sword. (All personal weapons were confiscated by order of the government on October 6, 1795.) Afterwards Josephine called to thank the general and he told his friends later that he found her 'seductive'. Several days later they met again at one of Paul Barras' dinner-parties; and then on a regular basis. Hortense de Beauhar-nais particularly recalled another Barras dinner in January, 1796 when she was seated between Napoleon and Josephine. 'In order to speak to her, he constantly thrust himself forward with such force that he tired me out and made me draw back. He spoke with fire and was solely preoccupied with my mother.' Meanwhile Barras himself – his lustful eyes now focussed on Madame Tallien – encouraged the affair, and later claimed to have made Napoleon Commander-in-Chief of the Army of Italy as a wedding present.

The marriage took place at a civil ceremony in a hotel along the Rue d'Antin on March 9, 1796. Present as witnesses were Tallien, Barras, Josephine's lawyer Calmelet, and eventually Napoleon's ADC Lemarois. Also, according to Anthony Burgess, 'there was a faint odour of scorched varnish from the wooden leg of the acting registrar asleep by the fire'. *(Napoleon Symphony)* The general arrived late. He strode in at ten o'clock, his head still buzzing with plans for the Italian campaign, pulled Josephine's ear, kicked the registrar's leg out of the fire and ordered: 'Begin!' Josephine was thirty-three, he was twenty-seven, but the certificate recorded both as being twenty-eight.

Two days later Napoleon set out for Italy and the battles which made him a hero. From there he wrote his wife the passionate love letters which Sainte-Beuve has said 'come near to being national epic'. Josephine joined him at Mombello, near Milan, in the summer of '97.

She became as popular with the troops as she was later to be with the French people, visiting dignitaries and heads of state. Conversely there were the other members of the Bonaparte family. Envy and spite always motivated their behaviour towards her, and never more so than following Napoleon's return from Egypt. Josephine, accompanied by Louis Bonaparte, had set out to meet him by the wrong route. Consequently he came home to an empty house and a deafening family chorus of his wife's alleged affair with the young army captain Hippolyte Charles. He locked the bedroom door against her. Eventually though, after much pleading and the intercession of Eugène and Hortense, a reconciliation was achieved. (To the absolute fury of the Bonaprtes!)

To begin with Josephine admitted to being both 'frightened' and 'in awe' of her husband. She now loved him with a devotion which nothing and no-one would ever shake. In Jacques Louis David's huge painting of the coronation ceremony of 1804, she looks both stunning *and* submissive: and at forty-one still remarkably youthful.

The divorce which the Bonaparte family had so longed for came about in 1809 only because the Empress had failed to produce an heir. But after the near-hysteria when the subject was first broached, she eventually submitted. And Napoleon, who found it equally painful, was even more generous than usual. She retained the rank of 'Empress-Queen'. Her annual income was the equivalent of £80,000 from public funds, plus £40,000 from Napoleon's own. And he gave her Malmaison.

She said: 'I make this sacrifice for France.' Nevertheless her signature on the divorce document shows that she was trembling.

Josephine continued to be his greatest supporter as well as a moderating influence upon his policies. He discussed affairs of state with her in an informal way that he never managed to achieve with Marie Louise.

Josephine retained her popularity with the French nation. And within the army. Veterans of the Imperial Guard, especially, grumbled that the Emperor's luck had deserted him after the divorce. At Malmaison she tended her roses, received friends and read the future of France in the fall of her playing cards.

Her health began to fail in 1814. Napoleon was on Elba, but William III of Prussia and the Tzar Alexander who visited her paid tribute to her beauty and sweetness. After her death on May 24, when Napoleon heard the news he called it 'the most awful grief' of that fatal year. And later, when during the Hundred Days he revisited Malmaison with Hortense, he said: 'Poor Josephine, she inspired me through that wonderful campaign of 1796. She had her failings, her extravagance... but she would never have abandoned me!' Embedded in this statement lies his everlasting condemnation of Marie Louise.

MARIE LOUISE, the second Empress (1791 – 1847)

Married to Napoleon by proxy at Vienna on March 12, 1810. The match was a hoped-for political solution to the longstanding warfare between France and Austria, but even more, it was intended to produce the heir which Napoleon so desperately desired.

She was the daughter of the Emperor Francis I. She was tall, fair, blue-eyed and agreeable in manner but without Josephine's vivacity.

Caroline Murat was sent to escort her into France, and the intended meeting place with Napoleon was Compiègne. However, wearing a new coat he'd had made by the fashionable tailor, Léger, he rode on to Soissons; where he entered the bride's carriage and she told him he was more handsome than the picture she'd received. The marriage was then consummated; with a religious ceremony following in Paris in April. The Duchess of Montebello, widow of Marshal Lannes became the principal lady-in-waiting to the new Empress, with the Countess of Luçay as first lady of the bedchamber.

Marie Louise never succeeded in acquiring the great popularity in France that Josephine enjoyed – although Napoleon announced that he was more than satisfied with his new bride.

In the light of subsequent developments it is unlikely that she came to love him in any other than the most superficial way. She respected him and her life in France was exemplary. On the first night of their honeymoon, having enjoyed their lovemaking she promptly invited the Emperor to do it again! She liked rich food (lobsters in cream sauce and chocolate cake), waltzing and she had some talent as a painter. On the other hand she had been brought up more strictly than Josephine, believed in ghosts and wouldn't go to bed unless there were a dozen candles burning in the room. Napoleon who liked to sleep in the dark, used to make love to her and afterwards go back to his own room.

The birth of the son-and-heir, the King of Rome, took place on March 20, 1811. It was evidently a difficult confinement and forceps had to be used. Napoleon told the gynaecologist Dubois to save the mother's life even if it meant sacrificing the child; an order Marie Louise always remembered with gratitude. Josephine, generous as ever, sent her congratulations and Napoleon, who had shed some tears after the birth, wrote her: 'My son is plump and healthy. He has my chest, my mouth, my eyes . . .'

Marie Louise accompanied the Emperor to Dresden the following year and shone socially there – although it was clear that she took no part in politics.

During the 1814 invasions of France she retired with the King of Rome to Blois and never saw the Emperor again. Back under the influence of her father (and Metternich) she ignored Napoleon's plea that she join him on Elba and made her way instead to Vienna: in the company of Count Adam Albrecht von Neipperg, an officer of whom she was growing increasingly enamoured.

Although granted the duchies of Parma, Piacenza and Guastalla she did not leave Austria again. She later went through a form of marriage with Neipperg and bore him four children.

Other Loves, Mistresses

When Napoleon was first commissioned as an officer with the artillery in 1785 he put on his best boots and went round to pay a courting-call on the two daughters of Madame Permon, Cécile and Laure (the future wife of Junot). Their mother was a Corsican;their father an army commissary. The new officer, aged sixteen, was feeling proud of himself. But was quickly deflated when they laughed at his gauche appearance in uniform. 'Clearly you're just a couple of schoolgirls,' he told them, visibly annoyed. 'And what about you?' they cried, 'You're just a puss-in-boots!'

After this incident, in taking up his military duties and with a mother and his younger brothers and sisters to support, there was little time and certainly no money to spend on further dalliances. However, while stationed with the city garrison at Valence he addressed four letters to one Caroline du Colombier – although he preferred to address her as 'Emma'. They were simply innocent love-letters and nothing more occurred between them.

He seems to have had his first physical experience with a woman in 1787 – on the evening of Thursday, November 22 to be exact. (The details come from his own notebook.) He doesn't name her but states she came from Nantes, had been deserted by one officer and was now the mistress of another away in London on business. Napoleon picked her up in the garden of the Palais-Royal. 'Her shyness gave me the courage to speak to her. Yes I spoke to her, though more than most people I hate prostitution and have always felt sullied just by a look from a woman like that. But her pale cheeks, the impression she gave of weakness and her soft voice at once overcame my doubts.'

Nothing new in his love-life is recorded until after the Siege of Toulon, by which time he was twenty-five and already a general of a brigade. This next affair did not involve any sex; on the contrary it was based on much tenderness, a regular exchange of letters and on at least one occasion a proposal of marriage. Bernardine Eugènie Désirée Clary (1777 – 1860) was the daughter of a Marseille textile millionaire, recently deceased. The young general fell for her brown curls and large, dark-brown eyes. They also shared an enjoyment in music. He penned a romantic novella for her and added: 'Remembrance and love from one who is yours for life'!

Meanwhile Joseph Bonaparte had courted and married her elder sister Julie; an event which prompted the mother to remark: 'One Bonaparte in the family is enough'. Not that this would have been sufficient to put an end to the affair. It was his posting back to Paris and there being dazzled by

Josephine which finally put an end to it. Napoleon did his best to let her down gently. 'Softest Eugènie,' he wrote, 'you are young. Your feelings are going to weaken, then falter; later you will find yourself changed. Such is the realm of time. I don't accept the promise of eternal love you give in your latest letter. Rather I substitute it for a promise of inviolable frankness. The day you love me no more, swear to tell me. I make the same promise.'

He wrote her only three more letters after this.

Désirée, as she was always addressed at home, continued to love him. And – because she couldn't have him – did everything in her power to go against and frustrate his own as well as France's best interests. She referred to Josephine as 'that old woman'. Meanwhile Napoleon's endeavours to arrange a marriage for her with General Duphot also came to grief when the young officer was killed in a riot at Rome (December 1797).

In 1798 she contracted to marry General Bernadotte – and probably influenced his decision not to help Napoleon through the events of 18/19 Brumaire. (This didn't prevent her asking the new First Consul to stand as godfather to her son. He agreed and gave the child the name Oscar: a reference to his admiration of the Celtic poet Ossian.) She seems not to have cared in any great depth for Bernadotte. But she was only too willing to conspire with him against Napoleon – who for his part, no doubt due to his lingering feelings of guilt, continued to show the most remarkable tolerance towards her activities. Of Bernadotte though he said later: 'He can thank his marriage for his marshal's baton, his principality of Pontecorvo and his crown. His treacheries under the Empire were overlooked on the same grounds...'

In 1810 when her husband became Crown Prince of Sweden, Désirée hated the country on sight. She very quickly returned to Paris, plotting this time with Talleyrand and Fouché – and again getting away with it. Until her death, at the age of eighty-three and in the house given to her by Napoleon, she was still treasuring his love-letters – and her grudge, even towards his memory.

That Josephine remained the overall love of Napoleon Bonaparte's life has never been contested by anyone since. Apart from his desiring her and enjoying her actual company, she undoubtedly possessed everything which suited him best in a woman. She was intensely, exceptionally feminine, and affectionate, and above all she never nagged at him or tried to interfere in affairs of the state. It is true that he had other affairs, but these were few and far between and only one lasted for any length of time. Moreover, apart from Marie Walewska he treated each of these affairs very lightly. Josephine could have spared herself the periodic worries. Napoleon was temperamentally incapable of becoming a daily philanderer like Paul Barras. The divorce, when it came, was for dynastic reasons, not because of another woman.

The first infidelity occurred in Egypt with Pauline Fourès, a pretty blonde from Carcassonne. She was the bored wife of an infantry officer and

Napoleon, although married, was still not absolutely sure of Josephine's love for him. The affair was short, pleasant and did not interfere with what the soldiers referred to as Napoleon's 'real mistress', the new *Institut* of Cairo. Josephine heard about Pauline from her son Eugène, who as ADC in Egypt was distressed at having to ride behind his stepfather's carriage. However with correct *sang-froid* Josephine refused to be perturbed by the affair. Her husband had been a lonely officer out on campaign, and back in France, although he organised an annuity for Pauline, never saw her again.The next two were actresses. First, the startling Marguerite Josephine Weimer (1787 – 1867), better known by her stage-name as 'Mademoiselle George'. This time Josephine did show some alarm, but Napoleon laughed it off. 'She's always afraid that I'll fall deeply in love and can't understand that its not like that with me. For what is love? Its just a passion that renounces the whole world in favour of one beloved object. Well, such exclusiveness isn't in my nature.' Mlle George claims the affair lasted for two years: which is doubtful. Born at Bayeux, she first appeared on the Paris stage in 1802 and, when Napoleon met her, was a tall, well-built girl 'with burning eyes'. Having been impressed by her performance as Clytemnestra in his private theatre at St.-Cloud, the First Consul sent his *valet-de-chambre* to arrange a rendezvous. She came, stayed the night, and then subsequently on several more occasions. Napoleon nicknamed her 'Georgina', invented for her a new type of garter, made of elastic because he found the buckled variety difficult to undo, and when the affair was ending – on the eve of the Ülm-Austerlitz campaign – he stuck a roll of 40,000 francs down between her breasts. She remained a confirmed Bonapartist and during the Hundred Days came to the returned Emperor's assistance by passing on a number of treason-filled documents from Fouché, which had accidentally fallen into her hands.

Giuseppina Grassini was an opera singer as well as an actress. She was no less than the prima donna at La Scala, Milan. First the voice drew him; then the body. But she wasn't prepared to play a supporting role, not even to an Empress. She agreed to sing in Paris and in double-quick time found herself another lover.

The affair which Josephine took most seriously was with Marie Antoinette Duchâtel. There were tears and recriminations, and Hortense and Eugène joined her in pleading with Napoleon to break it off. Marie Antoinette had been a lady-in-waiting to Josephine, another blonde – and with blue eyes said to be almost as beautiful as Josephine's own. In the end France's ruler consulted his wife on how most easily to terminate his relations with the girl.

The Murats, persistent troublemakers, introduced Napoleon to Eleonore Dénuelle de la Plaigne, a tall delicate brunette aged 18. She became pregnant by him, but then Napoleon went off on campaign and never resumed their affair. His liaison with Emilie Pellapra of Lyon was even shorter and troubled Josephine hardly at all.

MARIE WALEWSKA, (1789 – 1817)

After Josephine and his mother, Marie Walewska was the one other woman who loved Napoleon both generously and most sincerely. According to reports she was attractive without being pretty, but once having fallen for the Emperor she loved him with a deep passion and always remained loyal to him.

The daughter of a Polish nobleman who died when she was only five, (of wounds received at the Battle of Maciejowice against the Russians) she then had a lonely upbringing on the impoverished family estate at Kiernozia. She escaped this after a fashion by marrying Count Anastase Walewska, the regional governor; a man forty-nine years older.

On New Year's Day, 1807 Napoleon passed by Kiernozia on his way to Warsaw, the imagined liberator of Poland from the country's traditional oppressors and occupiers, the Russians and Prussians. Marie, wearing peasant costume, presented him with flowers – and the message, 'Welcome, Sire, a thousand times welcome to our land'. As they drove on Napoleon said to Duroc: 'That child was absolutely charming, exquisite'.

Later they met again at a ball and the romance between them developed – encouraged by Napoleon's many adherents and supporters in Poland. He by this time was 37: the fair-haired Marie just 20.

Talleyrand had said that Poland was not worth a single drop of French blood, but Napoleon promised Marie that her nation would be reborn. Back in Paris he wrote to her: 'The thought of you is always in my heart and your name often on my lips'.

A child was born of their relationship, Alexandre Florian Joseph Colonna, and in 1810 Marie brought the boy to Paris where Napoleon made a great fuss of him and insisted he be taken for daily walks in the fresh air: his recipe for good health. (Alexandre, who lived until 1868, was destined to become a naturalised Frenchman and a duke, but also he remained very active in Poland's struggles against Russia. Napoleon III employed him as a special envoy to Florence, Naples and London. He became a Frnch senator and briefly a minister, Number Two at the Foreign Affairs department.)

Marie visited the exiled Emperor on Elba although for political reasons she did not become his mistress again. Napoleon was delighted to see her and played a lot with Alexandre, but he didn't wish to compromise the hopes that his second Empress might be allowed to rejoin him on the island. Marie even tried to follow him to St.-Helena, but the Allies prevented this.

THE KING OF ROME, Napoleon Francis Joseph Charles, Duke of Reichstadt (1811 – 1832)

The Emperor's legitimate son and heir.

Today he seems an almost shadowy equivalent to the young Dauphin, son of Louis XVI, who disappeared during the Revolution. But to the more fanatical Bonapartists he was a focus for the restoration of the Empire and his death (of natural causes) at age 21 struck them a terrible blow.

The issue of Napoleon's second marriage to Marie Louise, he never really knew his father, although it did appear that in his young way he had inherited certain typically Leo-Napoleonic characteristics. It was hoped, of course, that he would become the second in a ruling dynasty; and at the birth itself there was national rejoicing. But in the years which followed the Emperor was embroiled in the struggles with Russia, then in the battles for Germany and France, after which he never saw the boy again, despite his efforts to do so. At the time of the first abdication Napoleon II (as he came to be referred to) was with his mother at Blois. From where, for political reasons, he was whisked away to Austria. There were various ploys to get him back to France during the Hundred Days, none of which stood much chance of succeeding, and after Waterloo and Napoleon's captivity on St.-Helena he was granted the title Duke of Reichstadt.

His first tutor, and a good one, Count Dietrichstein found him to be precocious and 'very interested in military affairs'. Everything French as he grew up was quite deliberately removed from his surroundings: nevertheless he continued to embarrass his tutors with a string of questions about his father. He asked one, Foresti, if it was true as the Austrians said that Napoleon had been 'a great criminal and a waster of human life'. 'It is not for us to judge him', the tutor replied. 'Continue to love him and to think well of him.'

He was indifferent to religion and disliked mathematics (at which Napoleon excelled). But he had the Emperor's firm mouth and chin and something of his penetrating glance. Also he was fiery and ambitious, with 'a lively imagination and a quenchless thirst for action'. Obviously he had not inherited the essential dullness of the later Hapsburgs. And, writes one of his biographers, 'he never lost a chance to show his independence of mind'.

Upon the news of his father's death, he wept. Then he began privately preparing himself as a future Emperor of the French. He had high hopes that after the Revolution of 1830 he would be called upon 'to take his rightful place as France's head of state'; and indeed this was what many Frenchmen were hoping too. However there was not the slightest chance of Metternich letting him out of Austria: a policy shared by the royal family in Vienna who were considerably alarmed by the young man's repeatedly referring to himself as a French prince.

Meanwhile the Duke devoted himself to the study and pursuit of military affairs, which in the end brought about his early death. He went in for exercise and tests of endurance far beyond the limits of his constitution. He suffered from catarrh, then a fever which turned to pneumonia: nearly always a terminal illness in those days.

Although he died in the castle at Schönbrunn his remains are now at Les Invalides, in the Church of the Dome near to his father's.

=4=
Top Brass: The Marshals and the Near-Marshals

I am impressed by nothing save success
– Napoleon

When Napoleon came to power as First Consul there were no Marshals of France. The rank had been abolished by the Revolution (when the existing marshals of aristocratic descent were guillotined).

During the years of his consulship this policy remained official (although without further executions!) It was only upon his becoming Emperor that the marshalate was revived. An empire required a new nobility, new titles, and who better to lead it than a group of his most distinguished senior officers. After all, despite the *coup* of 18/19 Brumaire Napoleon owed his own elevation to his feats of arms. It was only logical therefore to view the generals who had given France security in the face of repeated attacks from the rest of Europe as the most deserving in the land.

In all the Emperor created twenty-six marshals – of which only three were technically foreign-born: Ney (in Germany, where his father had served France under Louis XV), Masséna (at Nice, then separate from France) and Poniatowski (in Poland, although his descendants are now naturalised French). Of these twenty-six eighteen were promoted to coincide with France becoming the First Empire. Napoleon believed them all militarily up to the job, and was swift to express his dissatisfaction when they later made mistakes. Berthier, his longstanding Chief-of-Staff headed the list. A majority of the others had also served under him in Italy: Masséna and Augereau, Jean Lannes, Bessières and Murat, even Moncey (a former royalist). Ney was promoted from the northern armies and while he enjoyed a brilliant reputation one also assumes that this was done for political reasons: gaining the allegiance of a former friend of the Emperor's rival, General Moreau.

Four marshals were made up for their special services to France in the early days of the Revolution: Kellermann, Lefebvre, Pérignon and Sérurier:

but of these only Lefebvre continued in a fully active capacity.

Of the eight generals promoted to marshal after the 1804 list Macdonald and Poniatowski received their batons actually on campaign and Grouchy during the Hundred Days when several of the earlier marshals had gone over to the Bourbons. As time revealed, not all of those chosen felt permanent gratitude for the rank, titles and money Napoleon showered upon them. Sometimes they acted like bad children. But not one could be said to lack interest.

AUGEREAU, Pierre François Charles, Duke of Castigione (1757 – 1816)

Not one of Napoleon's favourite marshals, and he would repay his former leader with some very bitter words at the end. At least though he'd been promoted on apparent merit and on one occasion the Emperor admonished a person criticising him by saying, 'Ah, but remember what he did for us at Castiglione'

Born in Paris, the son of a fruit-seller in the Faubourg St.-Marceau and a chambermaid, he had little or no formal education. He grew up to be rough-mannered and personally brave, but also touchy and frequently involved in scrapes and duels. He became a professional soldier at age 17, although twice to begin with he bought himself out of the army. He wandered about the Levant selling watches, saw service with the Prussians against Austria and again with the Russians against the Turks.

Destined, it seemed, for the life of a footloose mercenary, we next come across him in 1786 as an instructor to the army of Naples and Sicily; then in Portugal where he'd eloped with a Greek girl. But on the outbreak of the Revolution he returned to France and became an officer with the volunteer troops. After showing some ability in La Vendée against the rebels (Les Chouans) he was promoted general of brigade and in the subsequent Spanish campaign general of division.

Following this he was transferred together with his men to the Italian front under Napoleon: where he made his real reputation. On November 24/25, 1895 he distinguished himself at Lonato. On April 10, 1796, after two days' forced marching he seized the passes at Montenotte to effect a vital junction with Mesnard and Joubert. (Which led to the surrender of an entire Austrian division.) Five days later he captured the strongpoint of Millesimo and then moved on to overrun the Piedmontese at Céva. Next he took Alba, Casale and at the Battle of Lodi (May 10, 1796) his turning movement did much to win the day. At Bologna he captured four hundred of the Pope's mercenaries as well as the papal legate and his staff.

But it was at Castiglione (August 3, 1796) against Würmser that his fighting spirit showed up best. In a day-long battle Masséna was in great danger of being surrounded. The other French generals were already considering retreat. Only Augereau carried on – and eventually carried the

68

French to victory. Later still, at Arcola, when the French were once more in trouble, Augereau was seen to grab a standard, hoist it above his head and dash at the enemy as if prepared to fight them on his own. Not surprisingly therefore, after the fall of Mantua Napoleon dispatched him to Paris with the sixty colours captured from the Austrians.

Around this time too he evidently developed certain political ambitions. He was the 'key' general in the *coup* of 18 Fructidor (September 4, 1797). As military commander in Paris he entered the hall of the Legislature, tore the *épaulettes* off Colonel Ramel and arrested General Pichegru and over a hundred other members. He had hoped to be created one of the new Directors. But Barras had duped him; all the places were filled, he said. Augereau shouted and threatened to no avail. He was posted to the Army of the Rhine and Moselle instead.

The later campaigns never quite recaptured the speed and intrepid displays of Italy. From 1805-7 he commanded 7th Corps. He won over Jellachich at Feldkirch and received high praise for his intervention at Jena on October 4, 1806. However, on February 6, 1807 – the day of the nearly disastrous Battle of Eylau – he had a fever and asked to be excused his command. Napoleon persuaded him to stay on: which he did, strapped to his horse and held upright by his *aides* – only to witness his corps nearly annihilated and to be badly wounded himself (an arm wound which he never really recovered from). After the battle he was vividly outspoken on the way it had been fought: resulting in his being excluded from court on all but the most important Imperial occasions.

His military performance in Spain was mediocre, similarly at Leipzig and in the subsequent battles for France he lost at St.-Georges (March 18,1814) and he abandoned his HQ at Lyon five days later. By now there was some suspicion of treachery, and in April he declared for the Bourbons. In a published proclamation he abused and insulted the Emperor for 'having sacrificed the welfare of France to his own insatiable ambition'. The returning Louis XVIII awarded him the Grand Cross of the Order of St.-Louis and appointed him military commander in Normandy.

During the Hundred Days Napoleon struck his name off the list of marshals and upon the Restoration he was again in trouble: his excuse of illness being considered no excuse for his refusing to join the court-martial of Michel Ney. For this he was disgraced and banished to his estate at La Houssaye (Seine et Marne).

Although foul-mouthed on the battlefield and in barracks, nevertheless he was a conscientious and firm general who would behave well when there were ladies present as well as being – perhaps more surprisingly – a good dancer.

BERNADOTTE, Jean Baptiste Jules, Prince of Pontecorvo (1763 – 1844)

The marshal who went on to become Charles XIV, King of Sweden and

Norway (from 1818) and founder of the present royal house of Sweden. Not a particularly distinguished soldier; but certainly a very political one.

Born at Pau (Pyrénées-Atlantiques), the son of Henri Bernadotte, an attorney and one Jeanne St.-Jean. The family name had been changed from de Poney in the 17th Century.

Bernadotte enlisted at seventeen in the Regiment de Brissac and his first tour of duty, oddly enough, was in Corsica. In 1788, having transferred to a regiment of marines and become a sergeant-major, he saved the life of his colonel when attacked by a Marseille mob and was promptly promoted to lieutenant. Even so, he remained at this time an ardent Republican himself and had the words 'Death to Tyrants' tattooed on his arm.

From 1792 to 1797 he served with the Army of the Rhine and that of the Sambre et Meuse, mostly under Kléber. He fought at Fleurus and afterwards was promoted general of division: a rank which, militarily speaking, should have been his limit. He then went to Italy, where he met Napoleon and fought with distinction at the passage of Tagliamento. Already ambitious to enter politics, he realised that Napoleon's was the genius he would always in future have to contend with – but the latter trusted him at this stage and after the Treaty of Campo Formio generously allowed him to take the remaining captured Austrian colours back to Paris.

On January 18, 1798 he was dispatched as France's ambassador to Vienna, his objective being to reassure the Austrian Emperor that in marching on Rome the French army had no designs on the Papal States. However, a week after his arrival the news came through that Switzerland had been invaded and Rome declared a Republic by Berthier. Puzzled and angry, the long-nosed, curly-haired Gascon had to witness an Austrian mob, overjoyed to be at war with France, invade the embassy and tear the Tricolour to shreds. He believed – justifiably – the Directory had again mismanaged events and quit Vienna the following morning.

On August 16, 1798 he married Désirée Clary, Napoleon's former sweetheart and now the sister-in-law of Joseph Bonaparte. The match was guaranteed, given Désirée's feelings, to alienate him from the future First Consul still further. He would take no part in the events of 18/19 Brumaire.

But first there was his brief, stormy period as Minister for War.

Paul Barras had hoped to find in him a military man rather than a political one. Instead of which he sent letters to all the generals urging their patriotism and loyalty to his office. He also instituted enquiries into the conduct of the various governors who had surrendered their Italian fortresses. And he began remodelling the divisions of the army under senior commanders thought to be his adherents. (Bonaparte, of course, was away in Egypt.) Barras showed considerable alarm – and on September 4, 1799 Bernadotte was removed from the ministry on the pretext that he was needed in the field. Instead of which he retired to the country and sulked. Although, when Napoleon landed back in the Republic at Fréjus, Bernadotte wrote to Barras that he ought to be proceeded against for having abandoned his army...

Under the Consulate he was appointed Councillor of State and Commander in Chief of the forces operating in La Vendée against the remaining Chouans (literally 'screech-owls', the royalist rebels). On June 6, 1800 he prevented the English landing at Quiberon. However, he endeavoured to turn the unrest in western France to his own advantage, probably as the first move in a conspiracy against Napoleon who, hearing of it, posted the intriguer away as ambassador to the United States. Bernadotte now skilfully delayed the equipping of the frigates to take him to America until the appointment was postponed indefinitely. In 1804 he was named as being party to the Moreau conspiracy: but again Napoleon spared him, it is believed on account of his last, lingering guilt-feelings over Désirée.

In fact he continued to promote the ungrateful general. In May, 1804 he was appointed Governor of Hanover, then a marshal and in February 1805 decorated with the Grand Eagle of the Legion of Honour. Finally (on June 5, 1806) Napoleon created him Prince of Pontecorvo and Grand Dignitary of the *Couronne de Fer* of Italy.

During the campaign of 1806, on October 14 Bernadotte kept his 1st Corps totally inactive between the twin-battlefields of Jena and Auerstadt. His subordinate generals expected him to be shot, and Napoleon signed an order for the Prince's court-martial but later cancelled it. 'I believe he has enough honour to recognise that he has performed a disgraceful action.'

But this would continue to be the pattern of his fighting under the Empire. To take part in and win minor actions, as at Nossentin in November, 1806 against Blücher – and at Lübeck the same month, where his men looted the city while the Prince (according to Marbot, then his ADC) put himself out to be agreeable to his Swedish prisoners: a calculated *politesse* which is said to have led to his being nominated as heir-apparent to the childless Charles XIII.

At Wagram in 1809 he again failed miserably – or deliberately. In command of 9th Corps of the Grand Army, after being driven back and also failing to pin the blame on his Saxon troops Napoleon – who as it happened had ridden over and witnessed his performance – decided enough was enough. 'Is this the kind of telling *manoeuvre* you boast will force the Archduke Charles to lay down his arms?' He fumed at him. 'I herewith remove you from the good corps which you have handled so persistently badly. Leave my presence now – and leave the Grand Army within twenty-four hours!'

Once more though Bernadotte was destined to fall on his feet. On April 21, 1810 the Swedish parliament adopted him as their new Crown Prince – provided he accepted the Protestant religion – and Napoleon, somewhat reluctantly, agreed to let him go: another major mistake.

Because from now on Bernadotte would throw in his lot with the Allies and in 1813 he led the Swedish army in the field against the nation of his birth. He continued to dither as a general but heavily outnumbered, he defeated Oudinot at Grossbeeren on August 23, and then defeated Ney at Dennewitz in September. He took a back-seat at Leipzig ('The Battle of the Nations') because of planning his invasion of Holstein, after which he compelled Napoleon's ally the King of Denmark to cede Norway to the Swedes (the Treaty of Kiel, January 14, 1814).

After Napoleon's first abdication he entertained some hopes of replacing him; until it was pointed out that the majority of Frenchmen considered he was nothing other than a traitor.

Having been crowned King of Sweden as Charles XIV he went on to make an excellent ruler: a moderate who improved the living standards of the Swedes and enjoyed their company rather more than he had that of the French.

BERTHIER, Louis Alexandre, Duke of Valangin, Prince of Neuchâtel, Prince of Wagram (1753 – 1815)

Napoleon's celebrated Chief of Staff; and named first in the promotions to marshal of 1804. His abilities as a fighting general were strictly limited (as revealed by the muddled way he commanded at the start of the 1809 campaign). But as an organiser, in his grasp of detail and above all by being able to interpret his master's military mind, he was unequalled within the Grand Army. Or within any army of the time. He stammered and bit his nails; he had an oversized head with frizzy hair; he was usually lovesick. And he was irreplaceable.

Nicknamed 'The Emperor's Wife' by the troops, he was in fact fifteen years older than Napoleon and had been born into an army family posted at Versailles. His father, an officer with the engineers, made sure he got a sound education, especially in mathematics which greatly contributed to his later success. He enlisted at fourteen (as an *ingenieur geographe*), then saw service with both the infantry and in the Prince of Lambesq's dragoons before going to America on Rochambeau's staff (1781). He returned with a colonelcy and the Order of St.-Louis. Various staff positions and a mission to Prussia occupied him until the outbreak of the Revolution when he was Chief of Staff with the National Guard at Versailles. As such Berthier assisted in the escape from there of the aunts of Louis XVI, but otherwise he espoused the Republican cause, serving under La Fayette, as Chief of Staff to General Luckner, and in the Argonne campaign under Dumouriez and Kellermann. In helping to put down the Vendéean revolt he again showed great administrative talents – until suspended during 'The Terror'.

Reinstated in 1795 with the rank of brigadier, he was next appointed Chief of Staff to the Army of the Alps and Italy and promoted general of division, in which capacity he first met Napoleon Bonaparte and formed a remarkable military partnership with him lasting all of eighteen years. Napoleon was quick to appreciate Berthier's knowledge, his mastery of logistics and, not least, the thoroughness of all his work. From now on his Chief of Staff would become a part of the living legend: serving throughout sixteen campaigns in Italy, Egypt, Central Europe, Prussia, Poland, Russia and France, rarely separated from his Commander in Chief for more than a few days at any one time. He received all of Napoleon's instructions and transmitted them to the different army commanders. He always accompanied the First Consul/ Emperor in his coach where they examined the order-books and reports on the troop movements. Berthier then noted down Napoleon's decisions, made out the fresh orders and at the next station they came to would dispatch them via his teams of couriers – or, if especially important, with a senior ADC. His drafting was precise, his handwriting clear. No marshal or general could claim the instructions he received were less than explicit...

After the brilliant Italian campaign of 1796 and the Peace of Campo Formio he was left in charge of the army, fell desperately in love with Giuseppina Visconti at Milan and then set about organising a Republic in Rome (1798). In Egypt his pining for Madame Visconti reached ridiculous proportions. He kept saying he would have to resign; also he designed a special tent, carried by three mules, which when erected housed her portrait and incense burners. Otherwise though he functioned as normal.

After the events of 18/19 Brumaire he was for a time Minister for War. But his talents were soon required again on the battlefield. The Austerlitz, Jena and Friedland campaigns were near-miracles of French organisation; and so, after a shaky start, was the Wagram campaign of 1809. Nobody could move troops and artillery about or order up supplies like Berthier. He then seemed to know exactly where every division had bivouacked and how long it would take the field-kitchens and wine-wagons to cater for their needs. Such speed and efficiency regularly gave the Grand Army an advantage of surprise over the more cumbersome movements of the enemy.

Nor did his work go unappreciated by the Emperor. By 1809 he was receiving over a million francs a year, was made a duke, a prince twice over and had been decorated by nearly every ruler in Europe. But Napoleon finally lost patience with his mooning over Madame Visconti; he arranged for Berthier to marry a niece of the King of Bavaria.

The Chief of Staff carried on through the Russian campaign of 1812 – although he was patently unhappy when the Emperor left the Grand Army at Smorgonie and he had to serve under Murat. He then poured all of his considerable abilities into the German campaign of 1813 and the subsequent battles for France. However, he admitted to feeling tired. 'I'm being killed by work,' he complained. 'An ordinary soldier is better off than I am. Yes; I have a big fine house in Paris – but when do I sleep there?' Upon the first abdication, in common with most of the marshals, he agreed to submit to the Bourbons.

Louis XVIII was delighted. He made Berthier Captain of the 5th Corps of Guards, a peer of the realm and a commander of the Order of St.-Louis.

Moreover, unlike Ney and Soult, the marshal did not go back on this particular oath of allegiance. Upon the escape from Elba he escorted King Louis to Ghent. He would not fight against Napoleon; nor did he return to him. Instead he went to Bamberg in Bavaria. The returned Emperor was genuinely distressed. 'Berthier's desertion has broken my heart! My old friend, my comrade in arms,' he said sadly.

On June 1, 1815, just as the Waterloo campaign was beginning to gather momentum, so Berthier's death occurred under the most mysterious circumstances. Savary in his *Mémoires* claims that the former Chief of Staff was involved in a plot to assassinate Napoleon: an unlikely story – especially since it is supported by the notoriously inaccurate, opium-ridden fantasies of Madame Junot. Others report that he was murdered by six masked men. The more acceptable theory – since Berthier was always an honourable man – is that upon the sight of Russian troops marching to invade France, he flung himself from the balcony of his hotel in a fit of remorse.

BESSIÈRES, Jean Baptiste, Duke of Istria (1768 – 1813)

The cautious cavalry commander whose advice the Emperor took at Borodino and which lost the French the advantages of victory there. Otherwise a brave soldier and one of Napoleon's truest friends.

Born at Prayssac (Lot), he served first as a private in the short-lived Constitutional Guard of Louis XVI (in 1792) and is said to have saved several members of the Royal household from the mob. He then joined the battalion of Jacobins St.-Dominique of the National Guard and took part as an NCO in the war with Spain. In 1796 he was posted to Italy and promoted to captain.

This brought him to Napoleon's personal attention. One day at Cremona his horse was killed under him. Undeterred he attacked an Austrian gun-crew with just his sabre. By the time help arrived he had captured the gun. Napoleon now chose him to command his newly formed company of Guides; in which capacity Bessières fought with distinction at Rivoli and La Favorita and had the honour of carrying the captured Austrian standards back to Paris.

A tall, slender figure who never cut off his cavalryman's *queue*, in Egypt he took part in the Siege of Acre and the Battle of Aboukir.

Following the *coup* of 18/19 Brumaire he was given command of the Horse Grenadiers of the Consular Guard, and for the remainder of his life he would always have special responsiblity for the cavalry of Napoleon's Guard. He charged in splendid fashion at Marengo (in 1800) and was promoted to brigadier. Two years later he became a general of division and in 1804 received his marshal's baton. Perhaps he owed this to the Emperor's friendship, but then so did Jean Lannes.

At Austerlitz he captured a large part of the Austrian and Russian artillery and again distinguished himself at Jena. He charged with the cavalry of the Guard at Eylau and later at Friedland. Napoleon rewarded him with the Grand Eagle of the Legion of Honour and annuities worth nearly 300,000 francs. He was also decorated with the Grand Cross of Saxony and the Golden Eagle of Württemberg.

Bessières was extremely popular with his men. At Wagram in 1809 he was hit and thought dead. Neither Nansouty nor Walther would charge without him. As he was borne from the battlefield on a litter his men were in tears. All vowed to avenge him. 'It was a finè shot, Bessières,' the Emperor remarked later. 'It made my Guard cry... but it also cost me twenty thousand prisoners which you would have taken!'

Before Wagram though, he had fought in Spain and done rather well; at least by comparison with several of his colleagues. He won convincingly over Cuesta and Blake at Medina del Rio Seco and this cleared the way for King Joseph's entry into Madrid. 'A wound received by Bessières at this moment would give the whole army lock-jaw,' Napoleon said in his praise. He won again at Guadalajara and assisted in the pursuit of Sir John Moore to La Coruña.

After the Wagram campaign he was given command of the Army of the North and successfully put paid to the British Walcheren expedition, retaking Flushing. Napoleon then posted him back to Spain as Governor of Castile and León. After his death the inhabitants of the towns under his administration offered up masses for him: a rare display of affection in view of how the French were generally regarded in Spain.

However, in Russia at Borodino his judgement was definitely at fault. After the sledgehammer blows by Davout, Ney and Murat had the battle won in the centre, eager to exploit their position, Ney begged Napoleon to commit the reserves. They could then overrun the Russians. Napoleon, ill and holding a box of throat pastilles, hesitated; he turned to Bessières. 'Will you risk your last reserves eight hundred miles from Paris?' the commander of the Imperial Guard replied. Unfortunately the Emperor acted on this advice and the larger part of the Russian army got away. It was the bloodiest victory of the Napoleonic era, with over thirty thousand French casualties, including forty generals.

In April, 1813 Bessières was again given command of the Guard. But on May 1, just before the battle of Lützen he was engaged in forcing a narrow defile near Poserna. He advanced into the line of fire from a laid cannon and the ball took off his hand before entering his chest. He died instantly.

Napoleon was deeply distressed by his passing. He arranged for the dead man to be buried at Les Invalides, while the King of Saxony raised a monument on the spot where he was killed.

BRUNE, Guillaume Marie Anne (1763 – 1815)

The one marshal Napoleon ought to have made more a friend of; a fact he realised when it was too late. Brune was a genuine revolutionary, then a convinced Bonapartist – despite a period of being under suspicion – and ultimately his beliefs cost him his life.

He was born at Brive-la-Gaillarde (in Corrèze), the son of a lawyer, and logically enough started out as clerk to the local *procureur*. His father was determined to give him the right education and consequently sent him to Paris to continue studying law. But the young man, bright and of imposing stature, had other ideas. He had Revolutionary ideas and he wanted to be a soldier. He began to write political journalism and became the friend of Danton. By 1789 he was a captain in the National Guard.

Promoted general of brigade (1793) he had a victory at Pacy-sur-Eure to his credit and also fought at Hondschoote. In 1796 he was sent to Italy and fought under Masséna at Arcola and Rivoli. Napoleon noticed his abilities here and promoted him general of division; confirmed by the Directory in 1797. (N. 'This general has received seven musketballs in his clothes, none of which wounded him: this is to enjoy good luck!') The following year he was given command of the French army on the Swiss border, putting down revolts in Berne and Fribourg. Next, he was summoned to the defence of Holland, where he smashed and put to flight an Anglo-Russian expeditionary force led by the incompetent Duke of York. His prompt action and realistic withdrawal terms led to 8000 French and Dutch troops being released from English prisons.

Brune was made a Councillor of State (in 1799) but rarely sat in this capacity. He was busy with the Army of the West putting down royalist revolts in La Vendée. Then he was sent by Napoleon to Dijon and then on to Italy for the Marengo campaign. He took over from Masséna and won actions at Monzembana, Mincio, Verona and Vicenza, which led to the armistice at Treviso in 1801. In nineteen days he had killed 10,000 Austrians and taken some 20,000 prisoners. In 1804 he was acting ambassador to Turkey when the news reached him that he had been raised to the new marshalate. By 1805 he was back in France and Napoleon invested him with the Grand Eagle of the Legion of Honour.

The 'trouble' between the Emperor and his marshal happened, for rather stupid reasons, during 1807. Brune had been created Governor-General of the Hanseatic cities and with orders to deal 'with that archfool, the King of Sweden'. In July he took Stralsund. Then, in talks with the Swedish army, he is alleged to have made reference to the 'French army' instead of 'the army of His Imperial Majesty'. This reached Napoleon's ears as gossip; together with other, completely unfounded, stories of Brune's general untrustworthiness. After this he remained unemployed, and did not, like his fellow-marshals, receive a dukedom.

In 1814 the returning Louis XVIII created him a chevalier of the Order of St.-Louis. But this and despite his poor treatment did not shake his belief in Napoleon being the best leader for France. During the Hundred Days he immediately rallied to the Emperor's side. Napoleon, realising his earlier mistake, embraced him warmly and appointed him commander of the Army of the Var as well as Governor of Provençe. He also made him a peer of the realm.

Brune defended the South vigorously against the invading Austrians and even after Waterloo still kept the Tricolour flying at Toulon. The infuriated Bourbons of the 'White Terror' ordered his arrest and probably planned his murder. A prisoner, he was dragged from his coach at Avignon by royalist extremists, shot at point-blank range, stabbed a hundred times and then flung into the Rhône, where his body was used for target practice.

DAVOUT, Louis Nicholas, Duke of Auerstädt, Prince of Eckmühl (1770 – 1823)

He has been described by several respected authors as the finest soldier Napoleon ever promoted. All the facts point to their being correct.

Behind a dour and cold exterior, and a brusque manner, he was completely loyal – even to the extent of defending Hamburg in the Emperor's name *after* Napoleon's first abdication was known to him. Moreover he was very gifted. If only Davout had been Chief of Staff at Waterloo instead of Soult the outcome might have been different again. Napoleon would have listened to him; taken his advice. Davout together with Ney could have made it into a French victory.

He had most of the frontline fighting abilities of Ney and Jean Lannes, and the same tactical skills, but with a better grasp of strategy than either. Also, he was brilliant at administrative work. He was bald and short-sighted, and, although of noble birth, seems to have lacked charm. But the mind was first-class, and he had the courage to go with it. To the Austrians, Prussians and the Russians he proved a deadly opponent. As things turned out though, Wellington never came up against him.

Born at Annoux (Yonne), he was the scion of a major in the royal army and has sometimes been called Davoust...

He attended the Military School at Auxerre, the Royal Military School in Paris and was then posted back to his father's regiment at Hesdin as a sous-lieutenant, (where he was almost immediately in hot water over his Revolutionary principles). At one point he spent a number of weeks under close confinement at Arras.

Once the Revolution broke out, though, his merits were soon in evidence. He served in Belgium under Dumouriez (and tried to have the latter arrested for lack of Revolutionary zeal!) Next he helped to overrun Luxembourg, was promoted general of brigade and in 1793 assisted Desaix brilliantly in forcing the passage of the Rhine. At that time he seems to have been earmarked for the Army of England, but Desaix brought him to Napoleon's attention who took him to Egypt instead. So impressive was his sense of detail during the battles at the Pyramids and Aboukir that the soon-to-be First Consul now made every effort to keep Davout attached to him. In 1800 he promoted him general of division and the following year even arranged his marriage, to the sister of General Leclerc.

In 1804, as well as being created Marshal of France and awarded the Grand Eagle of the Legion of Honour, he also became a colonel-general of the Imperial Guard: a sure sign that Napoleon trusted him implicitly.

At Austerlitz, in command of the right wing of the French Army he covered himself in glory. And on October 14, 1806 he won an even more amazing action at Auerstädt. While the Emperor was enjoying a numerical superiority at Jena, Davout with only 26,000 men suddenly found himself up against 60,000 Prussians under the Duke of Brunswick, despite which, and after a six hour battle, he gained the victory and Brunswick was killed. After this, and after Eylau, his 3rd Corps had the honour of leading the army into Berlin. Davout himself became Governor-General of the new Grand Duchy of Warsaw.

He was extremely fortunate not to be involved in the events and inter-marshal feuds of the Peninsular war. Instead he remained in Germany, based upon Hamburg. In 1809 he effectively won at Eckmühl and fought at Wagram where he survived having his horse shot from under him. Already created Duke of Auerstädt, Napoleon now named him Prince of Eckmühl. Although a firm (and sometimes severe) disciplinarian, in these years his corps gained the reputation for being the best run and equipped in the whole of the French army.

During the Russian campaign he fought with great courage and determination during the first part of the Battle of Borodino, despite his disagreement with Napoleon's conduct of the battle. This time he had two horses killed under him and was wounded himself; being carried from the field thought dead. But he recovered to fight again at the crossing of the Berezina.

Following the campaigns of 1813 and 1814 – and his not surrendering Hamburg until May 27, 1814 – the Bourbons banned him from visiting Paris. But he was back in the capital in 1815, as the returned Emperor's Minister for War. 'I can entrust Paris to no one but you,' the Emperor told him. Perhaps; but it kept Davout there when he could have been at Waterloo...

Following the second restoration the Bourbons exiled him to Louviers; also depriving him of his pay and titles. These were returned to him in 1817 – although he never again held a military position.

He doesn't appear to have worried that people thought him harsh and lacking in the social graces. In reply to the Duchess Augusta of Saxe-Coburg's complaint that his ADCs were as 'unamiable as the marshal himself' he would probably have replied that, like him, they were soldiers and had a job to do. On the other hand, he enjoyed a happy marriage and was untainted by corruption.

78

GOUVION SAINT-CYR, Laurent, Marquis (1764 – 1830)

One of the ablest of Napoleon's senior commanders; a gifted administrator, also sound in tactics and strategy. But at the same time a cold man: cold and selfish and generally unhelpful towards both his fellow officers and those serving under him. Marbot in his *Mémoires* recalls once finding him shut up in his tent playing his violin when he could have been visiting the wounded. He was known in the army as 'The Owl'.

Born at Toul (Meurthe et Moselle), he enlisted in 1792 in a volunteer battalion (1 Battalion of *Chasseurs Républicains*) and within two months was promoted captain. From then until 1797 he served with the Army of the Rhine, almost immediately demonstrating that he possessed considerable abilities as a soldier. Further promotions came quickly. By 1794 he was a general of division, confirmed by the Committee of Public Safety on September 2. At the Siege of Maintz and the subsequent storming of the *Merlin* redoubt he so impressed Kléber that the latter gave him command of four divisions. And for several weeks in 1793 he actually commanded the whole Army of the Rhine: when General Hoche lay dying (it was suspected, after being given poison).

He was then switched to the Italian front, replacing Masséna at Rome. In 1798 General Brune dismissed him for insubordination. For a time he was Governor of Genoa and after taking prompt action at Albaro (December 15) received a sabre-of-honour.

Back on the Rhine, he won the action at Biberach (May 9, 1800) but again became involved in quarrels with his superiors and doubts now arose regarding his character and reliability. However, since his immediate commander was Napoleon's arch-rival General Moreau the First Consul preferred to excuse Gouvion. He made him a councillor of state and gave him command of the (first) Franco-Spanish invasion of Portugal. Later he became French ambassador in Madrid.

With the change to Empire it was speculated that he might be included in Napoleon's first creation of marshals; but this was not to be. Instead he had to be content with Colonel-General of the Cuirassiers and a Grand Eagle of the Legion of Honour. (Although in 1808 Napoleon also made him a Count.) It is probable that soon after this France's leader too was having doubts about Gouvion's loyalty and application to the task...Doubts which were realised in the course of the Peninsular War (a graveyard for reputations among the high command). Placed at the head of 7th Corps – 30,000 men – and charged with the subjection of Catalonia, Gouvion at first enjoyed several successes. He took Rosas (December 5, 1808), relieved Barcelona a fortnight later and won at Molin de Rey (December 21) and Valls (February 25, 1809). But then, evidently peeved at being ordered to hand over the Siege of Gerona, he abandoned his positions before his successor could take over. Furious, Napoleon relieved him of his command.

He remained in disgrace until 1812 when the Emperor recalled him to lead the Bavarian Corps for the invasion of Russia. Yet again he quarrelled with his superior – Oudinot this time – but at Polotsk on August 18, with Oudinot wounded, Gouvion (who was wounded himself) took over and won the action. His handling of the 6th Corps against Wittgenstein's defences had been masterly and in effect secured the whole of the French left flank for the army's advance. At last he was given a marshal's baton.

In the final stages of the retreat from Moscow he was principal adviser to Prince Eugène who was in command of the Grand Army. In 1813 he commanded the French centre at the battle of Dresden and afterwards Napoleon entrusted him with the defences of that city. It proved difficult to hold against the again-advancing Allies. On November 11 Gouvion surrendered and was taken prisoner.

Returning to France in 1814, and still dedicated to his own self-centredness, he adhered to the Bourbon cause. In 1815 he was given the army formed at Orléans to check the Emperor's return. But the troops deserted him. Upon the second Restoration Louis XVIII appointed him Minister for War, then Minister of Marine and in 1817 he was created a marquis and received the Grand Cross of the Order of St.-Louis. As a minister he proved both energetic and efficient; setting in motion a total overhaul of the armed forces as the one way to block their reverting to an area of Bourbon privilege. Also to his credit he did his best to obtain a sentence of deportation on Marshal Ney instead of the eventual execution.

He spent the last ten years of his life at Hyères in the Var, tending his garden and composing the four volumes of his *Mémoires*.

GROUCHY, Emmanuel, Marquis (1766 – 1847)

The last of the twenty-six marshals to be created (in 1815) and the officer to whom most of the blame is still attached for the defeat at Waterloo. A number of Bonapartists have even accused him of treason, but this is unlikely. After all, he too suffered exile under the Restoration. And he was not allowed back in France until 1821. No; the truth seems to be that he was a brave soldier, and throughout the Empire an excellent cavalry commander, but after Ligny he failed to appreciate what was required from him in the areas of tactics and strategy.

Born in Paris, of a noble family, at age 13 he became a cadet at the School of Artillery in Strasbourg. He didn't enjoy being a gunnery-officer and in 1784 transferred to the cavalry. Two years later he joined the Scots Company of the Royal Guards.

Also by this time he was embracing Republican principles and continuously in trouble with his superior officers. Only the Revolution itself saved him from expulsion; but then he achieved rapid promotion (to general of division) – until the Decree of the Convention excluding nobles from future military employment. He had just beaten Charette and the Vendéeans outside Nantes when this occurred. Undeterred, he joined the National Guard as a private. 'If I am not allowed to lead a column against the enemy, no one can prevent me shedding my own blood in the cause of the People!'

He was reinstated upon the fall of Robespierre, served as Chief of Staff to Hoche in finally putting down the revolt in La Vendée and then took part in the ill-conceived expedition to Bantry Bay in Ireland (December 1796 – January 1797).

Few French officers can have seen service on so many fronts. In 1799, we discover he was in Italy and in the action at Novi sustained fourteen wounds – as well as being captured. In 1800 he then fought alongside Moreau, Ney and Richepanse through the decisive battle of Hohenlinden. After this – and despite having reservations about 18/19 Brumaire – he took part in every one of Napoleon's campaigns: serving loyally and with great courage in Austria, Prussia, Spain, Poland and eventually Russia. He manoeuvred his cavalry with particular brilliance at Eylau, where again he was wounded, at Friedland and also Wagram, following which he succeeded Marmont as Colonel-General of Chasseurs. The Emperor rewarded him with the Grand Cross of the Order of Bavaria, the Grand Eagle of the Legion of Honour and he became a member of the *Couronne de Fer*.

In Russia, at Borodino and while leading one of the four cavalry corps, he was wounded in the chest by a blast of grapeshot... but recovered in time to command the Emperor's bodyguard, the *Bataillon Sacré*, during the retreat from Moscow. Later, in the 1814 battles for France, he fought at Brienne, La Rothière, Vauchamps, Montmirail, Troyes, Braisne (receiving yet another wound) and Craonne, where he was shot through the thigh. Under the first Restoration he was stripped of all titles and honours.

Inevitably though with Grouchy one must finally focus upon the events of the Waterloo campaign. Created a marshal (on April 15) and a peer of France, the Emperor then entrusted him with the entire right-wing as the army moved forward into Belgium. He had good troops and a number of distinguished subordinate generals: Vandamme, Exelmans, Gérard, Pajol. Following Napoleon's near-rout of Blücher at Ligny (the Prussian commander had been rolled upon by his own horse and narrowly escaped capture), Grouchy was charged with the pursuit as the enemy fell back in an untidy mess on the village of Wavre. However, he vacillated and then botched it, halting most of his 30,000 troops around Wavre when he should have pressed on and mopped up the Prussian reserves.

On the fateful morning of June 18 only Thielmann's men were facing him across the river. Ziethen, Bülow and Pirch had regrouped and were beginning to move off in the direction of Mont St.-Jean. When the cannonade opened up to the west Grouchy was sitting in the pleasant green summerhouse of the Notary of Walhain St.-Paul, M. Hollert. He was topping off his breakfast with a dish of strawberries and cream. If at this vital stage he had roused himself, got some of his troops across the narrow river and struck north-eastwards the French would have cut the Prussian advance in two. Instead he did nothing. Soon Count Gérard rode up and urged him to march towards the sound of the Emperor's guns. At least they could provide him with a valuable strategic reserve. Grouchy calmly finished off his strawberries. His orders, he said, were to dislodge the Prussians from Wavre and then pursue them towards Brussels. So the French right-wing never did see action at Waterloo: a disaster.

In the two days following Napoleon's defeat Grouchy conducted a skilful but ultimately useless retreat upon Paris – before escaping to America. He was amnestied in 1821 and made a peer again in 1830. By this time he was a broken man. Reviled by the Royals and Bonapartists alike, his efforts to justify his conduct in the last parts of his five-volume *Mémoires* merely reminded everyone of what he might have achieved.

He died at St.-Etienne.

JOURDAN, Jean Baptiste, Count (1762 – 1833)

His principal task as a marshal under the Empire was the unenviable one of serving as military adviser to King Joseph Bonaparte during the Peninsular War. Other than this his appointments were comparatively minor and sometimes simply honorary. He had been a leading general under the Revolution and is best remembered today for his vital (France-saving) victories at Wattignies and Fleurus. Dark and saturnine, he was not an intimate of the Emperor's. Moreover, although an enthusiastic Republican to begin with, he proved quite adept at changing his political hats.

Born at Limoges (Haute Vienne), the son of a surgeon. He became a soldier in 1778, with the *Régiment d'Auxerrois*, and in the American War of Independence was present at the (unsuccessful) siege of Savannah. Back in France, upon the outbreak of the Revolution he became a captain of the National Guard and then earned swift promotion with the Army of the North, fighting at Jemappes, Neerwinden, Hondschoote (where he was wounded in the chest) and finally, as a full general, defeating Frederick, Prince of Saxe-Coburg at Wattignies (October, 1793) and even more soundly at Fleurus (June 26, 1794), driving the enemy back to the Rhine. Appointed commander of the New Army of the Sambre et Meuse, he next took Brussels and in July, Namur.

Under the Directory, as Deputy for Haute Vienne in the Council of Five Hundred, he opposed the events of 18/19 Brumaire. But he quickly saw which way the new wind was blowing, and escaped disgrace (and possible deportation) by changing sides and then served under Napoleon with mixed feelings of loyalty until 1814. Listed fourth on the creation of marshals in 1804, in the following year the Emperor decorated him with the Grand Eagle of the Legion of Honour.

Jourdan's unhappy involvement with Joseph Bonaparte started in 1806 when Napoleon appointed him Governor of Naples. However, Naples was quiet: an easy posting. Spain from 1808 onwards was an altogether different affair. Jourdan was Chief of Staff there as well as Governor of Madrid, and at one stage he had to take over 4th Corps from Lefebvre. His tactical plans and overall strategy for fighting the *guerillas* and Sir Arthur Wellesley were invariably brought to nought because King Joseph wouldn't or couldn't control the other marshals, especially Soult, Victor and later Marmont. Victor and Jourdan suffered a bloody repulse at Sir Wellesley's hands near Talavera in 1809, but Jourdan redressed the balance somewhat by winning at Almonacid a month later.

The war in Spain dragged on, it seemed, interminably. But it swung finally and decisively in the newly-created Duke of Wellington's favour after his defeat of Marmont at Salamanca on July 22, 1812 – and was concluded by his rout of King Joseph and Jourdan at Vittoria the following June. Jourdan had argued against this battle. If they waited a few days, he urged, and chose a different place, then their 20,000 troops would be augmented by the 30,000 under Clausel and Foy. But on the day King Joseph, the worst kind of military amateur, pushed his ill-luck. Afterwards, as they rode away from the scene of Wellington's triumph, Jourdan remarked with some bitterness: 'Well Sire, you've had the battle you wanted...and it seems to have been a defeat...'

At Vittoria Joseph lost his kingdom, his last shreds of reputation, 8000 Frenchmen and a silver chamber-pot. However, he was still the Emperor's brother. Jourdan lost something far worse personally: Napoleon's further trust, no matter who was to blame.

After the first abdication he immediately threw in his lot with the restored Bourbons and became a chevalier of the Order of St.-Louis; also Governor of the 15th Military Division. Then, surprisingly, he adhered to Napoleon during the Hundred Days: to be appointed Governor of Besançon and France's eastern borders. Amazingly, after Waterloo, the Bourbons forgave him. He became President of the Council of War which failed to court-martial Marshal Ney and in 1830 Governor of Les Invalides.

KELLERMANN, père, François Etienne Christophe, Duke of Valmy (1735 – 1820)

He had fought his way in to France's history books long before the rise of Napoleon. The oldest of the first creation of marshals under the Empire, he was commissioned in 1754 and distinguished himself in the Seven Years War (in the reign of Louis XV). It was said of his promotion to marshal that it was because of his past, but one must avoid being too simplistic here. Until 1814 (when he sided with the Bourbons) the Emperor continued to seek his advice on matters of the army's well-being and administration. And he regularly employed him in defensive areas. As late as the battles for France of 1813 Kellermann was still commanding the Corps of Observation of the Rhine.

Kellermann was born at Strasbourg. As a fully-fledged general officer (trained in France and Poland) he was to prove of vital importance to the Revolutionary government, and never more so than at Valmy in September, 1792. The Duke of Brunswick and his force ('splendid in their uniforms and old-fashioned beliefs', according to Goethe) had boasted they would overrun 'this unkempt rabble of France' who waited for them on Valmy ridge, near the windmill. Following which they would 'stroll on' to Paris. How different it turned out to be! To everyone's surprise, except Kellermann's, the French withstood the five-hour cannonade and then put the enemy to flight. Dumouriez was the nominal commander, but as the government realised, Kellermann's tenacity, tactics and leadership had brought about the victory: and in effect, saved France.

However this didn't prevent him being relieved of his command in November, 1792, 'Insufficient Revolutionary spirit' being given as the reason. A week later, back in favour, he was given the Army of the Alps. In mid-1793, after clearing the enemy from Lyon and Savoie he was dismissed again, and this time imprisoned. Such were the fortunes of war – and of the chaos. But under the Directory he commanded in the Alps and along the Italian border from 1795-97.

Later in Paris Napoleon appointed him President of the Senate. Promoted marshal in 1804, the following year he was awarded the Grand Cross of the Legion of Honour and in 1808 made a duke (after the most famous of his battles).

However – and unlike his son who performed with such spirit in Italy and at Waterloo – he never became a true Bonapartist. He accepted the idea of Empire, he gave his professional advice and he fulfilled his regional commands, but he was not one of the enchanted. (This explains his opting for the returned Bourbons: who then honoured him in every way they could, including making him a peer.)

In this last capacity – to his discredit (whether under pressure or not) he was one of the five marshals who voted for the death of Marshal Ney. Of Marmont and Victor what could one expect? Of Pérignon, Sérurier and Kellermann there were better things to be expected.

LANNES, Jean, Duke of Montebello (1769 – 1809)

Jean Lannes was – with Michel Ney – one of the two fiercest frontline fighting marshals to serve with the Grand Army. He also possessed great tactical skills, an extraordinary logistical foresight and the ability to improvise with speed and imagination in a difficult situation. Above all, he had the courage and determination of an Achilles; but tempered by magnanimity, warmth and a sort of rough but genuine compassion. Although a firm patriot, his personal loyalty to the Emperor came before everything else. They had been boon companions in Italy – as well as, coincidentally, being born in the same year. At one point Lannes even dreamed of marrying Caroline Bonaparte – only to witness her affections go in the direction of Murat.

Napoleon loved him. He was the first of the Grand Army's marshals to die in battle – a disaster in itself – and the Emperor had never previously shown so much distress, not even over Caffarelli.

Born at Lectoure (Gers) under the sign of Aries, he grew up to be handsome and energetic, blond with large, round blue eyes. He was of extremely humble birth (the son of a groom) and had been apprenticed to a dyer before serving as a volunteer with the Revolutionary armies. Within a year he was a major, saw many actions along Les Pyrénées and survived one at Banyuls when a musket-ball passed clean through his arm.

But it was after his transfer to Italy that the name of Lannes came to be associated with such an intrepid, absolutely fearless officer. Even his new-found friend General Bonaparte was amazed at the number of his successful interventions: at Loano, Millesimo, Dego, the first Frenchman over the bridge across the River Po at Plasencia, Lodi, Pavia and San Giorgio. Napoleon promoted him general of brigade. He took two colours at Bassano and a musket-ball at Governolo; then three more musket wounds at Arcola. In the evenings he drank with Napoleon, talked politics or army affairs, and addressed his commander as 'thou' instead of 'you': a rare familiarity he would be allowed to do still under the Empire.

He distinguished himself throughout the Middle Eastern expedition (Napoleon had taken him from the intended Army of England). Having stormed Alexandria and captured Rosetta, he next stormed Jaffa and was shot in the neck during the siege at Acre. Napoleon promoted him general of division; after which he suffered a leg-wound at Aboukir.

One of the officers chosen to return to France with Napoleon in 1799, he played a decisive role in the events of 18/19 Brumaire. As commander at HQ inside the Tuileries and also *commandant extraordinaire* of the 9th and 10th Military Divisions, he virtually ensured that his blood-brother and mentor didn't have to keep looking over his shoulder when he made his bid for power.

Napoleon being Napoleon, naturally such loyalty brought its rewards. Lannes was appointed Inspector-General of the Consular Guard, given the first of several large pensions and entrusted with the Army of the Reserve in Italy. But he continued to repay his master with interest in victories and feats of arms. In 1800 he forced the Great St.-Bernard Pass, won the battle of his future dukedom at Montebello and at Marengo withstood the Austrian attack for seven hours – for which the First Consul awarded him a sabre-of-honour.

In 1802 Napoleon also tried him out as a diplomat: on a mission to Portugal to try to gain for French shippers special rights in using the port of Lisbon. However, on this occasion he failed. Never a courtier, he strikes one as being an equally unlikely ambassador.

In any case his abilities were soon to be required again in more familiar surroundings. First, though, there were to be more rewards: as the tenth marshal named in the creation of 1804; recipient of the Grand Cross of Portugal (despite his rebuff there) and Grand Eagle of the Legion of Honour in 1805; and made a commander of the Iron Crown of Italy in 1806.

From 1805 until his death the Lannes story is one of uninterrupted gains, militarily. All I can do here is list them and marvel. He shared in the capture of Ülm and the surrender of General Mack with his army. He then commanded the French left at Austerlitz. Before the battle the Emperor had said; 'I've got them! They won't escape me now...' Lannes' corps, stationed on a rocky prominence with Murat's cavalry, formed the strategic reserve, until, upon Napoleon's order, they swept down and cut the enemy's battle-line in two. No wonder the Tzar left the field weeping!

Next he defeated Louis Ferdinand of Prussia at Saalfeld and maintained the Emperor's centre at Jena. He helped seize Danzig, clinched the Battle of Heilsberg and steadied the French centre again while Ney won the battle at Friedland. Napoleon made him a duke, ribbed him over his snappy dressing, put up with his store of barrack-room jokes and took him off to fight in the Peninsular War.

Lannes defeated Castaños at Tudela, immediately afterwards was thrown off his horse into a ravine – when Chief-Surgeon Larrey had him sewn up in a fresh sheepskin – and finally, in devastating fashion, finished off the siege at Zaragosa: after which the city-walls resembled those of Jericho.

Still no rest though. Napoleon now needed him for the Aspern-Essling-Wagram campaign. At Abensberg (April 20, 1809) he flung in a typically Lannes-style attack, took Landshut a day later, helped Davout win at Eckmühl – and then stormed Ratisbon, as at Zaragosa, like an architect of the modern *blitzkrieg*. The end occured with casual suddenness. At Essling, in command of 2nd Corps, he had held out all day and was resting in the early evening when a stray shell came over and struck him on the knees. With one leg amputated, infection set in and he died on the way to Vienna. The body was taken back to France, and the Emperor in his grief assembled no less than one hundred thousand men to form the *cortège* before the burial of Lannes' remains in the Panthéon.

LEFEBVRE, François Joseph, Duke of Danzig (1755 – 1820)

A tough-as-old-boots veteran of the Revolutionary wars, who went on to serve Napoleon remarkably well.

Gruff, outspoken, essentially a straightforward soldier without the intellectual capability to master an overall front or campaign, nevertheless at corps level and anything less he was a truly formidable fighting general. He had the qualities of being brave, loyal and not forever trying to reinterpret orders. In view of the number of actions he took part in his dukedom under the Empire was even more deserved than his baton. As he pointed out while cutting down to size some young whippersnapper who had referred to his big house and many possessions: 'Go and stand in the garden. I'll take sixty shots at you. Far fewer than have narrowly missed me in battle. If you live through those sixty shots you can have everything I own!'

Born at Rouffach in Alsace, in 1755, he enlisted in the *Gardes Françaises* and in 1782 held the rank of sergeant. In 1789 he rescued several of his officers from the mob; was promoted lieutenant and then, appointed to the National Guard, wounded while protecting the Royal Family on its return to the Tuileries from St.-Cloud. During the Revolutionary wars he was transferred to the Army of the Centre (Moselle), promoted captain and on December 2, 1897 to general of brigade. From now on he took part in nearly all of the actions in the North: at Fleurus, Bracquignies (where he turned a near-defeat into victory), along the Rhine, at Stokach and for several months in 1797 he commanded the famous Army of the Sambre et Meuse when Hoche had been wounded.

However, at Pfallendorf on March 21, 1799 he collected a musket-ball in the arm, was invalided back to Paris, appointed commander of the 17th Military District (virtually the military governor of the capital) and so was ideally placed to assist Napoleon during the events of 18/19 Brumaire. Napoleon presented Lefebvre with the sword he had carried at the Battle of the Pyramids. The big man grunted his appreciation. 'I'm ready to throw those buggers of lawyers into the river,' he said.

Under the Consulate he became President of the Senate; then in 1804 one of the four honorary marshals of the new Empire. Unlike the other three though he was eager to go on fighting, and in fact remained on active service up until 1814. Decorated with the Legion of Honour in 1805, he took command of 5th Corps of the Grand Army in September 1806 and the infantry of the Imperial Guard a month later. He fought at Jena, and then – in command of 10th Corps plus a necessary complement of sappers and engineers – laid siege to Danzig. After four months the city surrendered on January 23, 1807. Napoleon was so delighted he created Lefebvre the first of his Imperial dukes.

For years the ex-sergeant had been married to Catherine Hubscher, once a laundress and now known to the court as 'Madame Sans Gêne' (rough and ready). Upon their next visit to the Tuileries she went loaded with every jewel she possessed, *and* flowers *and* furs. 'I want the lot on!' she said. The chamberlain Beaumont indicated that he thought this unduly ostentatious. But he then forgot to add the title 'Duchesse' to that of 'Maréchale' and Napoleon reprimanded him for it. 'There's one in the eye for you, my boy,' she smirked.

Lefebvre did reasonably well in Spain as commander of 4th Corps. He beat the Marquis de la Romaña at Durango (1808), took Santander and won the action against Blake at Guenes in the same year. Then in the Austrian campaign of 1809, in command of a Bavarian corps he won at Arnhofen and assisted Davout at Eckmühl. Switched to the Army of the Tirol he defeated General Jellachich and captured Innsbruck.

He again distinguished himself in Russia commanding the infantry of the Guard. He was at Borodino and also actively engaged in trying to sort order out of chaos at the crossing of the Berezina. But when his only son Marie Xavier was killed at Vilna some of the fight went out of the old campaigner. With a frozen white beard and baton in hand he harangued the Guard: 'Look at the Old guard that was once the terror of Europe. See what condition it is in. Not one of you will ever see France again!' Murat gave him permission to return to Paris ahead of the remnants.

Even so, he recovered sufficiently to take part in the battles for France. He fought at Champaubert and Montmirail, and again with great distinction at Montereau where he led the seizure of the all-important bridge. According to Captain Coignet who served under him, the marshal 'fought so hard he was foaming at the mouth. And we swept everything before us!'

At Fontainebleau he joined the group of marshals who were urging Napoleon to abdicate and under the restored Bourbons was created a peer of the realm. But during the Hundred Days he pledged his support for the returned Emperor although he was too tired to fight. As a result, after Waterloo he wasn't allowed to resume his seat as a peer until 1819.

MACDONALD, Jacques Étienne Joseph Alexandre, Duke of Taranto (1765 – 1840)

MacDonald was, with Poniatowski, one of the only two marshals to receive his baton while actually on the battlefield. This happened after he had settled the outcome at Wagram in 1809, when the Emperor – who previously had distrusted him – grasped his hand and said: 'Come, in the future we must be friends!'

He was an able officer and a good corps commander who always fought with bravery and loyalty. But he needed to be under the orders of a first-class strategist, as his defeats at Katzbach in 1813 and later in the battles for France clearly showed. With Napoleon's eye directly upon him his abilities bordered on the magnificent; and he was also noted for his honesty and directness.

Born at Sedan (Ardennes), he was the son of one Neil MacEachain of the Macdonalds. Apparently at the time of the Jacobite rising in 1745 his father was a schoolmaster on South Uist in the Hebrides who, while not in fact fighting for Bonnie Prince Charlie, befriended him and helped him escape after the disaster at Culloden. It is also claimed he was a cousin of Flora Macdonald's; he certainly published some verses about her.

The younger Macdonald (his mother was a Frenchwoman) encountered no difficulty in entering the Bourbon's service. The traditions of the Auld Alliance were still strong and he was accepted in to the *Legion Irlandaise* in 1784. In the following year he was seconded to the Dutch Army, but by the outbreak of the Revolution, he had returned to France and held the rank of *sous-lieutenant.* A keen Republican he underwent his baptism of fire at Jemappes in November 1792 where he was ADC to General Dumouriez, and afterwards he was looked on favourably by the government in Paris for refusing to desert with Dumouriez to the Allies. Carnot promoted him lieutenant-colonel immediately and in August, 1793 general of brigade.

At the battle of Tourcoing in Holland under General Pichegru he played a significant role in dividing (and then defeating) the disorganised Prince of Saxe-Coburg from the incompetent Duke of York. In November 1794 Carnot promoted him to general of division.

He next had a somewhat chequered period in Italy (the results of which formed Napoleon's initial prejudice against him). In 1798 as Governor of the Papal States he fell out with his military commander General Vachier (Championnet) and then, after defeating the King of Naples at Atricoli he was himself caught and defeated on the Trebbia.

Still worse was to come. Through 1801 and 1802 he served Napoleon as Minister Plenipotentiary to Denmark. But in 1804 he was publicly disgraced for seeking support for General Moreau against the government's corruption charges. (Macdonald sincerely believed Moreau to be innocent.) Napoleon would not employ him again until 1807 when officers were badly needed for the Neapolitan service. In 1809, in command of the right-wing in Italy under the Viceroy, Prince Eugène, he crossed the Isonzo to take Laibach. Later he was wounded at Piare (May 8).

However, it was to be at Wagram in July that his full rehabilitation took place. And in glorious fashion. With so many marshals and generals tied up in Spain the Emperor decided to trust Macdonald with a corps; and after Masséna had borne the brunt of the day's fighting it was Macdonald's 8000 infantry, formed square, moving at breakneck speed and supported by Lauriston's gunners who finally cracked the Archduke Charles' centre. French casualties were high, but the soldiers had performed almost super-humanly and none more so than their commander.

Napoleon certainly made generous amends to the new marshal: Grand Eagle of the Legion of Honour; a pension of 60,000 francs on the Kingdom of Naples; and on December 9, 1809 a dukedom. [I've long felt that his ducal-title, Taranto, has a somewhat Gilbert and Sullivan-ish ring to it, but in reality it was thoroughly deserved.]

In 1810-11 he was in Spain: on purely policing duties in Catalonia. Then on the 1812 expedition to Russia he had command of 10th Corps, which in effect meant the whole northern flank – although he failed to take Riga after a siege lasting from August to December.

In 1813 he fought superbly in command of the right-wing at Lützen and Baützen, and in-between won an action at Bischofswerda on May 12. But on August 26 he suffered a terrible defeat (in fact, more like a rout) at Katzbach. Separated from the Emperor and pushing ahead rashly, the marshal allowed Blücher to wheel and drive back into his advancing columns. The French suffered 15,000 casualties and prisoners, plus the loss of 100 cannon.

This was not his lucky period. Having fought with great courage at the Battle of the Nations, he only got away by swimming the River Elster (where Poniatowski drowned). And his involvements in the various battles for France were generally in retreat. However, although in favour of the first abdication and charged with Ney to take the signed documents to the Allies, he remained personally loyal to the Emperor and in fact went to salute him on his departure for Elba. 'I could not be more touched than I am by your conduct,' Napoleon said to him. 'You, who owe me nothing, have remained true.'

But he did not return to Napoleon during the Hundred Days...

Afterwards he was kept busy disbanding the Imperial Guard; the remnants of which had retreated behind the Loire. Also he was created a peer of the realm, always voting as a moderate. His final military appointment was as Honorary Commandant of the Royal Bodyguard, although for most of his later years he preferred being on his estate at Courcelles-le-Roi (Loiret) to the social round in Paris.

MARMONT, August Frédéric Louis Viesse de, Duke of Ragusa (1774 – 1852)

In the French language, at least to Bonapartists, the verb *raguser* derived from Marmont's ducal title means to betray. That he did so was a particularly cruel blow to Napoleon, since of all the marshals – and after the death of Lannes and Bessières – the Emperor had regarded him as a familiar and friend. He was a good soldier and thoroughly merited his promotion; although except under the Empire he could never have risen so high. Unfortunately, in the end, loyalty lost out to his personal ego.

Born at Châtillon-sur-Seine (Côte d'Or), the son of an army officer with Republican sympathies, he was always intended for a military career and joined the garrison forces at Chartres while still only fifteen. He then became an officer cadet at the Artillery School of Chalons and first met Napoleon on a visit to Dijon. He met up with him again during the Siege of Toulon where he gained promotion to captain. He was just nineteen. Afterwards he served under Desaix with the Army of the Rhine and was mentioned in dispatches for having conducted himself with great bravery at

Maintz (October, 1795). But Napoleon took him along as an ADC to Italy and from this moment their personal friendship seemed secure. Marmont fought well at Cherasco and Lodi. At the bridge of Arcola, when Napoleon's wounded horse bolted with him into a swamp, it was Marmont together with Louis Bonaparte who pulled him out; and after the Siege of Mantua the young artillery officer was given the honour of taking twenty-two captured Austrian colours back to the Directory.

Promoted to brigadier, he next served with Napoleon on the Egyptian expedition. At Malta he captured the banner of the Order of the Knights of St.-John and later fought with distinction at Alexandria and during the Battle of the Pyramids. Selected to accompany his commander in the rush back to France, he was therefore in a position to assist Napoleon during the *coup* of 18/19 Brumaire and as a result the new First Consul made him a councillor of state.

Vain and foppish, even effeminate-looking with long eyelashes and brown, wavy hair, nevertheless Marmont was both ambitious and very much a thinking soldier. After his skilful handling of the artillery at Marengo in 1800 Napoleon promoted him to general of division. He helped force the passage of the Mincio and on the Consul's behalf signed the armistice at Treviso (January 16, 1801). In the following year he was made overall Inspector General of Artillery and later Commander in Chief of the artillery belonging to the six separate camps of the Grand Army at Boulogne.

It must have come as a big blow to his ego that he wasn't included in Napoleon's first list of promotions to marshal in 1804; and the probable initial cause of his resentment. Instead the new Emperor appointed him Colonel-General of the Hussars and Chasseurs and decorated him with the Grand Eagle of the Legion of Honour. He commanded 2nd Corps of the Grand Army at Ülm, won at Weyer (November 3, 1805) and was then posted to Italy as Governor-General of Dalmatia. He routed the Russian Admiral Siniavin at Ragusa and a delighted Emperor created him a duke with that name.

Marmont revealed himself to be a gifted administrator in Dalmatia. The province was backward, the peasantry illiterate, but he set about his tasks with real determination. He put an end to torture, improved prison conditions, made provisions for education and started a whole new public building programme. Most important of all though he gave the area its first proper road system. He had one stretch of sixty miles from Knin to Split constructed in only six weeks. The locals joked that the Austrians only talked about road-building, whereas Marmont jumped on his horse, rode off and before he'd dismounted the road was there!

He also took time off to do battle. Wounded at Gradschatz in Croatia (May 17, 1809), he recovered to win at Göspich only three days later. He captured Fiume, Graz and then joined the Emperor in time for the Battle of Wagram. On July 9 he won convincingly at Znaim after things had seemed to be going badly for the French. This finally earned him his marshal's

91

baton.

The first setback in Marmont's military career occurred in Spain. Masséna had been relieved of his command, Marmont was sent to take over and while the French were still manoeuvring Wellington caught them at Salamanca (July 22, 1812). The marshal was severely wounded as well as defeated; a piece of shell shattering one of his arms. However, he pulled through to fight at Lützen, Baützen, Dresden, Leipzig and Hanau as commander of 6th Corps and in the subsequent battles for France. The latter to begin with went well for him. He fought at Brienne, La Rothière and Champaubert, won at Montmirail and Gué-à-Tresmes. But he was heavily defeated at Laon and again at La Fère-Champenois and La Ferté-Gaucher.

Still in high favour though, he was now entrusted by Napoleon with the 'key-role' in the defence of Paris; leading to the events which have made his name a permanent blot on the history of France. The Emperor was a hundred miles to the east with Ney, Macdonald and Lefebvre, busy cutting the enemy's lines of communication. If Paris held there was a real chance of the French forcing their invaders to seek terms. Marmont had command of 20,000 troops and the pick of France's artillery. Mortier was not far away with a further 15,000 men, while Moncey was organising the defences inside the city. So the position looked good, with the Allies scattered and not knowing where Napoleon's roving commanders would hit them next. But then Talleyrand came hurrying with propositions from the Bourbons. A hostile Senate had decreed Napoleon must go, he shrilled triumphantly, (which counted for nothing, other than an excuse.) Ever the intriguer he flattered Marmont's ego until suddenly the marshal felt he had the destiny of all Europe in his hands; which in effect he did. He wrote to the Tzar: 'I am ready to leave with my troops the army of the Emperor Napoleon on the following conditions, of which I insist on having from you a written guarantee...' Lavalette, sensing treachery, dashed off messages of warning to the Emperor – but already it was too late. Marmont agreed the surrender; soon the keys to the capital were in the Tzar's possession. Worse, the marshal had duped his own troops. Before they realised what was happening more than 12,000 of them were the Allies' prisoners and the Emperor's enforced abdication a certainty.

'Unhappy man, I loved him!' was Napoleon's comment when the news came through. But the man he had raised to fame and fortune was now about to receive even more. Instead of thirty pieces of silver he was given 450,000 francs, a peerage and command of the household troops. During the Hundred Days Napoleon struck his name from the list of marshals, but following the second Restoration he became a major-general of the Royal Guard and was soon to be made Minister of State. In keeping with his behavioural pattern meanwhile he voted for the execution of Marshal Ney.

Under Charles X he was appointed Governor of Paris, a member of the War Council and he also acted as the King's special representative at the coronation of Tzar Nicholas I (April, 1826). However, during the Revolution of 1830 he backed the wrong side and the new king, Louis Philipe who was an admirer of Napoleon seized the opportunity to exile Marmont for life.

His later years (he was the last of Napoleon's marshals to die) were deservedly Cain-like. He wandered through Russia, on to Turkey, Egypt and finally to Venice, where he died, very much alone and still an outcast. In the nine volumes of his *Mémoires* he labours the point that Napoleon had become a despot. But far from justifying his actions, it is his own vanity and self-seeking which predominate in the books.

MASSÉNA, André, Duke of Rivoli, Prince of Essling (1758 – 1817)

Despite his humble origins and lack of any formal education the little general from Nice has to be judged one of the most brilliant soldiers in the French army up to and including the Battle of Wagram. After this his weaknesses of the flesh tended to take over; leaving Napoleon no choice but to dismiss him from command following a series of bungled actions in the Peninsular War.

The son of a wine-seller (and also thought to have some Jewish blood), he ran off to sea as a cabin-boy, in 1771, crossing the Atlantic several times to trading posts in the Guianas. But he threw this up in 1775 to join the Royal Italian regiment (later the Royal Chasseurs of Provençe) which proved equally frustrating. Within two years he was a sergeant. However by 1789 there were still no prospects of his obtaining a commission so he obtained a discharge instead. Having married a Mademoiselle Lamarre, a surgeon's daughter, he now opened up a shop selling dried-fruit. But, it is claimed, this was merely a façade for his smuggling activities. He had a nose for profit and over the next two years he never once got caught: which says something for his brightness and cunning as well as his avarice!

As with so many men lacking noble birth though, the real 'open sesame' for him came with the Revolution. Joining the 2nd Battalion Volunteers of the Var, with his special knowledge of drill and how to discipline men, especially the ragged, down-at-heel troops of the Republic, he quickly became a lieutenant-colonel. By 1893 he was a general of brigade and in August, 1894 in delayed recognition of his courageous assaults on the forts of Lartigue and St.-Catherine at Toulon the government promoted him general of division.

Assigned to the Army of Italy, in his first action at Saorgio he captured no less than seventy Austrian guns, then went on to defeat the Austrians and Sardinians convincingly at Laono (November 23-25, 1795). Even so, by the date of General Bonaparte's arrival as Commander in Chief (March, 1796), French morale had fallen to an all-time low. Still ragged but now half-starved as well and months without being paid, the soldiers seemed more interested in lounging about and playing cards than fighting the Austrians.

There then followed a remarkable interview between Masséna, Augereau, Sérurier and Napoleon. The three older men refused to doff their hats to the new commander and the swarthy Masséna with his glittering black eyes tried to stare Napoleon out. The latter removed his own hat, obliging them to do the same. He then replaced his hat firmly on his head and glared at them defiantly. From this moment on it became clear who was master. 'Now gentlemen,' he said to them pointedly, 'Let us get on with the business of instilling some spirit into this army—'

In the great campaign of northern Italy which quickly took shape as the result of Napoleon's inspired strategy and organising genius, Masséna was easily the next most successful French general. Although duly deferential to his commander's orders, nevertheless he revealed an extraordinary ability to improvise tactics, plus the tenacity to hold on to what had been gained. And he liked to lead from the front. He was Napoleon's principle subordinate at Montenotte, Dego and Cherasco, the first over the bridge at Lodi and also into Milan and Verona. In August he won at Lonato, relieved Peschiera and the following month, after suffering his only reverse of the campaign at Due Castelli, won again at San Giorgio. After Arcola, in 1797 he won at St.-Michele, in devastating fashion at Rivoli and La Favorita and finally in April at Neumarkt/Unzmarkt. Not a bad tally for the one-time smuggler! And of course he was kept too busy to indulge his taste for plunder...

Masséna didn't join the Egyptian expedition. Which is just as well because in Napoleon's absence he found himself called upon to fight a battle absolutely vital to France's security. This was at Zürich on September 25/26, 1799 when he pulled off a classic victory against what had been a three-pronged attack by the Austrians under Archduke Charles and the Russians under Generals Suvorov and Korsakov. Having brought the Austrians to a gory standstill, he then left Soult to contain them on that side while he threw his remaining forces against the Russians. The outcome was their total rout, with the French taking 5000 prisoners and 200 cannon.

His ultimate military triumph in the years leading up to the Wagram campaign was the heroic defence of Genoa (from April to June, 1800). The French had been bottled up there by superior Austrian forces while Napoleon, now the First Consul, was still recruiting. But in no way would Masséna give up. His men were reduced to eating loaves backed with starch, hair-powder, wood shavings, linseed-oil, cocoa, nuts and weevil-infested flour – and only then if they carried a musket. There was a typhus epidemic and the English under Admiral Lord Keith were bombarding the town from the Gulf. It is estimated that 20,000 French and Italians died of famine and typhus, but Masséna kept calm and held on. He had intelligence that Napoleon's new French army was nearing the Lombardy plain. When he did finally agree to surrender it was only on condition that the French marched out with the honours of war. Masséna rode out though, on a barebones horse said to be the only one in Genoa not killed for food. Meanwhile the siege had fulfilled its purpose: it had kept the Austrians static. Ten days later

Napoleon broke them at Marengo and the struggle for northern Italy was over.

There were now quiet times ahead for Masséna; also honours: a marshal's baton; Grand Eagle of the Legion of Honour; a sabre-of-honour and a large annuity. But he remained much more interested in loot than decorations. He took advantage of the comparatively easy invasion of Naples (in 1806) to help himself to nearly everything in sight. And once Joseph Bonaparte was installed there as King, Masséna felt free to devote himself to a life of bribe-taking and even selling licences to help the Italian merchants evade the Emperor's Continental System! When the corruption was at its height Napoleon stepped in and confiscated most of the fortune Masséna had amassed. In view of the latter's character this must have been for him the equivalent of undergoing major surgery.

However, real surgery would soon become necessary. In March, 1808, the Emperor created Masséna Duke of Rivoli – and further increased his annuities, although this did nothing to lessen the marshal's greed. The Emperor also invited him to a shooting party, in the course of which he managed to put out one of the marshal's eyes, (only to blame it on Berthier: The Grand Huntsman!)

Wearing a black eyepatch, in the European campaign of 1809 Masséna got just about everything right. He fought at Landshut and then, in support of Davout at Eckmühl, captured the fortress of Ebersberg and displayed great skill in taking the village of Aspern. After the Battle of Aspern-Essling (where he more than anyone saved the day) he conducted a masterly withdrawal onto the island of Lobau in preparation for what would be the decisive action of the campaign at Wagram on July 5/6. Here he was in command of the French left-wing and on the second day effected a vital breakthrough while MacDonald pressed the attack in the centre.

The battle won, a triumphant Napoleon created Masséna a prince (of Essling). He also offered him as a gift the château of Thouars, south of the Loire. This the marshal declined. Although now a franc multi-millionaire, his meanness matched his pursuit of wealth. (It would cost too much to repair, he said.) And another story survives of him after Wagram. He had been driven about the battlefield in a light carriage: the result of a fall from his horse three days before. He proposed to reward the coachman and postillion who'd shared his dangers with 200 francs apiece. 'You mean in the form of an annuity?' one of his ADCs murmured politely. Masséna promptly blew his top. 'What!' he shrilled. 'I'd rather see you all shot and get a bullet through my own arm. If I listened to you I'd be ruined. RUINED, d'you hear!'

The accounts of what followed in Portugal and Spain make sorry reading. 'Your reputation alone will be sufficient to finish the business,' Napoleon said in appointing him. But Masséna was fifty-two and looking it. His failure to control the supposedly subordinate marshals; the taking along of his current mistress, Madame Lamberton, wearing a dragoon's uniform; an ill-advised frontal attack against Wellington at Bussaço: ending in a bloody repulse; the French looting of Coimbra; failure to penetrate the Lines of Torres Vedras before Lisbon; then the ignominious retreat: followed by an indecisive and broken-off counter-attack at Fuentes de Oñoro in the May of 1811. Not even his earlier prestige could save him from the Emperor's wrath. 'Well, Prince of Essling? So you are no longer Masséna!' he fumed at him in Paris upon his recall.

He decided the marshal must be put out to grass: or more specifically to garrison duties at Toulon. And there Masséna stayed until the end of the Napoleonic wars; apart from two weeks in 1815 when he commanded the Paris National Guard.

One thing he had not lost though and that was personal courage. He seemed set to receive a number of honours under the restored Bourbons; perhaps even enjoyment of high office. Instead of which he refused point-blank to sit in judgement of Marshal Ney (despite their quarrels in Spain). It meant the finish of his career – but unlike Marmont and Victor he had no intention of joining a jackal-pack.

Masséna met up with Wellington in Paris during the allied occupation. 'You turned every hair in my head white!' he told the duke. Wellington smiled. 'We were pretty even,' he replied. But by this time the Frenchman was already a very sick man – albeit still a rich one. He died in his bed on April 14, 1817.

MONCEY, Bon Adrien Jeannot de, Duke of Conegliano (1754 – 1842)

Born at Besançon, the son of an *avocat* who gave him a first-class education. At an early age he enlisted in the *Champagne-infanterie* as a volunteer, didn't like it and six months later his father bought him out. In 1774 he enlisted again, this time in the *Gendarmes Anglais*, and this time he bought his own discharge, returning to his native Doubs and taking work in his father's office, which proved equally uncongenial. So he rejoined the army, and in 1791 (on April Fool's Day) was promoted captain.

From 1793 to 1795 he served along the Pyrénées, rising to general of division and Commander in Chief of the Western Pyrénées. His various operations there (in defeating the Marquis of St.-Simon at Arquinzun; in seizing San Sebastian with all of its 200 guns and in winning the protracted siege at Tolosa) were impressive. But when on July 19, 1795 he took Bilbao his name in Revolutionary circles was definitely that of a new 'star'. However – and such is political and military fortune – someone close to the government then denounced him as a royalist and he remained unemployed until 1800 when Napoleon took him to Italy.

He played a large part in getting soldiers, horses and cannon over the difficult St.-Gotthard Pass at speed. (He had the guns hand-hauled in hollowed-out tree-trunks.) And he distinguished himself in the 1801 campaign – despite being nearly relieved at one point by Brune for letting the remnants of the enemy give him the slip. Late in 1801 he was appointed Inspector-General of the *Gendarmerie* and in 1803 went with Napoleon on his tour of the Low Countries. He was Number Three in the Emperor's first creation of marshals on May 19,1804, also being invested with the Grand Eagle of the Legion of Honour. Napoleon then appointed him 'Commander of the Corps of Observation of the Coasts' (a cunning title for the intended involvement in the affairs of Spain and Portugal) and created him a duke.

But the *imbroglio* of the Peninsular War witnessed his first military setbacks.

He began with a minor victory at Los Capreros. But then what should have been his victorious march upon Valençia ended prematurely outside the city's walls. In his haste he had arrived without a siege-train and the defenders were in a mood to defend. Consequently, when the news came over that Dupont had surrendered at Baylen, he realised his position was untenable. He redeemed himself somewhat at Tudela on November 23, 1808. Castaños and Palafox were routed, losing 26 cannon and suffering nearly 6000 casualties. But here Moncey was fighting under the overall command of Jean Lannes. Later, in the protracted and costly Siege of Zaragosa his leadership was described as stodgy and unimaginative. Not surprisingly therefore, since the Emperor's war-machine was fuelled on successes, he received no new independent command\between 1809 and 1814. Instead he was appointed to the comparative calm of administrative work in Belgium and northern France.

On the other hand, after Berthier, Murat and finally Ney were created princes, Moncey became the *doyen* of the marshalate. And by January, 1814, with French forces faltering, Napoleon needed him again. He was appointed Commandant of the National Guard of Paris, hastily put the capital's defences in order and then personally led a spirited resistance to the Allies at the *barrière* of Clichy (March 30). Following Marmont's treachery and the subsequent surrender he assembled the remainder of his force on the Champs Elysées and led them off to rejoin the Emperor at Fontaine-bleau. If he wasn't a great fighting general at least he was a man of honour...

Louis XVIII retained him as Inspector-General of the Gendarmes and made him a peer of the realm. But during the Hundred Days he refused to take sides. And a further scandal arose when he refused to preside over the court-martial of Michel Ney. The returned royalists were beside themselves! Moncey was stripped of his rank, his titles and sent to prison for three months at the fortress of Ham (Somme).

However, by 1819 he was back in favour; and then, in the war of 1823 he pulled off the very victories in Spain which would have pleased the Emperor so much had they happened earlier. He trounced the *guerilla* leader Mina and in a whirlwind campaign conquered the whole of Catalonia. Honours now showered down upon him. Grand Cross of the Order of St.-Louis, governorship of Les Invalides, chevalier of St.-Esprit and the *Couronne de Fer*, Grand Cross of Charles III of Spain and Grand Cordon of St.-Vladimir of Russia (1st class).

Perhaps a suitable epitaph for Moncey is the one provided by his former adversaries, the Junta of Oviedo. 'We know that this illustrious officer detests the conduct of his companions. And so we beg him to aid us with his talents and bravery. If his nature will not allow him to do so, yet he shall be considered by us a just and honourable man. Our esteem will follow him wherever he goes.'

MORTIER, Édouard Adolphe Casimir Joseph, Duke of Treviso (1768 – 1835)

The marshal everybody liked.

He was an able corps commander, loyal, dependable when given clear orders and a big man who smiled a lot and was popular with all those who served under him. He was also half-English and the last of Napoleon's marshals to die under violent circumstances.

Born at Cateau-Cambresis (Nord), the son of a cloth-merchant and an English mother. He studied at the Collège des Anglais in Douai until the outbreak of the Revolution and grew up to speak English as well as French. Meanwhile his father had been elected the deputy for Cambresis in the States-General.

In 1791 Mortier became a captain with a volunteer regiment. He fought at Jemappes under Dumouriez and also during the storming of Namur in November, 1792. He then fought at Neerwinden, Hondschoote and was wounded at Dourlers.

After many more actions against the Coalition powers (which included serving as Chief of Staff to Lefebvre at Mainz) he was finally promoted to general of division under Masséna in 1798.

In May, 1803 he completed the occupation of Hanover in such an impressive manner that Napoleon decided to add him to the first list of marshals created in the following year. (The entire Hanoverian army had surrendered to him at Arlenbourg.) He was decorated with the Grand Eagle of the Legion of Honour and from August 1805 commanded the infantry of the Imperial Guard: a sure sign of trust.

In the Ülm campaign he fought with remarkable distinction at Dürren-stein on November 11, 1805, leading his men sword in hand. In 1807 he occupied Hesse and Bremen and then commanded the French left-wing at Friedland. It was after this that Napoleon created him Duke of Treviso with an annuity of 100,000 francs (to be paid, ironically, by the British sovereign territory of Hanover).

In the Peninsular War he was successful throughout two campaigns. He won at Somosierra, helped Jean Lannes at the Siege of Zaragosa, was wounded at Ocaña, took part in Soult's conquest of Andalusia and won the Battle of Gebora (February 19, 1811).

In Russia he commanded the Young Guard and fought with distinction at Borodino. But the unpleasantest task of his career was when Napoleon made him Governor of Moscow. As such he had to fight the fires and order the summary executions of the incendiarists.

In 1813 he commanded the Young Guard at Lützen, Baützen, Dresden and Leipzig and in the battles for France of the following year he shared the defence of Paris with Marmont.

Mortier escorted King Louis XVIII to the Belgian frontier at the start of the Hundred Days, but then he adhered to Napoleon – although he was too ill (with sciatica) to take part in the Waterloo campaign. There were signs that the restored Bourbons wanted him back in their service, but he refused to take part in the court-martial of Marshal Ney and was promptly cashiered, not to be restored to his rank until 1819. Charles X made him a chevalier of the Order of St.-Louis in 1825 and a member of the supreme War Council in 1828. And at the coronation of Louis Philippe in 1830 he presented the new king with the traditional sword.

For the next two years he served as ambassador to Russia and was clearly very high in Louis Philippe's favour. He was popular and admired by all those around him; but his fate was to be killed on the parade ground. He had accompanied the king to a review of the National Guard when Fieschi set off his bomb. The intended victim was the king himself, but Mortier died instead.

MURAT, Joachim, Prince of the Empire, Grand Duke of Berg and Clèves, King of Naples and the Two Sicilies (1767 – 1815)

Second on the list of marshals Napoleon created in 1804 and if not the best, then certainly the best-known of the Grand Army's cavalry commanders. In battle he was both optimistic and opportunistic, usually overdressed and totally without fear. Also he had the ability to get men to charge with him in a moment of crisis. However, as Savary remarked in getting him out of trouble at Heilsberg: 'It would be better if he had slightly less courage and a bit more common sense!' And as time went on his defects became increasingly obvious. His personal ambitions knew no bounds. Add to this his quick temper and its hardly surprising that he made a dangerous friend; as the Emperor found out to his cost . . .

Born at La Bastide-Fortunière in the Périgord (since the Revolution in the Lot and today renamed La Bastide-Murat). His father was an innkeeper who also managed an estate for the Talleyrands, and through the influence of that family Joachim – the youngest of six children – obtained a bursary to the seminary at Cahors. He then went on to study theology and canon-law at

the University of Toulouse: only to fall victim to his own erratic temperament and, after many instances of indiscipline, to find himself expelled. On
an impulse he joined a regiment of *chasseurs* passing through Toulouse and
his remarkable military career now began. This was in 1787. He proved to be
a natural horseman and two years later had become *maréchal des logis* (a
sergeant-major). However in 1790 he was dismissed from the army for
insubordination and returned to La Bastide where he took charge of his
father's stables.

In 1792 he was one of three citizens from the Lot selected to join the
Constitutional Guard of Louis XVI (in which he first met Bessières) and this
acted as a stepping-stone to his re-entering the *chasseurs* and – promoted to
captain – becoming ADC to General d'Urre de Molans. He fought in
Argonne and along the Pyrénées, but before long he was in trouble again.
Having declared himself in loud terms a committed Jacobin (even announc-
ing he wanted to change his name to Marat!), with the fall of Robespierre on
9 Thermidor, Murat was denounced 'for his extremist views', cashiered and
briefly imprisoned. Eventually, though, the colonel of the 16th Chasseurs
gave evidence that he wasn't really a terrorist and his commission was
restored.

The incident which catapulted Murat to political prominence was soon to
follow. During the rising (by the mob and other dissidents) of 3-5 Vendémiaire (October, 1795) against the Convention, it was Murat, at the head of
300 horsemen, who whisked the forty guns from the artillery-park at Les
Sablons from under the noses of the insurrectionists and galloped back with
them through the night to General Bonaparte at the Tuileries. Napoleon's
use of the guns (the celebrated 'whiff of grapeshot') put paid to the revolt
and the government of Barras and Carnot was safe. Murat's reward was to
be promoted colonel (of the 21st Chasseurs). But more importantly he went
to Italy as Napoleon's ADC: with the opportunity to make his name as an
intrepid and at times quite dazzling leader of cavalry.

It is very likely that the future First Consul recognised Murat's vanity and
ambition from the beginning: in his taste for elaborate and exalted uniforms,
for instance, which led to Napoleon comparing him with Signor Franconi,
the famous circus rider. Also in his mad desire to capture enemy standards.
But at the same time his courage under fire was obvious; likewise his skill in
manoeuvring squadrons of horsemen to gain a quick advantage. Moreover
while under the eye of his Commander in Chief he appeared perfectly
content to be subject to his will. All of which (plus the fact that he was
cheerful and friendly) now gained him rapid advancement.

Murat's battle honours read like an itinerary of the first great Italian
campaign. Dego, Ceva and Mondovi (after which he took the captured
colours back to the Directory in Paris and was promoted general of brigade),
Borghetto, the River Adige and Fort St.-Giorgio (where he was wounded),
the Tirol, Tagliamento and a short spell in command at Rome (1798).

The Egyptian expedition followed, where again the cavalryman covered himself in glory. Before Alexandria, in the Battle of the Pyramids and at Aboukir, his charges were always outstanding. During the last action he was shot through the jaw and·found himself in a hospital bed beside his fellow-Gascon Jean Lannes: but the two men had already taken a dislike to each other. In Syria Napoleon promoted Murat a general of division.

Like Lannes he was one of the small band of officers chosen to accompany their leader in the rush back to France and the political triumph of 18/19 Brumaire. It was Murat who put the sixty grenadiers into the Orangery at St.-Cloud to smash windows, overturn benches and tear down the cloaks and togas of the Council of Five Hundred. The latter were bundled outside; the Directory was finished. Afterwards Napoleon placed Murat at the head of the Consular Guard and – to the anger and frustration of Jean Lannes – now agreed to the general marrying his sister Caroline.

It seems the two had met while Caroline was on her way to Rome, when she'd immediately fallen for the tall, handsome Gascon with his black, curly hair and dark-blue eyes; also very likely his resplendent uniforms! The marriage (celerated on January 20, 1800) proved happy enough in its first few years, with Joachim keeping quiet about his occasional affairs. In any case until 1808 he remained under Napoleon's close observation and direct influence. It was only after this the Murat's intriguing began...

In the Italian campaign of 1800 the cavalry leader received a sabre-of-honour for his courage at Marengo. Later, on Napoleon's orders, he occupied the whole of Tuscany, ejected the King of Naples and his army from the Papal States and seized Elba. This time his reward was to be made Governor of Paris: in which capacity he organised the court-martial leading to the execution of the Duke of Enghien, although apparently proceeding with much reluctance. In the same year (1804) as well as being promoted to marshal, he was decorated with the Legion of Honour, created a prince and appointed, of all things, Grand Admiral!

In the European campaigns from 1805 to 1807 he again frequently distinguished himself. But, as Napoleon soon realised, only when entrusted with the cavalry charges. His tactics were primitive to say the least; his strategic sense virtually non-existent. At Ülm he completely misunderstood the situation involving Mack's Austrians and the French victory was only achieved after some prompt improvisation by Marshal Ney. At Dürrenstein Murat was so eager to press on and be the first into Vienna that Kutuzov was able to attack Mortier's unprotected flank. The Emperor was justifiably angry. 'You proceed like a bewildered idiot,' he told his brother-in-law. 'Do you think I issue orders for the fun of it?'

Nevertheless he redeemed himself at Eylau (February, 1807). The French in the centre of the battlefield were coming close to defeat when Murat put in his 80 squadrons. They cut the Russian army in half, sabred the gun-crews and then wheeled to charge the infantry again from the rear. It was the finest achievement of his military career and Napoleon, quick to forgive, showered him with gratuities amounting to hundreds of thousands of francs.

101

In 1808, on May 2 (*Dos de Mayo*), Murat's bloody suppression of a feeble demonstration in the streets of Madrid sparked off what would be the long and (for France) disastrous Peninsular War. The Murats had entertained hopes of becoming King and Queen of Spain in place of the deposed Bourbons. But apart from having united the Spanish against the previously popular French forces, they now found themselves posted to Naples as replacements for the Emperor's first choice of a king for Spain, his brother Joseph.

They were formally proclaimed the rulers of their new country in August: amidst much pomp and ceremony, and in Murat's case the inevitable new uniform. On the whole they had inherited a remarkably well-run little kingdom. Joseph Bonaparte had done a good job in overhauling its adminstration, improving roads and public services and adding much to the liveliness of Neapolitan social and cultural life. Caroline, too, possessed abilities as an administrator; which left her husband free to invade and capture Capri from the English (who were led by Sir Hudson Lowe, later Napoleon's gaoler on St.-Helena). He also readied his forces for an invasion of Sicily where the ousted Bourbons still lurked. However they were protected by an Allied fleet and Murat never did succeed in crossing the Straits of Messina.

Napoleon at this stage left them very much to their own devices. With the Peninsular War and the Wagram campaign to occupy his mind all he wanted to hear from Italy was that things remained quiet there. What he couldn't possibly know was that a joint self-interest had reunited politically the Murat's flagging marriage and seriously undermined their loyalty to both France and himself. From now on they would scheme to hold on to their newly-acquired kingdom at any price...

In 1812 Murat was recalled to the Grand Army for the invasion of Russia. He fought tremendously well at Borodino and, signalling with his golden wand, was one of the first to enter Moscow. In contrast, his behaviour during the retreat can only be described as unforgivable and a mockery of what is regarded as a soldier's duty. Charged by Napoleon at Smorgonie with supervising the last stages of the retreat, at Vilna on December 9, he callously abandoned 20,000 of the Grand Army's wounded. Then on January 18, 1813, he announced that he was handing over the command to Prince Eugène and leaving for Italy. Eugène was simply speechless, Ney coldly contemptuous and Davout exclaimed with an oath that this was downright desertion. But Murat left anyway.

He had some suspicions that Caroline might be intriguing to take over the government of Naples completely, and so he entered into secret negotiations with Great Britain and the Austrians. He hedged his bets by fighting with the French in 1813: at Dresden and Leipzig. But then he deserted for a second time, signing treaties with the Allies and raising troops for a push north against Prince Eugène on the Mincio. 'The conduct of the King of Naples is infamous!' Napoleon stormed. 'And that of my sister the Queen even worse. I hope to live long enough to avenge such an outrage and such ingratitude—'

In the end though the whole of the Murat's scheming came to nothing. Far from honouring their treaties the Allies left the Bourbons free to chase the couple out of Naples and then out of Italy. Rather naïvely the prince offered his services to France for the Waterloo campaign. Napoleon didn't even bother to reply and Murat found himself at the dockside in Toulon with a price on his head. In desperation he now endeavoured to recover his former kingdom by way of an invasion at Pizzo in Calabria: with a mere 30 men. Alas! for those involved this was far from being another Elban escape. Upon landing there was no popular rising in their favour; only capture, and for Murat a court-martial, followed half an hour later by his execution in front of a firing squad (October 13, 1815).

Vainglorious still, he requested that they aim at the heart and avoid damaging his head.

NEY, Michel, Duke of Elchingen, Prince of the Moscowa (1769 – 1815)

Having said in an earlier piece about Jean Lannes that Ney was Napoleon's other best frontline fighting general, it is ironic to be adding here that he is best-known for a defensive action; and a period of inspired improvisation. But he had been trained for the retreat from Moscow: by having to get Masséna's rearguard out of Portugal ahead of Wellington. And at Waterloo? Well, despite the various mistakes, at one point he had the battle all but won...

Ney came comparatively late into the *élite*; and although he then fell under Napoleon's spell, he was never what one would call an intimate of his leader like those officers of the Italian campaigns and Egypt. He was a distinguished product of the northern armies, needed and valued by Napoleon for his bravery and tactical skills, but also for the important political reason of drawing him away from the ambitious General Moreau, Ney's superior at the decisive Battle of Hohenlinden (December 3, 1800). What then occurred over the years in the convoluted relationship between master and subordinate is one of the most fascinating and ultimately tragic stories of the Napoleonic era.

Contrary to a number of popular accounts Ney was better-educated than a lot of the other marshals. Born in Germany (at Saarlouis), the son of a barrel-maker who fought for Louis XV at Rossbach, he went to school at the nearby Collège des Augustins. He was afterwards placed in a law-office; his father's idea being that this was the right stepping-stone to an influential job with the *Procureur du Roi*. Michel grew up to be bilingual in German and French (hence his later usefulness to Napoleon in the creation of a modern Switzerland) and in his spare time he practised the flute. Otherwise he was

103

bored, (especially when he saw the troops marching through Saarlouis towards Central Europe), so he took his idea of a stepping-stone towards a chosen career: running the office at the Apenwarler iron-mines, then becoming an overseer at the Saleck works where he had the opportunity to study cannon-construction. After three years at Saleck he joined the *Régiment Colonel Général des Hussars* (February, 1787).

He was tall for the period, five feet eleven, with bright auburn hair and high colouring (gaining him the nickname *Le Rougead*). As a hussar he rode magnificently and he had a big bellowing voice which would soon become used to command. Above all though, he had immense courage and the desire to know everything he could about his profession, leading on to genuine military skills.

Although joining the army while France still had a king, Ney quickly adapted to the new Revolutionary ideas. He took part in so many actions before finally meeting Napoleon in 1801 that I can only include reference to the more important ones. He had his baptism of fire as an officer on the ridge at Valmy in 1792. He fought at Neerwinden in 1793 and then as a cavalry commander under Kléber, the first senior officer to recognise his true abilities. At this stage Ney got a reputation for refusing promotions, stating he wasn't yet ready. But after collecting his first wound (in the shoulder) during the siege at Maastricht; charging down the *émigrés* at Opladen; storming the citadel of Würzburg and distinguishing himself again at Forcheim, both Kléber and the Committee of Public Safety insisted upon his promotion to general of brigade (August 1, 1796). He was wounded again (twice) during the capture of Mannheim and promoted a general of division. (This was after his accidental capture at Giessen, when Hoche ransomed him.)

However, he recovered to take part in the Battle of Hohenlinden, the action which effectively knocked Austria out of the field until 1805.

The strategic credit for Hohenlinden belongs to General Moreau; but Ney's heroic defence against the enemy onslaught in the centre, while all the time Richepanse's men were creeping down through the forest to attack the Austrian rearguard, was crucial to the victory.

Summoned to Paris now, Ney's first meeting with Napoleon did not go well. Both men felt awkward, and in the end it was Josephine more than anyone who brought the tough northern general into the *élite*. Having personally charmed him, she then proceeded to gain his loyalty through marriage: to Hortense's great friend Aglaé Auguié. Meanwhile Napoleon had learned something important about the newcomer's character. A keen student of warfare Ney might be, also contemptuous of politicians; but he had a natural thirst for what the French call *La Gloire* and would willingly attach himself to its success...

In 1802 Ney's prompt action in Switzerland completed the First Consul's plans for that country and the general stayed on for a time as Minister Plenipotentiary, signing the Act of Mediation on February 19, 1803. In 1804 the new Emperor named him twelfth of the first creation of marshals and decorated him with the Grand Eagle of the Legion of Honour in the following year.

In the campaign of 1805/6 – probably the greatest in France's military history – the marshal disobeyed an order of Murat's (on the advice of his ADC Jomini) in order to conform with Napoleon's overall strategy against the Austrians at Ülm. His 6th Corps took and held the bridge at Elchingen which brought about the surrounding (and then surrender) of General Mack with 30,000 men.

He took no part at Austerlitz because the Emperor had detailed him off to occupy the Tirol; but before the battle Napoleon was heard to remark: 'I wish I had my Ney with me now!' He was then rebuked at Jena for rashness. 'The Emperor said a few words to him on the subject – but delicately.' (Savary). However, he went on to capture Erfurt (12,000 men, 100 cannon) and at Eylau, although arriving late, he effectively helped clinch the day. But his greatest feat of arms was at Friedland on June 14, 1807. In command of the French right-wing, his corps smashed the Russians and drove them back into the River Alle with an estimated 10,000 casualties out of their original force of 46,000. After this Napoleon was able to proceed to the Peace of Tilsit and dictate terms to the Tzar...

1808-11. Ney had a bad Peninsular War, (although nothing to do with his fighting abilities). He took Bilbao; chased Sir John Moore towards Coruña; beat the Marquis of La Romaña out of the Asturias; besieged and captured Ciudad Rodrigo and also Almeida (where one of his gunners ignited a trail of powder leading to the main magazine inside the cathedral and the whole centre of the town went up!) and in the end conducted the most masterly retreat out of Portugal which filled even the frustrated Wellington with admiration. But the quarrels with his overall commander Masséna were a serious breach of discipline. Ney had disagreed with the frontal attack at Bussaço, where his troops were thrown back by the British. Masséna, though, had insisted on the uphill charge. Once out of Portugal there were more rows. Corrupt and slipshod Masséna might have been, but he was still the commander – so Napoleon felt he had no alternative but to take Ney away from the war and post him to the camp of Boulogne. (Masséna's sacking soon followed.)

Rehabilitation came with the Russian campaign of 1812. The marshal fought magnificently at Borodino in the storming of the Grand Redoubt. Deliberately he fought in his dress-uniform so the troops could see he was sharing their dangers. Miraculously no sniper's bullet reached him. On the other hand, there was the notoriously angry outburst when the ill Napoleon refused to commit his reserves and a large part of the Russian army got away. 'What is the Emperor doing there at the rear? If that's what he wants to do, then let him go back to the Tuileries and leave the generals to finish the war!'

But the retreat from Moscow in the teeth of a Russian winter and against the marauding Cossacks saw a very different kind of general: a patient, gritty and resourceful one. No wonder Napoleon forgave him his earlier insubordination. 'I have millions in gold in Paris,' the Emperor said, 'but Ney is worth more.' After the crossing of the Berezina he took full responsibility for the French rearguard, outwitting the Russians at every turn, fighting when he had to, otherwise moving men and guns at dead of night until even his opponents had to admit the brilliance of it all. 'A marshal of France never surrenders!' he retorted to an envoy of his pursuers. 'One does not parley under the fire of the enemy.'

He was the last Frenchman to quit Russian soil: unshaven, in a dirty fur-coat and still clutching a musket. 'I'm damnably tired,' he said to an innkeeper in Prussia, 'bring me some soup!'

Napoleon created him Prince of the Moscowa and awarded him a pension of 800,000 francs. But Ney continued to fight: at Baützen, Dresden, Dennewitz (which he mismanaged) and throughout the battles for France. Afterwards though, he urged Napoleon to abdicate and was one of the officers authorised to negotiate with the Allies.

He served the restored Bourbons, but unhappily. He busied himself with the internal reorganisation of the army, in particular the cavalry, and then retired from the court following an outburst after the Duchess of Angoulême insulted his wife. He was surprised and amazed by Napoleon's escape from Elba. He thought France faced the prospect of civil war and informed Louis XVIII he would bring back the Emperor in an iron cage rather than see this happen. Instead of which he found his soldiers eager to go over to Napoleon and decided to join them...

In the Waterloo campaign he commanded the left-wing at Quatre Bras and was overly cautious when he could have overrun Wellington's outposts. (However Soult's bad staff-work was a contributory factor.) At Waterloo itself he blundered badly by not supporting his great cavalry charge with infantry and so Wellington's squares held firm. But later in the battle, after the capture of La Haye Sainte, his gunners had the English in real rouble. Only now the Emperor himself hesitated and neglected to send in the Imperial Guard until after Wellington had been reinforced. The final outcome was a rout.

Ney had four horses shot from under him in the course of the battle. His face was blackened with powder, his sword broken and his uniform in tatters. Afterwards though he was a marked man: the Bourbon's principal scapegoat. Several of the marshals refused to sit in judgement on him at a court-martial and Moncey was sent to prison for refusing. Meanwhile Ney could have escaped the firing squad on a legal technicality: his German birth. But he was too proud a French patriot by this date. The Royalist Chamber of Peers condemned him by 107 votes to 47.

At his execution, on Decmber 7, 1815 at the Carrefour de l'Observatoire in Paris where Rude's statue of him now stands, the marshal himself gave the order to fire. One of his four sons later challenged Wellington to a duel for not intervening to save him. No one knows why the Duke didn't use his influence. He also refused the duel.

OUDINOT, Nicholas Charles, Duke of Reggio (1767 – 1847)

The marshal who, as every French schoolboy is supposed to know, survived twenty-two serious wounds: more than any of his colleagues within the marshalate. Napoleon eventually came to regard his talents as mediocre, but like Lefebvre he was a good commander up to corps level – and in particular of infantry. Unfortunately, a profile of him is bound to read like one long medical bulletin!

He was born at Bar-le-Duc (Meuse), the son of a brewer who spent his first three years with the army (1784-87) in the *Rgiment de Médoc* as a private. On July 14, 1789 he became a captain and when the Revolution was fully established in 1792 he was promoted provisional colonel with the Volunteers of the Meuse. He made a very favourable impression upon the members of the Committee of Public Safety with his stubborn defence of Bitsch (in the Vosges) and his rank was confirmed to coincide with his transfer to the regular Army of the Rhine. He then collected his first wound – a musket-ball grooving his head – at Hagenau in December, 1793.

In 1794 he was promoted to general of brigade following his distinguished frontline fighting at Kaiserslauten and almost immediately was wounded again: shot in the leg at Trèves (August 8). Add the five sabre cuts and another musket-ball he received before being captured at Neckerau in October and his reputation as a great survivor was already well on its way. Exchanged in 1796, he was in command of a cavalry brigade when he collected four more sabre cuts and a shot in the thigh at Ingolstadt.

Promoted general of division on April 12, 1799, he was shot in the chest at Rosenberg, then in the shoulder-blade at Schwyz and in the chest again at Zürich. Following which he went to Italy as Masséna's Chief of Staff and took part in the heroic defence of Genoa. Afterwards Napoleon presented him with a sword-of-honour in recognition of his services there and also in forcing the passage of the Mincio at Monzembano (December, 1799).

In the renewed warfare of 1805 'Oudinot's Grenadiers' became the 1st Division of Lannes' 5th Corps. The general had picked and trained every man himself. With them he took the bridges at Vienna before being shot in the thigh at Hollabrunn in November. He assisted Lefebvre at the Siege of Danzig, then broke his leg when his horse fell on him – but he recovered to fight at Friedland.

At Wagram a bullet nearly took off one of his ears. He had it stitched back on and continued fighting. Already decorated with the Grand Eagle of the Legion of Honour and a count of the Empire, at Wagram (July 12, 1809) Napoleon promoted him to the marshalate only hours after Macdonald – and the following year made him a duke.

There then followed two and a half years of quiet: as the military governor of Holland. But with the invasion of Russia in 1812 he was soon back in action (as commander of 2nd Corps) and increasing his tally of wounds. Although he was winning at Polotsk his shoulder was filled with grapeshot so that he had to be relieved by Gouvion St.-Cyr. While at the crossing of the Berezina he was wounded in the arm – and again two days later defending the rearguard.

In 1813 he fought well at Baützen and Leipzig, but was caught and defeated by Bernadotte at Grossbeeren: which very much angered Napoleon who even considered relieving Oudinot of his command. But he was retained to take part in the battles for France – and to survive what were to be his final wounds. At Brienne he had a lucky escape when a cannon-ball grazed both of his thighs; and at Arcis he received a musket-ball full in the chest, but although knocked over the bullet had struck his Legion of Honour insignia.

Following the first abdication he decided to serve the Bourbons and as well as being made a peer of the realm he had command of the important 3rd Military Division at Metz. During the Hundred Days his troops deserted to Napoleon, but Oudinot did not join them. Upon the second Restoration Louis XVIII made him the military governor of Paris and a councillor of state.

His last active service was in Spain in 1823. Under Louis Philippe he became Grand Chancellor of the Legion of Honour in 1839 and in 1842 Governor at Les Invalides, where it is recorded that his favourite after-dinner recreation was shooting out the candles with his pistols.

PÉRIGNON, Catherine Dominique, Marquis (1754 – 1818)

One of four honorary marshals created in 1804. He held various administrative and defensive appointments under Napoleon but never took part in a major campaign after Novi where he was wounded and captured by the Austrians. His more distinguished fighting had all taken place under the Revolutionary government.

Born at Grenade (Haute Garonne), he was first commissioned in 1780 and then served with the *Grenadiers Royaux de Quercy*. He became Colonel of the National Guard of Montech in 1791 and promoted general of division in 1793. He won several engagements against the Spaniards and then went as ambassador to Spain (1795-7). In 1802 Napoleon appointed him 'Commissioner Extraordinary' to supervise the frontiers between France and Spain and on October 27 of that same year Vice-President of the Senate. He then invested him with the Grand Eagle of the Legion of Honour in 1805.

Following this and until 1813, Pérignon served mostly in Italy, first as Governor-General of Parma and Plasencia, then from 1808 as Governor of Naples under Murat – who eventually sacked him without consulting the

Emperor or General Clarke at the War Ministry.

Never a true Bonapartist, after the first abdication he immediately joined the restored Bourbons and accepted all their rewards: chevalier of the Order of St.-Louis, a peer of the realm, a governorship (of Toulouse) and a marquisate (in 1817).

In 1815, during the Hundred Days, Napoleon struck him off the list of marshals.

PONIATOWSKI, Josef Anton, Prince (1763 – 1813)

One of the most personally brave and gifted officers to fight on Napoleon's side. He was created Marshal of France in 1813 on the battlefield.

Although a lifelong Polish patriot and a sworn enemy of the Russians, he was actually born in Vienna, the son of a Polish general in the Austrians' service and a nephew of King Stanlislas (Augustus) II. He entered the Austrian service himself in 1780 and was immediately commissioned cornet in the 2nd Regiment of Carabiniers. He gained most of his initial military training under the experienced eye of Marshal Lacy.

In January 1788 he became ADC to the Emperor Joseph II and the same year saw action against the Turks. Before he set out he attended the first night of Mozart's *Don Giovanni*. Before the campaign was over he'd been wounded and promoted colonel.

From 1789 he devoted himself to the Polish independence struggles against Russia, first of all as commander of a division in the Ukraine, and finally, after many successful engagements – often against overwhelming odds – leading the rebel forces who would not accept the weak Stanislas II's giving in to the Tzar (the Confederation of Targowica). By the beginning of 1806 he was looking towards Napoleon and France as the only possible bastion to check Russian Imperialist expansionism. When the Grand Duchy of Warsaw was proclaimed he was the first governor of the capital, then Minister for War – and on June 2, 1807 he officially committed the 1st Polish Legion to the French service, with himself as its commander. In response Napoleon awarded him the Grand Eagle of the Legion of Honour and a pension of 30,000 French francs per annum. The Polish Legion received a subsidy of one million francs from the treasury of the King of Saxony.

The new alliance was now definitely on.

In 1809 an overconfident Austrian force invaded the Polish Grand Duchy only to be bloodily repulsed and to discover that meanwhile Poniatowski had invaded their own Galicia and taken the ancient city of Cracow. They sued for terms, leaving their victorious adversery to devote his energies to organising the new Polish state, founding schools of artillery, engineering works and hospitals.

In 1812 he furnished the Emperor with 36,000 troops towards the invasion of Russia, distinguished himself at Smolensk and performed with great success on the right-wing before Borodino, driving Russian regiments from the villages on the way to the Grand Redoubt. He was above all a cavalryman, and that was how he flushed out the opposition. He operated with equal bravery during the retreat from Moscow; and although wounded crossing the Berezina recovered in time to join the Emperor with 13,000 fresh troops at Lützen. A tall, slender figure, unusually dark for a Pole, he had by this time been taken to the hearts of the French general staff – despite his affecting the now out-of-fashion sideburns and luxuriant cavalry-man's moustache. ('But he's like Lasalle, that's excuse enough!') After their parallel fighting experiences at Borodino Marshal Ney had thought him 'wonderful'; so did Davout: an even more severe judge of military talent.

After Lützen he invaded Bohemia in the name of France, won actions at Lobau (September 9), Chemnitz (October 4) and Penig (October 8). The following day he was wounded again by a lance-blow, but still managed to join the Emperor for the crucial Battle of Leipzig (October 16-18, 1813). Placed in command of the French right, at the end of the second day's fighting he was created marshal.

On the 19th October, the French were in retreat due to lack of ammunition and reserves. Poniatowski was one of those cut off when the accidental blowing of the bridge over the River Elster occurred. Thirty French generals surrendered that day, including Lauriston and Reynier. But 'Pony' as the 'grumblers' referred to him affectionately, would have no part of it. (Certainly if there were Russians involved.) Wounded in several places, he cut his way through to the river and plunged in. He was exhausted; so was his horse. Before drowning the last words he shouted were: 'Poland' and 'Honour'.

His remains are buried in Cracow Cathedral, but his name is included on the east side of the Arc de Triomphe at the Place Charles de Gaulle in Paris. And, of course, his descendants have remained active in French domestic politics.

SÉRURIER, Jean Matthieu Philibert, Count (1742 – 1819)

The last of the four honorary marshals made up under the Empire and the last marshal to be named at the creation of 1804. From that time he saw no more active service but functioned as Governor of Les Invalides, the army's holy-of-holies in Paris.

Born at Laon (Aisne), like Kellermann he was a veteran of the Seven Years War; and also of the former French monarchy's 1762 expedition against Portugal, when he served as a lieutenant (having finally recovered from a shattered jaw: a wound received during the Battle of Warburg (July 31, 1760)). He later went on the Corsican expedition of 1770-1 and became a chevalier of the Order of St.-Louis in 1781.

Upon the outbreak of the Revolution Sérurier, by this time a colonel, was arrested as an instrument of the monarchists: only to be released and reinstated after the intervention of Paul Barras. He then performed a brilliant feat of leadership at Utelle (February 28, 1793) satisfying the Revolutionary government to the extent that he was promoted general of brigade – and in 1794 general of division, confirmed by Robespierre the following year.

He was now to add to his winning-streak serving under Napoleon in Italy: a handsome victory at Mondovi, concluding the Siege of Mantua and defeating General Provera at La Favorita (1797). Following this he became for a year Governor of Venice.

Already an army officer for over forty years, he began to think of retirement. Although never lacking in courage, he saw how warfare had changed and felt it time to go. However, Napoleon insisted on retaining him; first as Vice-President of the Senate, then in 1803 as President of the commission overseeing national boundaries, and finally, on becoming a marshal, at Les Invalides. He received the Grand Eagle of the Legion of Honour in 1805 and was created a count of the Empire in 1808.

The most spectacular event of his period of governorship occurred on March 13, 1814 when the Allies had reached the gates of Paris – and only a few days before Marmont's final betrayal. In the enormous courtyard of the Hotel 1,417 flags and colours captured from the enemy were burned in front of the assembled pensioners: weeping veterans of the Revolutionary wars and the Grand Army, many of whom had emerged the day before from their retirement to help Marshal Moncey defend the *barrière* of Clichy. At the height of this blazing *auto-da-fe*, ordered by Sérurier, the marshal personally threw on the bonfire the sword and sash of Frederick the Great of Prussia – a defiant gesture to say the least!

In view of his long service under the former monarchy the restored Bourbons were thought likely to keep him on at Les Invalides, but although they did vote him a pension and name him a peer, he was replaced as Governor by the ridiculous Duke of Coigny, created a marshal of France at age 79...

SOULT, Nicholas Jean de Dieu, Duke of Dalmatia (1769 – 1851)

Without question one of Napoleon's ablest commanders. He was a good frontline fighting soldier, but also a man who understood tactics and strategy. He liked a war of movement and manoeuvring, hated sieges and therefore it was with the former that his abilities showed at their best. Wellington rated him a worthy opponent. His two weaknesses were a predilection for plunder (especially paintings, preferably religious!) and an impatience with the necessary thoroughness of staff-work. As Chief of Staff at Waterloo he has to be judged a disaster. But if he had replaced Grouchy

111

on the French right wing...

Born at St.-Amans-la-Bastide (today technically Tarn, but formerly a part of the Languedoc), he was at first a baker's assistant, then threw the job in and enlisted in the *Régiment Royal-Infanterie* in 1785. During the Revolutionary wars he served under Hoche, Jourdan and Lefebvre, fought at Fleurus, also Altenkirchen and Stokach, but it was as a divisional general co-ordinating with Masséna in Switzerland against the Austrians and Russians that he really made his mark; especially in the great victory at Zürich. He was again with Masséna during the Siege of Genoa, ending up a prisoner of the Austrians and with a broken leg. However, his reputation had increased enormously. When Napoleon enquired about him Masséna made the comment that 'for judgement and courage he has scarcely a superior'.

He remained in Italy, part of the time assisting Murat in the south, until 1802 when he was recalled to Paris and appointed Colonel-General of the Light Infantry of the Consular Guard. From August, 1803 he served as commandant at St.-Omer, getting a name for himself as a strict disciplinarian and the following year was added to the first list of marshals.

He next distinguished himself at Austerlitz. He had command of 4th Corps: over on the right. The full weight of the enemy attack fell upon this wing, but Soult succeeded in storming and holding the Pratzen Heights which dominated the battlefield and thus largely won the day. Afterwards the Emperor described him as the best manoeuvring general in Europe. He commmanded the right-wing again at Jena, then the centre at Eylau and after the Peace of Tilsit he was created a duke.

Other honours soon came his way: Bavaria's Order of St.-Hubert; Spain's Order of the Three Golden Fleeces and Sweden's Order of the Seraphim, together with – and very importantly – money, of which he was inordinately fond. Napoleon gave him annuities worth at least 300,000 francs. But even this didn't prevent the marshal helping himself to paintings and fine furniture from the local big houses while on campaign.

From 1808 onwards his career was mainly bound up with the Peninsular War – and gradually, but increasingly, against Wellington. Together with Lannes and Victor and following Bessières' victory at Medina de Rio Seco he helped clear the way to Madrid. But this was of inferior Spanish forces. Against the British it was never going to be so easy. At Coruña in 1809 Soult's troops were thrown back in confusion by those of Sir John Moore, and although Moore died in the engagement the French failed to prevent the expeditionary force leaving.

Soult then invaded Portugal and occupied Oporto; only to be chased out of the country by Wellington. His subsequent occupation of Andalusia finally failed against Beresford at Albuera. He took Grenada but failed to relieve Badajoz which Wellington took.

After the Duke's great victory at Salamanca, Soult realised that to carry on in southern Spain was unrealistic. He abandoned the Siege of Cadiz, evacuated Seville and retreated upon Madrid, from where in 1813 he was recalled to France. Napoleon had need of him for the new German campaign. Depositing his large amount of personal booty in Paris, the marshal went on to fight at Baützen – and to take over command of the Imperial Guard following Bessières' death. But the news came through of Wellington's victory at Vittoria and Soult was posted back to take charge of the defence of the Pyrénées. It wasn't an enviable task. He was kept short of men and artillery. Also Wellington's troops had shown that the French could be beaten and their morale was high. Nevertheless the marshal fought with skill and determination and was still holding a line behind Toulouse at the time of the first abdication.

Adhering to Napoleon after the escape from Elba, he was appointed Chief of Staff for the Waterloo campaign, but proved an unfortunate substitute for Berthier. The muddled messages sent to Marshal Ney; the useless marching and countermarching by D'Erlon's corps; these must be blamed upon Soult. He did not know how to interpret Napoleon's mind and his drafted orders were far from clear.

After the battle he was, of course, a hunted man. His name was struck off the list of marshals and until 1819 he lived in exile in Düsseldorf. However his rank was restored to him in 1820 and in 1827 Charles X created him a peer of the realm. Under Louis Philippe he was the most favoured of all the marshals. Minister for War from 1830-34, he was President of the Council too for much of this time and was still holding office as a minister without portfolio in 1847. In-between he had attended the coronation of Queen Victoria in 1838 as France's Ambassador Extraordinary: when there was a pleasant meeting with his old rival Wellington. He was also one of the four marshals who survived to witness the bringing back of Napoleon's remains from St.-Helena. (Moncey aged 86, Oudinot and Grouchy were the others.)

However, probably the greatest moment of Soult's career came on September 26, 1847 when Louis Philippe promoted him to *Maréchal-General*, the only one of Napoleon's officers to be honoured in this way. It classed him with the mighty Turenne: no mean achievement.

SUCHET, Louis Gabriel, Duke of Albufera (1770 – 1826)

Widely regarded as one of the ablest of Napoleon's promotions to marshal – especially on the evidence of his period in the Iberian Peinsula where so many of the other marshals came to grief. The Emperor once remarked: 'If I'd had two Suchets I could have held on to Spain forever!' Which makes the fact that he made no use of him during the Waterloo campaign even more inexplicable...

Born at Lyon, he was the son of a silk manufacturer. An enthusiast for the Revolution, he became a voluntary cavalryman with the National Guard in 1791 and then moved on to the *Compagnie franche* of l'Ardèche. Elected colonel, he took part in the siege at Toulon and in December, 1793 gained credit in the eyes of both Napoleon and the government in Paris when he captured the British General O'Hara.

Following this he served for a number of years with the Army of Italy (apart from a brief period under Joubert and Brune in the Tirol and Switzerland, 1797/98). He saw action at Dego, Lodi and Castiglione, collected a musket ball at Cerea (on September 12, 1796) and then served as Masséna's deputy commander at San Giorgio, Arcoli and Rivoli. In 1799 he married Honorine Anthoine, daughter of the Mayor of Marseille and Marie Ann Rose Marseille-Clary, the sister-in-law to Joseph Bonaparte. A large, long-jawed man with a Roman nose and heavy lidded eyes, obviously it was a love-match because invariably he took her with him on his subsequent campaigns.

In 1800 he commanded the left-wing of the Army of Italy under Masséna. Although he failed in an attack on Monte San Giacamo (April 19) and again before Loano (May 1), when Masséna had got himself shut up and besieged in Genoa it was Suchet's troops retreating upon the Var who effectively prevented an Austrian invasion of south-eastern France. Napoleon promoted him to Inspector-General of Infantry (July 24, 1801).

In the Grand Army's campaign in Central Europe he fought at Ülm, Austerlitz, then Saalfeld, Jena, Pultusk and Ostrolenka. Napoleon decorated him with the Grand Eagle of the Legion of Honour, the Order of the Iron Crown of Italy and in 1808 made him a count. After which he posted him to Spain.

Suchet served continuously in the Peninsula from 1808 to 1814 and proved himself a brilliant administrator as well as a successful general. He not only put down the many revolts in Catalonia but gave the area sound and sensible government.

Having covered Jean Lannes' near-destruction of Zaragosa, he went on to rout General Blake at Maria and Belchite, then took Lerida and Tortosa, and in 1811 besieged and captured Tarragona: the event which clinched his marshal's baton. Having defeated Blake again at Benequasil he went on to capture Valencia (the city surrendered on July 10, 1812). Napoleon created him a duke, the only one of the marshals to receive a Spanish title.

He won various other battles in Catalonia before supervising a model retreat upon France in 1814. At the time of the first abdication he was Commander in Chief of the Army of the South and Colonel-General of the Imperial Guard: another sign of favour in Napoleon's eyes. So why during the Hundred Days did the returned Emperor give him nothing more than the Army of the Alps? Apart from invading Savoy his talents were wasted at this crucial moment in France's history. Suchet instead of Grouchy on the right wing at Waterloo? Or even replacing Soult as Chief of Staff? The speculation is tantalising.

Following the second Restoration he was stripped of his command, and titles and not readmitted to the Chamber of Peers until March, 1819. He died at the Château of Montredon near Marseille, leaving his *Mémoires* to be edited by the Baron St.-Cyr-Naques.

VICTOR-PERRIN, Claude, Duke of Belluno (1764 – 1841)

Napoleon's first promotion to marshal following the initial list of 1804. One is tempted to ask why? – since there were many more better-qualified candidates. As an officer he was brave enough, but certainly not imaginative; and also in the end he would betray the Emperor. However, the latter had known him from the Siege of Toulon onwards and the promotion was made in the euphoria which immediately followed the great French victory at Friedland.

Victor-Perrin, or simply Victor as he liked to be called, was perhaps the original example of the 'old chestnut' that a marshal's baton lies at the bottom of every drummer-boy's knapsack. He certainly enlisted as a drummer: with the Artillery Regiment of Grenoble in 1781. He had been born at Lamarche in the Vosges, the son of a notary, but all of his early military service was to be in the south. He next joined the National Guard at Valence as a grenadier; then – having declared himself a Revolutionary – he became a captain with the Volunteers of the Bouches du Rhône. When the Siege of Toulon started he had risen to colonel.

Victor led the attack on Fort Aiguilette (known as 'Little Gibraltar') and was wounded in the stomach. But the capture of this strongpoint led to a hasty English evacuation of the town and the harbour, and three days later he was promoted to general of brigade (provisional).

Having recovered from his wounds he then served under Pérignon along the Pyrénées before becoming involved over a long period in Italy. Under Masséna he fought at Borghetto, Loano, Dego and Roveredo. After La Favorita, Napoleon promoted him to general of division and he went on to beat the Pope's scrambled-together soldiery at the Senio which opened the way to Ancona. In 1799 he was wounded again at the Battle of Trebbia, but he was back in action at Montebello and for his bravery at Marengo received a sabre-of-honour.

In 1802 the First Consul was thinking of sending Victor as Governor of Louisiana, then changed his mind and kept him in Holland before posting him as Minister Plenipotentiary to Denmark in 1805.

In the 1806 campaign he served as Chief-of-Staff to Jean Lannes, fought at Saalfeld, Jena, Pultusk and then managed to get himself captured by the Prussians near Stettin. However within weeks Napoleon had arranged an exchange and then entrusted him with 1st Corps of the Grand Army (formerly Bernadotte's). It was in this position that he distinguished himself at Friedland in 1807.

Blond, ruddy-faced and now becoming portly, he had a spell of duty as Governor of Berlin before being sent to the Spanish Peninsula, where his career suffered its first setbacks. He started off in fine form against the local armies, defeating Blake at Espinosa (November, 1808) and Cuesta at Alcabon (July, 1809). But at Talavera against Wellington he experienced a bloody repulse, despite having superiority of numbers.

He was defeated again by the British (this time under Graham) in Andalusia in 1811; after which he was required for the Russian campaign, initially commanding 9th Corps. It was from this point on that the real defects in his character began to show up. Following the crossing of the Berezina during the retreat, there occurred a terrible quarrel with Marshal Ney which resulted in the latter taking on full responsibility for the rearguard. And although Victor fought again at Dresden and Leipzig, after the invasion of France he arrived so late for the action at Montereau that Napoleon relieved him of his command. He was then wounded at Craonne and his campaigning days were over.

But not his political activities. After the surrender of Paris he hurried off to ally himself with the restored Bourbons – and was made Governor of the 2nd Military Division (at Mézières). Having failed to prevent these troops rallying to Napoleon at the start of the Hundred Days he fled to join his new master at Ghent. Meanwhile in Paris his name was struck off the list of marshals.

Upon the second Restoration he was loaded with honours. A peerage, a major-generalship of the Royal Guard and membership of the Privy Council; plus huge gratuities and the inevitable decorations: Grand Cross of the Order of St.-Louis, Spain's Three Golden Fleeces and Portugal's Order of Christ. More significantly though, he became the Bourbon's principal 'witch-hunter', or as it was styled President of the Commission 'set up to examine the activities of officers during the campaign of Waterloo'. Included in a whole series of injustices he took the opportunity to pay off an old score in the most despicable fashion by arresting and helping to put on trial Marshal Ney. He also made sure of being present in the Chamber of Peers to vote for the death sentence.

Under Charles X he was at first Minister for War and still serving as a member of the War Council in 1830 when the mainline Bourbons were finally overthrown. Not surprisingly the new king Louis Philippe quickly removed him from public life. And in 1840 when Napoleon's remains were brought back to France, Victor did not receive an invitation to attend the ceremony, although living in Paris.

The Near—Marshals

DUROC, Géraud Christophe Michel, Duke of Friuli (1772 – 1813)

One of Napoleon's closest friends and intimates. He was entrusted with many diplomatic missions and also appointed Grand Marshal of the Palace. At the same time though he remained an active campaigning general, especially on the staff side, serving the Emperor most loyally in this capacity until his death after Baützen in 1813.

Duroc was born at Pont-à-Mousson in the Vosges. His family were poor and decided he should try for an army career. Their son was in full agreement, entering the artillery in 1792. He first met and became friendly with Napoleon during the Siege of Toulon. Later he accompanied the new star of the French army to Italy and conducted himself well in the action at Gradisca. In Egypt he took part in the battles at Aboukir, Jaffa and Acre, and following the events of 18/19 Brumaire was promoted general of brigade: still staying close to Napoleon though. In 1802, for instance, when the First Consul was beginning to look more and more like a sovereign, Duroc as his principal *aide-de-camp* was created Governor of the Tuileries, responsible for his master's personal safety and with a staff of ten senior adjutants and further junior officers. Four generals of the Guard were 'to be in constant attendance on the Consuls for ten-day periods by rotation'. Finally, in 1804, upon his coronation, Napoleon created him general of division and Grand Marshal of the Palace. After this the Emperor was the only man in France Duroc had to report to and – except for special missions – remained always in close attendance. On ceremonial occasions he wore a court-dress of red velvet and white satin and carried a sword and stick of office.

He was amiable but conscientious and proved popular as Grand Marshal. Tall and slim, he had dark hair and somewhat protuberant eyes. He had perfect manners and seemed to have a calming effect upon the new Emperor during some of his more irascible moments. He was good with the finances of the court and, following his marriage to a Madrid heiress, became an expert on Spanish affairs: invaluable when he handled the negotiations for the abdication of Charles IV.

But he remained by vocation a soldier; and in this capacity was a brilliant organiser. At Austerlitz he commanded the Imperial Guard, but was wounded just before Eylau. 'It's in my bad arm again', was his only comment. He served as principal ADC to the Emperor at Essling and Wagram, which led to his being sent to handle peace talks in St.-Petersburg, Vienna, Stockholm and Copenhagen. He concluded a treaty with Frederick William of Prussia and in 1808 the armistice of Znaim. Afterwards came Spain and his elevation to the high peerage. In 1813, after the retreat from Moscow, and his accompanying Napoleon back in the fast sleigh, he was created a senator as well.

He achieved wonders on the Emperor's behalf in helping to raise a new army against the advancing Allies and then cheerfully went off with his master to campaign in Central Europe. Again in command of the Imperial Guard, but still finding time to plan which tents the Emperor could use and what he would eat and drink. 'Soup, boiled and roast meat, vegetables; no dessert.' Yes, he even watched over Napoleon's figure!

His death occurred immediately following the Battle of Baützen. And more or less due to one of the flukes of warfare. As he rode away from the battlefield a late Russian cannon-ball ripped away most of his stomach. They carried him to a nearby farmhouse and the army's two top surgeons, Larrey and Yvan, hurried to examine him. But he knew he was done for and refused to let them dress the wound: he wanted the end to be quick. Napoleon was in tears. The front of his coat was wet with them. Duroc kissed his hand and begged for opium to ease the pain. 'I've spent all my life serving you,' he said, 'and I could still have been of use. That's why I'm sorry to die.'

'Wait for me in the next world,' Napoleon answered.

'Yes Sire. In thirty years, when you've beaten all your enemies and realised all France's hopes.'

Afterwards the Emperor bought the farmhouse and ordered a monument to Duroc erected there. Later, in his will, he made a large bequest to his Grand Marshal's daughter. Only Jean Lannes' death had moved him more.

JUNOT, Andoche, Duke of Abrantès (1771 – 1813)

He only had himself to blame that he never made Marshal of France. Certainly his friend and master gave him every opportunity. In reality though, while personally brave and in his way loyal, he wasn't much of a thinking soldier. Even worse, he was an inveterate looter – and except when under Napoleon's eye the campaign was likely to go badly wrong if there was potential plunder about.

Born at Bussy-le-Grand in the Burgundy, the son of a timber-merchant. He was educated at Châtillon, learned to write with a good hand and even entertained hopes of studying law. But then the Revolution came and Junot was a sergeant when he first met Napoleon at the Siege of Toulon. The Corsican took to him immediately and made him his secretary. He was cheerful, a willing subordinate and he had *sang-froid*. When an English shell landed nearby, nearly killing them and covering the order papers with earth, he exclaimed: 'Good! Now I won't need to sand the ink!'

He served as ADC to Napoleon throughout the subsequent Italian campaign. He also, upon their meeting, became infatuated with Napoleon's sister Pauline; but it was made clear to him that as a mere lieutenant he didn't stand a chance. 'You have nothing, she has nothing,' the First Consul told him. 'The total is nothing. Your children would be wretched. Best to wait!' Otherwise he remained in great favour. After the Battle of Millesimo he was chosen to carry the captured standards back to Paris and Napoleon used the Egyptian expedition as the reason to secure his promotion to brigadier.

In Egypt he displayed much personal bravery, but towards the end got involved in a duel on Napoleon's behalf with General Lanusse and was badly wounded: an eight-inch sabre slash across the belly. This caused him to be left behind when political events caused his superior to return to France in such a hurry. Later, making his own way home, he was captured by the English but almost immediately released and he reached Paris soon after Napoleon had come to power. The new Consul made him Governor of the capital.

Deprived of Pauline, Junot now married Laure Permon – who as a girl had laughed at Napoleon in his first officer's uniform – and the future authoress of the scurrilous *Mémoires ou Souvenirs Historiques* (in no less than eighteen volumes!) With his rough-shaped head, thick nose and untidy blond hair, the general didn't exactly look the part as a lover, but for several years at least the couple were happy enough. However Laure's extravagance showed signs of becoming more than just a nuisance and Junot's own previous cheerfulness had changed to bad-temper when he held an independent command. He was no longer popular with his junior officers. Napoleon too was beginning to have his doubts. He had promoted his friend to general of division, given him 100,000 francs as a wedding present and installed him in a fine house where the Junots regularly entertained and collected paintings and first editions. However, friendship was not to be confused with merit. Upon the change to Empire Napoleon hesitated, then decided against including Junot in the preliminary list of marshals...

In 1805 he sent him as ambassador to Portugal but no sooner had Junot arrived there than the news came through of the Grand Army's moves against Austria and the Russians. Immediately the general jumped on a horse and set off to rejoin his master: two thousand miles across Europe and just in time to fight at Austerlitz, where he distinguished himself in the battle.

This was sufficient enough for the Emperor to give him a very real opportunity to earn a marshal's baton. He then entrusted him with the 1807 expedition to Portugal. Junot, Laure and a force of 1,500 reached Lisbon on the day Napoleon had specified and for this the dukedom of Abrantès was bestowed. But Junot was frustrated in his efforts to seize the Portuguese fleet and his governorship of the city proved lamentable. (For administration read 'putting to sack'.) Meanwhile Laure's greed and extravagance knew no bounds. With the Portuguese thoroughly alienated, and the English under Wellesley welcomed back, the French stood little chance at the Battle of Vimiera. Junot's faulty and impulsive tactics only added to the disaster. Afterwards he was lucky to obtain a negotiated retreat – and even luckier to escape a court-martial (the fate of Dupont after Baylen).

Yet he tested the ties of friendship further still by entering into a liaison with Caroline Murat. It led to the most terrible dressing down. 'You compromise my sister,' Napoleon shouted at him. 'I know all the facts, which I am willing to look upon as imprudence only – but in them I also see serious faults in your character.'

Junot fought again in the Peninsular War under Masséna. When again there were notorious instances of looting. And a sharp rebuff from Marshal

119

Ney when Junot offered him a part of the spoils. He now received another bad wound and did not really recover until the Russian campaign: if then. He was riddled with rheumatism; his head was scarred and dented from too much frontline fighting, and his judgement could hardly be relied upon. At Smolensk the Emperor realised his old friend was spent. Under the circumstances he did the kindest thing possible, and posted Junot to Venice as Governor of Illyria: one of the few quiet provinces in the Empire. It was there, in the following year, that the general finally went mad. On one occasion he appeared in the streets naked except for his sword belt and *épaulettes*. The end especially was tragic. Crazily, he hacked himself about the body and then jumped from a high window.

LASALLE, Antoine Chevalier Louis Collinet, Count (1775 – 1809)

Probably the outstanding cavalry commander in the whole of the Grand Army, even ahead of Murat. Had he lived would undoubtedly have made marshal, being one of Napoleon's favourite and most inspired promotions. Sometimes off-duty he acted the swaggering bucko, but in action he combined phenomenal bravery with a cool head and a masterly grasp of tactics and mobility. By birth an aristocrat (although of the *petite noblesse*), he seemed ready-made to become a Bonapartist. He had *la gloire* as if within his soul and having found his chosen leader never afterwards swerved in his loyalty.

Lasalle entered the French army at age 11 and three years later was commissioned lieutenant. But on the outbreak of the Revolution his aristocratic background brought dismissal, so he enlisted in the ranks and regained his commission by bravery and sheer good-horsemanship.

He first came to Napoleon's attention with the Army of Italy and later went with him to Egypt where in one skirmish he saved Davout's life. In 1800 he was promoted to colonel and in the campaign of that year had two horses shot from under him and is said to have broken seven swords. He served at Austerlitz as general of brigade, then captured the fortress of Stettin with only 600 hussars and not even any artillery. For this Napoleon created him general of division. In the subsequent Polish campaign he helped form and then train the Polish light-horse, as well as saving Murat's life at Heilsberg. He led a distinguished charge at Eylau, but afterwards was switched to the Spanish front and under Bessières on July 14, 1808 led his Poles and the cavalry of the Imperial Guard in the destruction of a 21,000-strong Spanish force commanded by Cuesta and Blake at Medina-del-Rio Seco.

From Spain a junior officer wrote of him: 'It was in General Lasalle's school that we learned outpost duty. We have kept a precious memory of this general in whom all the lovable and imposing qualities of a born marshal were combined. He should have replaced the Grand Duke of Berg (Murat) to whom he was vastly superior.'

Meanwhile Lasalle himself had written the (somewhat chilling) words to the Poles' regimental march and would sing them as he led his men into battle:

> The French were once in Poland,
> Now the Poles have come to Spain;
> Europe will see them both command
> Her people without shame;
> What nation is so strong
> As to resist for long
> For Poles and Frenchmen in one breath,
> Could put all men on earth to death!

But his own death (a great loss, as the Emperor admitted) was near. In 1809, when the Austrians again took the field against France, the intrepid cavalry general distinguished himself in the decisive action at Essling and then during the great French victory at Wagram, only to be shot down in what was to prove the final charge of the battle.

LECLERC, Victoir Emmanuel, General (1766 – 1802)

Would probably have been created a marshal in 1804 had he lived – not so much for his military accomplishments, which were variable, but on account of his marriage to Pauline Bonaparte. After all, Murat, married to Caroline Bonaparte, became a marshal in the 1804 creation; and Pauline was the Emperor's favourite sister. While still First Consul Napoleon became godfather to the Leclerc's child and Leclerc's sister Aimée married Davout upon their leader's insistence.

Born at Pontoise, the son of a wealthy mill-owner. He seems to have been well-educated, joining the Revolutionary armies as a volunteer in 1791. He was with the Army of Italy as an adjutant-general when he married Pauline; at Mombello (1797). In the winter of 1800 he commanded the operations against Spain and Portugal. But it is clear he was unpopular with the troops, partly because he imitated the manner and even the clothes of Napoleon; also too because he was quite unnecessarily harsh. In anger he once caused an innocent solder to be shot out of hand because he'd failed to secure the conviction of two others.

In 1801 Napoleon organised an expeditionary force to put down the slave's revolt on San Domingo in the West Indies. (Its sugar and coffee production were considered of vital importance to France.) Leclerc was given command of the army; Villaret-Joyeuse the navy. It wasn't easy, facing the problems of the forests and swamps and the slave's hit-and-run tactics. Leclerc finally found here the bravery he had lacked in his earlier years. He also captured the main rebel, Toussaint l'Ouverture and had him shipped to France. But the climate eventually got to him. After a long series of fevers and infections, in the end he succumbed to cholera. Pauline had his body embalmed and accompanied it back to France, where Napoleon ordered a state-brial in the Panthéon.

=5=

Other Military Figures

Once Napoleon came to power there were few further French army promotions above the rank of colonel which he didn't make personally; and even those recommended by the marshals still had to be vetted and approved by him. However, such was his knowledge – and his ubiquitousness – that he made very few mistakes: perhaps a dozen altogether. To begin with he promoted largely from the officers of the Army of Italy. This was partly because he had got to know their abilities, but also due to his suspicions that those belonging to the Army of the Rhine and other northern groups were more loyal to his rival General Moreau. (His initial efforts to win over Michel Ney, for instance, were both militarily-inspired and overtly political.) As time went on though and his personal position became – or seemed – unassailable, so the promotions were made strictly on merit: and more often than not after Napoleon had witnessed an officer's performance on the battlefield. Junot, although a close friend, missed his baton for this reason. The retreat from Portugal simply confirmed what Napoleon already thought: that he just wasn't good enough.

On the other hand, with so large a body of men as the Grand Army it would be naîve to imagine that all the senior officers were Bonapartist to an identical degree. Probably not since Alexander the Great has personal loyalty to one man counted for as much: and loyalty to a man who knew as much about his army and so many of its officers, NCOs and privates, personally. Nevertheless many human factors entered into what is often summarised as devotion. Ambition, greed, love of country, the desire for fame, a wish to be associated with the principal European glamour of the moment, the need to go with success: all of these things come into it. Also sheer military professionalism. How else can one suppose that so many French officers emerged from the privations of the *débâcle* in Russia with the will and the capacity to fight again?

In the section which follows I have tried to identify the principal senior officers who were at the same time confirmed Bonapartists and owed their careers to the First Consul/Emperor. But professionalism still counted for a lot. It certainly appears to have motivated the gallant Jean Louis Reynier:

who served in Egypt, at Bussaço where he agreed with Marshal Ney's view that Masséna's tactics were wrong but still charged on cue; who survived the retreat from Moscow and didn't finally lay down his arms until captured at Leipzig...

Professional pride also played its part in the make-up of several of the younger generals who fought at Waterloo. Bachelu, Bailly de Monthion, Domon, Donzelet, Farine, Marcognet, Milhaud, Piré, Subervie and Travers are the ones who immediately come to mind. There is a tendency to assume that *all* who participated on the French side during the Waterloo campaign had to be Bonapartists. But by this time some officer's first loyalty was to the army itself; and when the mood of the troops was for rallying to the returned Emperor then they agreed to go along with it. The generals just named were not on the Bourbon's list of those to be proscribed for alleged treason. They were not considered Bonapartists through and through like La Bédoyère or the officers of the Imperial Guard. However, Piré, Travers and especially Milhaud had fought with such outstanding courage at Waterloo that questions were inevitably asked about them. Eventually they were pronounced 'sound'. Even the Bourbons realised they badly needed a general staff and capable commanders.

Another special case is that of General Jean Baptiste Eblé (born 1758), another count of the Empire. Evidently he was not politically-minded in any way, but his tough professional attitude included being loyal to France's chosen leader. In addition to which he was probably the most gifted engineer-officer in Europe. The crossing of the Berezina during the retreat out of Russia was his masterpiece. The river was 120 feet wide at Studianka where it was decided to make the crossing, fast-flowing and cluttered with lumps of ice. Oudinot was charged with protecting the work. Ney, Prince Eugène, Poniatowski and Davout were all with the rearguard. Eblé with 400 pontooneers of the Imperial Guard plus a handful of marines and gunners built the Grand Army a bridge. Even Murat thought he could never do it. He had a wagonful of nails salvaged from the boats at Orsha and he dismantled the timbered huts of two deserted villages to make trestles and rafts. Napoleon, very calm and collected, continually inspired the men with his presence. Most of these pontooneers were to die during or soon after the bridge's completion. Eblé too, having been working for hours on end and often up to his neck in the freezing water. He didn't complain though. There was a job to be done and he decided to set his men an example.

Finally forty thousand men with most of their guns got across his bridge. Meanwhile Ney and Oudinot had inflicted 20,000 casualties on the pursuing Russians.

Then Eblé set fire to the bridge. He died one month later at Koenisberg.

Like the majority of the officers now described he has become an unmistakeable thread in the overall Napoleonic tapestry.

BERTRAND, Henri Gratian, Count (1773 – 1844)

Of all the officers close to Napoleon, and of those few who shared the exile on St.-Helena, his loyalty was probably the warmest and deepest. Far from being the manifest declaration of an ardent Bonapartist like La Bédoyère, rather it was sure, steady and based upon his personal conviction that the Emperor was a genius who had saved France following the Revolution and made her great . . . therefore not a man to be deserted in adversity.

Born at Châteauroux (Indre). He was a student when the Revolution occurred, but immediately volunteered and served in the ranks to help defend the nation's borders against the First Coalition. Napoleon promoted him colonel during the Egyptian expedition, later general of brigade and after Austerlitz his principal ADC.

Although he took easily to staff-work, he'd first qualified as an engineer-officer and in this capacity performed outstandingly during the Aspern-Essling-Wagram campaign of 1809: which involved repeated bridging of the Danube and its many islands and tributaries. He never lost his cool. Before the Grand Army could be deployed at Wagram a makeshift pontoon of fourteen roped-together barges had to be floated across the river's notorious currents and whirlpools. 'How long?' the Emperor demanded of Bertrand and his assistant, Captain Heckmann. 'Fifteen minutes, Sire—' came the reply. 'I'll give you five!' Napoleon told them; and he borrowed Bertrand's watch to make sure. Fortunately the pontoon swung into place at the first go.

In the battles of 1813 he commanded 4th Corps and distinguished himself at Lützen, Baützen and again at Leipzig, where on the western flank he twice beat back the Austrian troops under Gyulai and then got his corps away before the fatal, accidental detonating of the bridge over the Elster. Also in 1813 the Emperor created Bertrand Grand Marshal of the Palace in succession to Duroc.

He was present at Fontainebleau during the first abdication and first raised the alarm after Napoleon's suicide attempt. He then accompanied his master to Elba; and later, on and off the battlefield at Waterloo. Although arrested, afterwards it was decided that he should be permitted to go with Napoleon into his final exile. (He received 500,000 francs under the Emperor's official will.)

In 1830 he was elected a deputy and in 1840 Louis Philippe chose him as one of the honoured few who brought back the Emperor's remains to Paris.

BONNEMAINS, Pierre, Count (1773 – 1850)

General of Division.

It is difficult to conceive of the tall, aristocratic Bonnemains belonging to the Bonapartist *élite*. With his high cheek-bones and severe glance, given the different uniform he might easily be taken for a German Junker. At least, that is how Couture portrays him.

Nevertheless he fought through most of Napoleon's European campaigns, was decorated with the Legion of Honour and then returned to fight under his old leader at Waterloo. The Emperor placed him in command of the 4th and 12th Dragoons of General Chastel's 10th Division (a part of 2nd Corps). He fought at Ligny and after Waterloo played a significant role in the preserved cavalry of France's right-wing halting the Prussians at Namur.

Following the surrender, as one of the officers close to Exelmans, he was suspected by the Bourbons of having been a party to Napoleon's escape from Elba. He went into exile but was pardoned in the later amnesty.

BOURMONT, Louis Auguste Victor, Count (1773 – 1846)

Thomas Creevey, who disliked Wellington but couldn't keep away from him, once asked the Iron Duke if the English could count on any desertions from Napoleon's army. Wellington was remarkably prophetic. 'Not a man from the colonel to the private in a regiment – both inclusive,' he said, 'we may pick up a marshal or two, perhaps; but not worth a damn!'

Well, they picked up two marshals: Marmont and Victor. Augereau, although he deserted Napoleon, never served under the Allies. Bernadotte had been fighting France for a number of years, while Murat was fighting to preserve his own kingdom rather than against his former friend and master.

But two prominent generals also deserted: Nansouty in 1814 and Bourmont in the thick of the Waterloo campaign. The latter was a more serious defection, because it occurred immediately before the action at Ligny and the general persuaded his HQ staff to go with him, seriously undermining the command structure of Gérard's 4th Corps.

Bourmont owed everything to Napoleon, including his title. And he later compounded his treachery by endeavouring to give prosecution evidence during the trial of Marshal Ney: which was demolished by the lawyers for the defence.

He became a court favourite under the restored Bourbons. In their North African campaign he took Algiers in 1830 and was promptly promoted to Marshal of France: for one month. After the revolution which followed in Paris the new king, Louis Philippe, exiled him for life.

When he walked into the Allies' camp before Waterloo, Blücher, who had every reason to hate Napoleon, growled: 'A cur is always a cur!'

BURTHE, André, Baron (1772 – 1830)

He was general of division, although he served at brigade-level in the Waterloo campaign, commanding the 5th and 13th Dragoons of the 2nd Cavalry Corps under Exelmans. Prior to that he had served in Russia, Germany in 1813 and then through the battles for France, when he was decorated with the Legion of Honour.

He took part in the fighting at Ligny and then, still under Exelmans, in Grouchy's muddled pursuit of the Prussians on June 17. (Which meant he took no part in the events at Waterloo itself.)After joining Grouchy's orderly retreat upon Paris, like many of the Bonapartist officers he was forced to go into hiding.

CAFFARELLI, Louis Marie Joseph Maximilien (1756 – 99)

A boon companion of the younger Napoleon, who called him 'Max', and a good officer. Had he lived would undoubtedly have risen to some high position under the Empire. Also a popular figure with the army as a whole. The enlisted men nicknamed him *Jambe de Bois* after the wooden substitute for the leg taken off by a cannon-ball.

Born in 1756, he first saw service along the Rhine under Kléber, specialising as an engineer-officer. He was a convinced Republican and on one occasion startled his colleagues by insisting that all property is a form of theft.

It was in Egypt that his close friendship with Napoleon developed. The latter took a keen interest in Caffarelli's workshops, which, apart from making cannon-balls, were turning out wooden *boules* and other things to give the troops recreation. The two men then went off to explore the sites of the ancient canal between the Mediterranean and the Red Sea. Their guides got them lost and they were nearly drowned, Caffarelli losing his wooden leg, (although he had a spare one back at HQ!)

During the siege at St.-Jean d'Acre it became a homesick joke to say: 'Caffarelli's all right. He's still got one foot in France!' However, in that same operation his arm was shattered by a Turkish bullet. After amputation infection set in. Napoleon was greatly distressed and visited him almost hourly. He read him Voltaire's preface to Montesquieu's *L'Esprit des Lois*, a favourite of both men. Gradually though his friend slid into unconsciousness and death. Napoleon wept. 'France has lost one of her best citizens and Science one of her most devoted servants,' he stressed.

Later he took Caffarelli's heart back with him to Paris.

CAMBRONNE, Pierre Jacques, later Viscount (1770 – 1842)

A French general, whose particular fighting abilities were usually matched by his salty language. Although captured during the final stage at Waterloo, when invited to surrender the last of his guardsmen he refused. 'The Guard dies but never gives itself up,' he is reported to have said. However other observers attest that his reply to the Allies was, quite simply: 'Merde!'

He was a Breton; born at Nantes into a comparatively poor family and lacking a good education. But he grew up to be handsome, tall and wavy-haired, and with fierce eyes in the Duke of Guise' style. He joined the Revolutionary forces in 1790 and served in most of the northern campaigns as an NCO. Later, having gravitated towards Napoleon, much of his time was destined to be spent with the Imperial Guard – first as a major with three citations and the Legion of Honour, then gradually working up to general of brigade and, finally, of division.

At the Battle of Dresden he commanded the 2nd Chasseurs. He was wounded at Hanau, but recovered sufficiently to take part in the action at Craonne, where he was hit four times but still stood firm at the head of his Guards.

One mission in which he failed – although through no fault of his own – was when Napoleon sent him to Orléans to collect Marie Louise and bring her to Fontainebleau. Metternich had got there first (in the person of Prince Esterhazy) and whisked her away to rejoin her father, the Austrian Emperor, at Rambouillet.

Cambronne was given overall command of the Imperial Guard on Elba (Napoleon was allowed 700 of them) and arrived there on May 26, 1814. His master had eagerly awaited him. 'Cambronne, I have passed many bad hours waiting for you, but at last we are re-united and they are forgotten.' He also made him Commandant of Portoferráio, the island's tiny capital, to supervise 'all that is police and security'. He also put him in charge of sanitation: a big problem, like the Elba mosquitoes. Cambronne examined everyone who landed on the island personally, and in his rough, but zealous way was often very abusive to visitors he suspected were instruments of the Allies. Meanwhile he kept his Guardsmen in peak condition. He knew some of them would soon be needed because he was party to the escape plans...

Once back on the mainland he led the vanguard of the advance from Cannes via Grenoble to Lyon. 'Cambronne, you will go ahead, always ahead. But remember, I forbid you to shed one drop of French blood in the recovery of my crown.' The vanguard consisted of only fifty grenadiers, but it was enough to frighten a whole series of mayors into opening up their towns and supplying money and provisions.

In the Waterloo campaign he led a charge at Ligny, was wounded again, but insisted on taking part in the action at Waterloo itself. Leading a division of the Old Guard, he fought with exceptional bravery. Reduced to the gory shambles of just one battalion he arranged his troops in triangles two ranks deep and continued to fire in retreat while other units were fleeing the field. Having uttered his famous reply, he was then shot in the head and left for dead; his command having been reduced to a mere 150 men.

After spending some time in an English prison, he then returned to France to face a court-martial. He was exonerated, but retired from the army in disgust – not taking up general duties again until after the Revolution of 1830.

He was another who benefitted from Napoleon's will.

CLAUSEL, Bertrand, Count (1772 – 1842)

One of the most fanatically pro-Napoleon members of the experienced officer corps; and a man prepared to die for his beliefs, although in the end he didn't have to and lived to become a marshal of France.

He was born at Mirepoix (Ariège in the Pyrénées) and joined the army as a boy soldier. He did well in the Spanish and Italian campaigns from 1791 to 1802. His frontline fighting abilities were first-rate and he was showing much promise as a tactician. Also at this time he became greatly attached to Napoleon, who decorated him with the Legion of Honour and later gave him a command in the Peninsular War, where he was one of the comparative successes in what was otherwise a sorry story. He defended Burgos with an absolute fury against Wellington and then managed to elude the British commander and skip the city. Later still, after the Battle of Salamanca, he replaced Marmont as overall commander and conducted a masterly retreat upon the Pyrénées. He did not get on well with King Joseph Bonaparte, but then no other professional on the French general staff did.

Once driven back into France he continued to retreat/resist stubbornly until the first abdication, when, to his surprise, he suddenly found himself being presented to Wellington – and was even more surprised when Wellington opened the door to his hotel room himself and offered him champagne as one soldierly colleague to another.

But if Clausel was impressed by the behaviour of his former British adversary he remained bitterly opposed to the return of the Bourbons. He is one of those claimed in the French army to have referred to the return of 'Louis the Pig' and upon Napoleon's escape from Elba was among the first to rejoin him. He was not present at Waterloo. Because of his special knowledge of the region the returned Emperor placed him in command of the Army of the Pyrénées, after which he was placed very high on the royalists' hit-list. However, he escaped to America, and on his return to France in 1819, later accepted an official pardon, was created Marshal of France and in 1830 commanded the French Algerian Expedition. He resigned his command though because of unsubstantiated but harmful criticism of his siege-tactics at Constantine, where his soldiers suffered numerous deprivations – although, he claimed, this was due to bad supplying by the French War Ministry. He chose to retire and eventually died at Secourrien, Garonne.

COLBERT DE CHABANAIS, Edouard, Count (1774 – 1853)

An outstanding cavalry officer and despite his aristocratic origins a convinced Bonapartist through to the end.

First commissioned captain of the Mameluks in the Consulate Guard, and later promoted colonel of the 7th Hussars. As a result of his part in the great charges at Wagram in 1809 he was decorated with the Legion of Honour. In command of the 2nd Lancers from 1812-14 he saw action at Gorodnia, fought with distinction under Bessières at Lützen (after which he was promoted general of brigade but kept with the Guard cavalry) and then took part without even the shortest rest in most of the battles for France. He joined the actions at Brienne, La Rothière, Gué-à-Tremmes, Craonne, Epernay, Arcis and St.-Dizier.

A tall, somewhat ascetic-looking man who always affected the cavalryman's heavy moustache, he viewed with distaste the returning Bourbons and their old-fashioned, no-lessons-learned ways. Adhering to the Bonapartist cause during the Hundred Days he was given command of the crack regiment of *Chevau-Legers-Lanciers* of the Imperial Guard. Wounded at Quatre Bras on June 16, 1815, he took part in the massive charge at Waterloo itself on the 18th with his arm in a sling.

Imprisoned for a time after the second Restoration, he was another of the select band of officers who later received money under the terms of Napoleon's will.

D'ERLON, Jean Baptiste Drouet, Count (1765 – 1844)

Again, despite an aristocratic background he proved to be one of the most loyal of the Bonapartists and as such after Waterloo only narrowly escaped execution.

General of brigade from 1799, Napoleon promoted him to general of division in 1803 and made him a count of the Empire in 1809. From 1810 he served in the Iberian Peninsula, to begin with under Marshal Ney, then later at the head of his own corps. In 1813 he was one of the principal commanders at the Battle of Vittoria, although the errors of the French *débâcle* were in no way attributable to his fighting abilities. He failed to hold the 'key' hill of Arinez, but by this time King Joseph had already lost the battle.

At the time of Napoleon's escape from Elba he had command of the garrison at Lille – and was arrested by local Bourbonist officers for rallying his troops to the returned Emperor's cause. However, he escaped and at Waterloo was placed in command of 1st Corps: 16,000 infantry, 200 field-pieces and Jacquinot's cavalry (1800 men). Due to faulty staff-work and several strange courier-messages he passed the day of Ligny/Quatre Bras marching and counter-marching in-between the two actions to no effective purpose. But at Waterloo itself his corps spearheaded the first French attack upon Wellington's lines.

D'Erlon was one of the last officers to quit the battlefield. In the end though, when the bleeding and powder-blackened Ney shouted at him, 'If they catch us, you and I will be shot', he took the advice and remained in Belgium. Louis XVIII issued an *Ordonnance* to the effect that 'the Generals and Officers who betrayed the King before March 23, or who attacked France and its true government *sword in hand*, and those who by violence seized hold of power, will be arrested and placed before Councils of War...' The list was headed by Ney and La Bédoyère, but D'Erlon was one of the other seventeen named. So he stayed put.

He returned to active service after the revolution of 1830 and was promoted to Marshal of France by Louis Philippe in 1843: a largely honorary appointment since his health was already failing.

DELABORDE, Henri François, Count (1764 – 1833)

The son of a baker at Dijon. He began as a revolutionary soldier, was promoted general of brigade and then present at the Siege of Toulon as Chief of Staff. Following this he was promoted general of division and served briefly as Governor of Corsica. He was on the Spanish frontier in 1794 and fought well at Bidassoa and Misquiriz. Afterwards the government posted him to the Rhine and he was a divisional commander under General Moreau in Bavaria in 1796.

Napoleon liked him a lot and used him frequently. He made him a commander of the Legion of Honour, then count when Delaborde was serving under Junot in Portugal in 1808. He extricated his men with great skill in the rearguard action at Roliça, earning praises from his distinguished opponent Sir Arthur Wellesley for it. In 1812 he commanded a division in Russia under Marshal Mortier as well as serving as Governor of Smolensk. Afterwards he was decorated with the Grand Cross of the Legion of Honour. In 1815, having recovered from a bad wound received during the Battle of Dresden, he was busy putting down a royalist revolt in the Vendée.

Following the Hundred Days the Bourbons court-martialled him and then put him on trial for his life. But he escaped due to a technical flaw in the charge. After this he retired into private life; badly crippled with gout.

DESAIX (Chevalier de Veygoux), Louis Charles Antoine (1768 – 1800)

Napoleon had numerous admirations for commanders of the past. He was not an assiduous student of military history for nothing. But of his contemporary officers in the period leading up to and including his total command of the French forces Desaix was the one man he regarded as possessing a genius for warfare. The two men became firm friends – and remained so until Desaix's death, which Napoleon then described as the greatest loss the new French army after the Revolution had so far sustained. He was born at St.-Hilaire-d'Ayot, of the *petite noblesse*, and into a family connected with the French army allegedly since the Middle Ages. His father put him into Marshal d'Effiat's military academy, from which – aged 15 – he entered the Regiment of Brittany as a sub-lieutenant. He espoused the cause of the Revolution and almost immediately began to reveal his natural abilities. (This, after nearly being guillotined merely because he happened to be on the staff of the executed Marshal Broglie!) Taken on by the Republican government, however, he quickly became general of division with the Army of the Rhine.

Lavalette in his diaries observed him closely at this time.

'He was', he says, 'tall in stature and his figure was singular. He had fine, black, fiery eyes, a nose that appeared to descend from the top of his forehead; and thick and unusually separated lips showing a set of teeth of sparking whiteness. His hair was flat and black as jet, surrounding a dark face. His gait was shy, as if betraying a want of knowledge of the world. Altogether he looked like a savage from the banks of the Orinoco dressed in French clothes. But such an appearance was easily overcome. His voice was soft and when once drawn out of his shyness, he delighted everyone by his real knowledge and the informality of his manner. He had none of the brutal faults of men accustomed to camp life. I never heard him swear or curse. In fact, an indecent word made him blush. On the other hand, since he was amiable and kind, his staff led a gay life and the pretty girls of the Palatinate thoroughly enjoyed visiting his officers' mess. One noticed though that he smiled at our pleasures without joining them. As if with the indulgence of a father who shuts his eyes to his children's odd pranks. I don't think I ever saw him dressed in the uniform of his rank. He generally wore a blue coat without lace and with sleeves so tight he might have worn it at his First Communion.'

But great military commanders – as Napoleon himself demonstrated – do not need to be clothes-horses...

In 1795 against the powerful Austrian forces and their assorted German allies Desaix commanded Jourdan's right-wing and never lost an engagement. Following the battles of Amberg and Würtzberg he was in charge of General Moreau's rearguard in the Revolutionary army's retreat and he successfully defended Kehl. In these situations he revealed himself as a fighter of the new order. He didn't just push his troops into hit or miss engagements. He saved men and won battles by clever tactical moves (a great influence upon Napoleon in the years to come).

The Paris authorities directed that he should go and join General Bonaparte in Italy; and there their mutual friendship grew. Napoleon next took Desaix with him to Egypt: and found he could be even more than a friend. Desaix performed with fantastic bravery at the Battle of the Pyramids. And yet...after the victory he had the character to win over many of the ordinary Egyptians who for so long had been subjected to near-slavery by the Mameluks. He gained the title 'The Just Sultan'. Baron Denon noted: 'How many wise ideas on civil government and philanthropy suggested themselves to his mind when the sound of the trumpet and the roll of the drum ceased to give him the fever of war!'

At this stage Napoleon considered Desaix and Kléber were 'his most distinguished lieutenants, both possessing great and rare merits'. Later he would add: 'The talent of Desaix was always in full activity. He loved *la gloire* for glory's sake, and France above all. Luxury and comfort he despised. He preferred sleeping under a gun in the open air.'

After the signing of the Treaty of El Arish Desaix handed over the command in Egypt to Kléber and returned to Europe, where almost immediately he was embroiled with Napoleon in a new campaign in Italy against the Austrians. Arriving with his two divisions of infantry at Marengo, just when the Austrians seemed victorious, he shouted: 'There is yet time to win another battle!' and went on and did so. His magnificent counterattack became one of Napoleon's greatest victories – although Desaix himself was mortally wounded in leading it.

Napoleon erected two Parisian monuments to his memory: one in the Place Dauphine, the other in the Place des Victoires.

DROUOT, Antoine, Count (1774 – 1847)

General of division and one of the officers most trusted by Napoleon. Following the first abdication he served as military governor on Elba and at Waterloo was Deputy Chief of Staff as well as commander of the Imperial Guard.

He trained for the artillery at the *Ecole Polytechnique*. By 1808 he was a lieutenant-colonel in charge of the Guard's light artillery. Wounded at Essling, he then took part with distinction at Wagram and in 1810 the Emperor made him a Baron. He served as a principal ADC during the Russian campaign, commanded the Guard artillery reserve at Lützen, Leipzig, Hanau and fought with great personal bravery at La Rothière, Craonne and Arcis. He accompanied Napoleon to Fontainebleau and went on to Elba with him at his own request.

A somewhat austere man, who for relaxation read the Bible, he complained that the discipline on the island was too lax. However, Napoleon pointed out that the men were bored. Give them a band and some dancing he advised. Meanwhile Drouot was charged with fitting out the ship, the *Inconstant* for their escape. Although being provisioned with french food and wine she was painted to resemble an English brig.

After the collapse at Waterloo he was arrested in Paris, tried and imprisoned.

Napoleon left him a sum of money in his will – and in 1830 Louis Philippe conferred on him the Grand Cordon of the Legion of Honour.

DUHESME, Philippe Guillaume, Count (1766 – 1815)

French general, born at Bourgneuf (Saône et Loire). He first became a military 'name' during the Peninsular War, where he commanded a line division. Then, early in 1808, he advanced upon Barcelona with 14,000 men. For a time he was highly successful, seizing the chief forts and the central citadel, but he was soon cut off from his supply-lines to Madrid by a general peasant uprising throughout Catalonia. To fight his way north to Perpignan he attacked the fortress of Gerona, but without success. This kept him blockaded in Barcelona for the next four months: until Gouvion St.-Cyr was sent to relieve him and their joint troops defeated the Catalans at Molins del Rey on December 21, 1808. Later Duhesme commanded a division at La Rothière in 1814. This battle against the Russians was fought in a blizzard, and eventually, after two days and 5,000 casualties, the French were forced to retreat over the Aube. However, Duhesme had been at the centre of a gritty resistance and Napoleon decorated him for it.

He adhered to Napoleon during the Hundred Days and was placed in command of the Young Guard. He fought at Ligny and helped extract 3rd Corps from a tricky situation at St.-Amand. He was killed at Waterloo near Plancenoit, dying on his horse, held upright by his faithful *tirailleurs*.

DUPONT DE L'ETANG, Pierre Antoine (1765 – 1840)

A General; and one of the brightest military figures under the Consulate and during the first years of the Empire. A high-flyer – even tipped as a future marshal – until he then had a remarkably swift, Icarus-like fall.

He first came to the fore at Valmy in 1793. He was promoted general of brigade and in 1797 general of division. He then came to Napoleon's attention during the *coup* of 18/19 Brumaire, resulting in his taking part in the Italian campaign of 1800. He fought at Marengo and again at Pozzolo, where he won the victory. Subsequently he fought under Ney at Ülm (in 1805); and then, so well under Ney again at Friedland (1807), that the Emperor decided to make him a corps commander for the big invasion of Spain.

He also created him a count of the Empire, after the occupation of Madrid. Following which – fatally as it turned out – he was charged with the subjugation of Andalusia...

Having beaten Castaños at the bridge of Alcolea, he then took Cordoba; making no attempt to stop his men looting it. However, on July 19, 1808, at Baylen, it was a different story. There the 20,000 French and with a disorderly, strung-out baggage-train filled with the spoils of Cordoba, found themselves suddenly surrounded by the resilient Castaños and a force of 35,000 Spaniards. Three days later a wounded Dupont agreed to surrender with all of his troops, including the marines of the Imperial Guard. It was the first time this had happened to a body of French troops since Napoleon's coming to power.

The Emperor was at Bordeaux when he got the news. Back in Paris, he cried when he spelled out the facts to the Council of State. But then he howled with rage: and again when he discovered the prisoners were being ill-treated and dying like flies.

Dupont – now nicknamed 'le Capitulard' – was court-martialled, stripped of his rank and title and imprisoned for the duration of the Empire.

Later he served the Bourbons, including a period as Minister for War and for all of twenty-five years as the deputy for Charente.

EXELMANS, Rémy Joseph Isidore, Count (1775 – 1852)

A brilliant soldier and destined to become a marshal of France – but not until after Napoleon's death. He had joined the army when he was sixteen – with obvious talents – and he soon distinguished himself in Italy serving under General Broussier. He took part in the conquest of Naples, where he first came to the attention of Murat. He became *aide-de-camp* to the latter in 1801 and subsequently served with him in Austria, Prussia and Poland from 1805 to 1807. His fighting abilities during the engagement at Wertingen, but even more so at Austerlitz brought him to Napoleon's attention, and after Eylau he was promoted to general of brigade. However in the Peninsular War he was unlucky enough to be captured and transported back to Britain. After three years he escaped and joined Murat in Naples where he was created Grand Master of Horse. Upon the invasion of Russia he returned to the main French Army, and as a result of his courage and endurance during the retreat from Moscow was created a general of division. He stayed very close to the Emperor during the first part of the retreat. At Krasny, with a contingent of the Old Guard he chased Ozharovski's cavalry out of the place. In the later battles for France he commanded the horse of the Guard at Montmirail, Château-Thierry, La Ferté and Craonne and upon Napoleon's first abdication he was banished from France.

Following the return from Elba (which he had conspired to bring about) he was made a peer of the realm. He commanded a cavalry corps of the Guard during the Battle of Ligny and supervised the cavalry's operations at Wavre. Later he was involved in the retreat upon Paris. Under the restored Bourbons he was exiled again for voicing his criticisms of the execution of Marshal Ney and lived in Belgium until 1819, when he was amnestied. He was restored to full honours by Louis Philippe and created a marshal by Napoleon III. He died from the effects of a hunting accident, (an irony, since he had never been unhorsed in battle).

FLAHAUT (de la Billarderie), Auguste Charles Joseph, Count (1785 – 1870)

Took the name of the Count of Flahaut although he was known to be the illegitimate son of Talleyrand. Not surprisingly perhaps, he cared little for his true father and grew up to be a Bonapartist through and through.

At the outbreak of the Revolution his mother took him abroad, but he returned to France as a volunteer and when only just sixteen fought at Marengo. It earned him promotion as junior ADC to Murat.

In 1805 he was wounded at Landbach, and later, while serving in Poland caused something of a scandal due to his liaison with the notorious Countess Potocki. But he returned to the battlefields of Europe, earning his commanders' praises during the Peninsular War and again in Russia where he was promoted general of brigade. In 1813 Napoleon made him one of his own ADCs and after the Battle of Leipzig, a general of division. By this time too he was a close personal friend of Prince Eugène and certainly the lover of Queen Hortense. (The Duke of Morny was said to be their offspring.)

During the Hundred Days he was sent by Napoleon to Vienna on an unsuccessful mission to try to secure the return of Marie Louise and the King of Rome. Then after Waterloo, when the Bourbon witch-hunts began, he escaped to England – eventually marrying Margaret Elphinstone, later the Baroness of Keith and Nairne.

FOY, Maximilien Sebastien, Count (1775-1825)

A good general both under fire and in the staff-officer capacity. Born at Ham (Somme), he entered the French army at age 16 and by 1800 had worked his way up to adjutant-general. From 1808 onwards he served in the Peninsular War. (Later he would write one of the better books on the subject: *Histoire de la Guerre de la Peninsula sous Napoleon*.) He served as a fighting general under Marshal Ney at Bussaço and then, with the vanguard of the advance, down towards the Lines of Torres Vedras. He was used as an emissary by Marshal Masséna and in particular in explaining this Commander in Chief's differences with Ney to the Emperor in Paris. Napoleon was so impressed by his abilities – even though Foy had opposed his taking the Imperial title – that he created him general of division.

In the final battle for the Pyrénées he was seriously wounded – and then deeply touched when Wellington stopped off at Cahors to shake his hand and talk about the war. 'Lord Wellington speaks French with difficulty,' he noted in his diary. 'He is slim, of medium build: he has an aquiline nose. His countenance is full of distinction, simplicity, kindness; just as one pictures our great Turenne.'

During the Hundred Days he proved an energetic supporter of the returned Emperor's cause and he served at Waterloo: first under Prince Jerome, then over on Ney's side of the field. He was badly wounded again after the capture of La Haye Sainte and this virtually ended his military career, although he was elected to the Chamber of Deputies in 1819 and incurred the displeasure of the Bourbons because of his outspokenly liberal views.

GALBOIS, Baron (1778 – 1850)

Another cavalry colonel who fought ferociously at Quatre Bras and Waterloo, he was commander of the 6th Regiment of *Chevau-Légers-Lanciers*: in Piré's division, attached to 2nd Corps. Already decorated with the Legion of Honour, had the campaign in Belgium ended differently his bravery and leadership would certainly have warranted further promotion.

GANTHAUME, Honoré Joseph Antoine (1755 – 1818)

Admiral ... and the one other naval figure after Decrès who seems to have been a familiar of Napoleon's.

Born at La Ciotat (Bouches du Rhône), he entered the French navy in 1781. He first saw active service during the American War of Independence. Later, off China, he was captured and held prisoner (albeit briefly) by the English.

Recovering from his wounds received in the 1794 sea-battle between Villaret-Joyeuse and Lord Howe, he joined the French Egyptian expedition, serving as Chief of Staff aboard the *Orient*. He then fought on land, was wounded again at Aboukir, but took part in the actions at Jaffa and St.-Jean d'Acre. Napoleon promoted him rear-admiral and in this capacity he transported the general and his selected band back to France in the *Muiron*. He was made Councillor of State in 1800, a vice-admiral in 1804 and a count of the Empire in 1810 – after which he commanded what remained of the generally-blockaded Mediterranean squadron.

He went over to the Bourbons in 1814, refused to rejoin Napoleon during the Hundred Days and upon the second Restoration became a peer of the realm.

GÉRARD, Maurice Etienne, Count (1773 – 1852)

General, later Marshal of France.

Born at Damvilliers (Meuse), he enlisted in 1791 and served under Dumouriez and Jourdan in the Revolutionary campaigns of 1792-3. In 1795 he served uder Bernadotte and in 1800 was promoted colonel. He impressed Napoleon at Austerlitz and again at Jena, and was promoted general of brigade and, after Wagram, a baron.

He was one of the few successes in the Peninsular War (a courageous contribution to the otherwise indecisive action at Fuentes d'Onoro) and later in Russia: at Smolensk and Borodino, where he was promoted general of division on the battlefield. His spirit and tenacity during the long ordeal of the retreat from Moscow were, it has been claimed, second only to Marshal Ney's. He survived to command a division at Lützen and Baützen; then created a count. He was severely wounded at Leipzig.

He accepted service under the restored Bourbons, also the Order of St.-Louis, but he adhered to Napoleon during the Hundred Days and was given command of 4th Corps with the Army of the North. He performed with less than his usual brilliance before Ligny, getting his troops into a muddle on the wrong side of the Sambre, then being tumbled off his horse into a ditch after a skirmish with Lützow's volunteers. The morale of his corps had been weakened by the defection of General Bourmont and several other officers: which brought the Count a personal rebuke from the Emperor.

However, in the aftermath to Ligny the mistakes were Grouchy's, not Gérard's. (Gérard had hoped to be promoted marshal before Grouchy.) But on June 18,1815 he did give his superior some sound advice. March towards the gunfire, he said. They were the Emperor's guns they could hear. Grouchy chose to ignore this advice and so botched what ought to have been his vital contribution to Waterloo.

After the battle Gérard retired to Brussels, not returning to France until 1817. In 1822 he became a member of the Chamber of Deputies and in 1831 he saw action again. Promoted to marshal at last, he greatly assisted the Belgians in their struggles for independence from the Dutch, driving the latter from Antwerp and then effectively back into Holland. In 1838 he was commander of the National Guard and finally, under Louis Napoleon, made a senator.

GIRARD, Jean Baptiste, Duke of Ligny (1775 – 1815)

French general. Born at Aups in the Var, he first saw service in Italy. He later distinguished himself at Austerlitz; was promoted general of division and created a baron.

He subsequently served in Spain, Poland, was wounded at Lützen and then fought at Dresden. But his main fame rests upon his heroic performance and death during the Waterloo campaign. During the Hundred Days he had been one of the first officers to desert the Bourbons for the returning Emperor. The latter immediately placed him at the head of a division: 'My Sacred Battalions' as he called the adhering troops. Before Waterloo Girard was, first of all, under Ney's command and chased the Prussians from Gosselies towards Fleurus. He then came under Vandamme's (and Napoleon's) command and proved to be one of the great individual successes of the Battle of Ligny. Here he led the 7th Infantry in their central push against Ziethen's troops and the village of St.-Amand. After his routing of the Westphalians the Emperor created him a duke on the battlefield. However, in pushing on beyond St.-Amand, at 4.00pm on June 16 he was shot through the body. He died several days later in Paris.

GOURGAUD, Gaspard, Baron (1783 – 1852)

General; who later accompanied Napoleon to St.-Helena. He seems to have been a witty and amusing conversationalist, but also vain and quick-tempered and upon his eventual return to France got involved in several duels, including one with Ségur. (On St.-Helena he had been rebuked by the Emperor for challenging Las Cases after a quarrel, and on another occasion he even considered challenging Sir Walter Scott over his hostile book: *Life of Napoleon*.)

Born at Versailles, the son of a musician at the Chapel Royal, he entered the artillery in time to take part in the campaigns of 1803 and 1805 and was wounded – although not seriously – at Austerlitz. He was briefly in Spain (the Siege of Zaragosa in 1808) and then fought through the whole of the Danube campaign of 1809, (which brought him closer to Napoleon). He was appointed an ordnance officer attached to the Emperor's staff immediately prior to the invasion of Russia. Entering the Kremlin ahead of the Emperor he discovered some booby-trapped barrels of gunpowder and defused them. Following this he was created baron and first ordnance officer. Later he fought at Leipzig and Hanau; again, it is claimed, saving his master's life by shooting dead the leader of a band of Cossacks who were charging the Imperial tent.

Probably his best fighting performance though was at Craonne in 1814 where he led two battalions of grenadiers in a spirited rearguard action alongside Marshal Ney. He was with Napoleon at Fontainebleau when the news came through that Marmont had surrendered Paris to the Allies.

Promoted to general during the Hundred Days, and serving as *aide-de-camp*, after Waterloo he was entrusted with the Emperor's letter of appeal to the Prince Regent for political asylum in England. But he was not allowed to land in England and so decided to go on to St.-Helena.

Evidently on the island he was less kindly treated by Napoleon than the other officers: perhaps because of his own irritable temperament...

Back in France he published his *Campagne de 1815* and from 1830 returned to active service. He was one of the officers who in 1840 brought back Napoleon's remains from St.-Helena and in 1849 became a deputy in the Legislative Assembly.

HARISPE, Jean Isidore, Count (1768 – 1855)

One wonders how on earth he ever managed to make Marshal of France; and yet all his earlier promotions occurred under the Emperor: 1807, general of brigade; 1808, baron; 1810, general of division; 1813, a count of the Empire. Napier calls him 'gallant' but in his only campaign as a general of division when the going got rough, (Soult's 1814 operations against Wellington along and behind the Pyrénées), he was wounded at Orthez and captured at Toulouse.

He adhered to the Emperor during the Hundred Days, although there is no record of his having been given a command in the Waterloo campaign. However, he must have been useful to Louis Napoleon Bonaparte (later Napoleon III), because he was promoted to marshal in 1851 – together with the far more gifted Exelmans and Ornano.

L'HÉRITIER, Samuel François, Baron (1772 – 1829)

General of division, and the cavalry commander who penetrated most dangerously between and around Wellington's otherwise impregnable squares at Waterloo.

Even among the toughest paladins of the Grand Army: those senior officers who had 'seen it all, been everywhere' under the Revolution, the Consulate and later the Empire, L'Héritier was still something of a living legend. Wounded at Marengo and in nearly every campaign which followed this, he had achieved what can only be described as a military 'high' at Znaim in 1809. After their defeat at Wagram the Austrians under the Archduke Charles had placed their cannon in the streets of the town in such a way that they thought it could never be enfiladed: until L'Héritier and his men risked their fire, jumped over the guns and began slashing into their crews from behind! Needless to say, he was wounded again.

He took the retreat from Moscow in his stride; helped defend Dresden; and was judged to have clinched the French victory at Brienne and then the minor one at Valjouan. At Waterloo he had command of the 2nd Division of the 3rd Cavalry Corps, his senior officer being the great Kellermann (the younger).

But Kellermann was absent from his command-post when the Emperor's order arrived for the Reserve Cavalry to go in, literally, on the hooves of the final waves of *cuirassiers*. However, the order had been given and L'Héritier spurred ahead. Kellermann eventually caught them up; he couldn't believe the order! Not with so much disorder going on up front. But by this time it was too late to turn them: and they were going through Milhaud's defeated and returning first squadrons.

L'Héritier found some little dips and gullies between Montplaisir and Hougoumont which allowed them to charge upwards towards Wellington without being touched by his gunfire. What remained of Milhaud's cavalry then reformed and charged again behind them.

They got up and went right through the Duke's lines, wheeling to fall on the British from the rear. But their horses were winded and although a number of squares caved in the majority held firm. With lancers L'Héritier could have stuck the enemy like pigs, however, his sabres were no match for point-blank musketry. The French knocked out several cannon, failed to spike others and eventually returned to base having covered a distance of more than four kilometres in a single action.

JERZMANOWSKI, Jan Pawel, Baron (1779 – 1862)

Lieutenant-Colonel (Or Colonel Major) in command of the squadron of Polish *Chevau-Légers-Lanciers* of the Imperial Guard.

A majority of Poles had entertained hopes that Napoleon was the one man capable of guaranteeing their independence after centuries of alternating domination (and often occupation) by the Germans and Russians. And the Emperor certainly made a start on the problem. By the Treaty of Tilsit in 1807 the area around Warsaw, the regional province of Posen and certain other tracts of land were formed in the Grand Duchy of Warsaw with Napoleon's ally the King of Saxony as its titular sovereign. After the peace at Schönbrunn in 1809 this area was greatly enlarged; which in turn brought many Polish officers and their men into the Grand Army. Its estimated that 60,000 of them took part in the invasion of Russia – and one of the reasons behind that invasion had been the Tzar's demand that Napoleon should formally promise never to reunite the whole of Poland and never to use its name officially...

The most famous Pole to fight under the Emperor was, of course, Marshal Poniatowski. But Jerzmanowski held a special place in the *élite* because his personal attachment to Napoleon made him, if anything, more fanatically Bonapartist than numbers of France's professional officers.

His lancers distinguished themselves in Russia – and especially during the retreat. Then, with his fellow Poles Prince Radziwill and Majors Chlapowski and Kozietulski, he served with the Lancers of the New Guard throughout the 1813-14 campaigns in Eastern Europe and in France. After this he was the Emperor's personal emissary in trying to persuade Marie Louise to join him on Elba.

The Pole then travelled to Elba himself, took over the squadron of lancers there (it consisted of 22 mounted and 96 dismounted cavalrymen) and remained close to Napoleon during the escape, the return to Paris and the Hundred Days. At the Célestin barracks in Paris the whole squadron slept in twelve small rooms without beds, tables or benches. At least, though, they were back at the centre of events!

At Waterloo the Poles were incorporated into the Red Lancers of the Guard under Colbert and took part in the main French cavalry charge of the day: making a brave but largely unsuccessful showing against the stubborn British.

After the battle he was a hunted man and a wounded one; and with the Tzar's seizure of Poland he was condemned to years of wandering around Europe. But he lived to be rehabilitated under Louis Philippe and to attend the big ceremony on December 15, 1840 when the Emperor's remains were landed on the banks of the Seine. He even survived to attend the funeral of Louis Bonaparte in 1846 – together with Arrighi and 400 other Guard veterans.

KELLERMANN, François, Count, later Duke of Valmy (1770 – 1835)

Son of the marshal, but also a brilliant cavalry commander and much more of a Bonapartist than his father.

He served under Napoleon at Marengo and took part in the final decisive charge. After this Napoleon promoted him rapidly. In the Peninsular War he led a cavalry division and at one stage was used by Junot as a negotiator with the British (after the defeat at Vimeiro). To Wellington's extreme chagrin Kellermann duped Sir Hew Dalrymple into giving the French far better terms than they deserved.

He commanded a cavalry corps at Lützen and again at Nangis.

Having returned to Napoleon he was very active during the Waterloo campaign as commander of 3rd Corps: 3,700 horsemen plus two batteries of horse-artillery. At Quatre Bras on June 16 he led a brigade of his cavalry against Wellington's infantry in possession of the vital crossroads. Ney had issued the command: 'The Fate of France is in your hands. Ride them down. Crush them!' But the Iron Duke's resistance held. Kellermann's horse was shot from under him. However, quick as a flash he grabbed two of his trooper's bits and ran off the field between them!

At Waterloo itself his force was in the second line of the massive and disastrous French cavalry charge. With pieces of black sticking-plaster on his face, he was still arguing aginst committing the whole of the cavalry when L'Héritier, his Number Two, received Napoleon's direct order and set off. Kellermann galloped after them but it was impossible to effect a turn and he became the enraged witness of several squadrons of his magnificent *cuirassiers* being reduced to a bloody shambles.

After the battle he only escaped arrest due to the personal intervention of his father.

KLÉBER, Jean Baptiste (1753 – 1800)

Had he lived, and provided no rivalry set in, he would undoubtedly have held some high position under the Consulate and the Empire: most likely as a marshal, perhaps even as Minister for War. On the Egyptian expedition he was not a close companion of Napoleon's like Caffarelli, Desaix or Menon; nevertheless he was greatly admired by him and ultimately, of course, became the caretaker-leader of the expeditionary force.

He had a very distinguished military career under the Revolution. He became a general in 1793 and fought in every one of the early campaigns along the Rhine; also in La Vendée, where he was rebuked for showing leniency towards the rebels. Although offered overall command of the Rhine armies in 1798, he preferred to retire and become an inspector of public works at Belfort. However, he was then persuaded to re-enter the army by Napoleon.

A short, plump man, always popular with the troops, he was wounded at Alexandria, but recovered in time to win a series of engagements during the Syrian campaign, the most notable being at Mount Tabor in April, 1799.

After Napoleon's return to France he achieved some spectacular results with little in the way of men or resources. When he attacked the Turks at Heliopolis he had under his command only 10,000 men, but completely routed the 60,000-strong force lined up against him. He then re-took Cairo, only on June 14, 1800, to be stabbed to death on the terrace of his house by a Muslim fanatic. (On the same day Desaix died on the battlefield of Marengo.)

Napoleon noted: 'Of all the generals I ever had under me Desaix and Kléber possessed the greatest talents...'

He was buried with much ceremony and the First Consul had a medal struck for him. It had his portrait on one side and on the reverse the words: 'Named, for his stature and intrepidity, the French Hercules. He braved death in the field a thousand times.'

LA BÉDOYÈRE, Charles Angelique François Huchet de, Count (1786 – 1815)

Best known for his sincere support of Napoleon, which amounted almost to hero-worship, rather than for any particular military skills.

Born in Paris, he was the scion of a long-established Breton family. After joining the army he was, first of all, a junior ADC to Jean Lannes, then to Eugène de Beauharnais. Promoted colonel by Napoleon in 1812, by this time he had become a fanatical Bonapartist. As a lieutenant he had served with the *élite* Household Troop of the Imperial Guard and been sabre-wounded during the Prussian campaign. After recovering he served as an orderly officer at Friedland, actually carrying the famous message to Mortier to finish off the Russians after Ney had broken their army in two.

During the retreat from Moscow he displayed the same courage and fortitude which had brought his colonelcy. Following this he fought at Lützen, Baützen and Kolberg.

But it was as a result of the Hundred Days that he became a public figure (and was put on the Bourbon's hit-list). Handsome, dashing and outspoken, he and his cousin Charles Flahaut had become the focus of a group of younger Bonapartists gathered around Hortense de Beauharnais. They openly disdained wearing the Legion of Honour, saying it had been dishonoured by the monarchy.

On Napoleon's escape from Elba, La Bédoyère was stationed at Grenoble in command of the 7th Infantry. Upon the arrival of Cambronne and the vanguard he immediately declared for the returned Emperor: the first major defection from Louis XVIII. Napoleon promptly promoted him to general and made him his principal ADC.

At Waterloo he did most of the Emperor's message carrying both verbal and written, and is generally blamed for getting things into a state of confusion, especially in his dealings with Marshal Ney. (He also angered the marshal by pretending to the troops that Marshal Grouchy would soon be arriving with reinforcements.)

But at least he evidenced bravery under fire and was one of the last to quit the battlefield. Back in Paris he took advantage of being an hereditary peer to rally support in the Upper Chamber for Napoleon's cause; even claiming that the French army remained unbeaten. He reminded the members of their former oath of loyalty. 'Shall we never hear anything other than perjuries in this place?' he cried scathingly. However, Ney, the Prince and hero of the Moscowa was also present that day. Following La Bédoyère he calmly and quietly informed the Chamber of what had really occurred on June 18.

Unlike Flahaut he did not leave Paris. (He was concerned for his wife and young child.) So he stayed and was arrested. His court-martial began on August 14, 1815 and was the first political trial of the new regime. It was a farce of course, and corrupt, but naturally the returning Bourbons wanted blood.

La Bédoyère was executed by firing-squad on the Plaine de Grenelle on August 19.

LALLEMAND, François, Baron (1774 – 1839)

General of brigade and within the structure of the Imperial Guard a personal *protégé* of Napoleon's. He was much in evidence during the big French cavalry charge at Waterloo where he commanded the *Chasseurs-a-Cheval* of the Guard.

He first came to Napoleon's notice as one of Bessières 'guides' (the troopers who escorted and protected the HQ of each field army) during the Italian campaign of 1800. A fresh faced, curly-haired youth, he soon felt the favoured pull on the lobe of his ear.

Eventually commissioned, he served throughout the European campaigns, staying with the Guard, and by the time of the first abdication had been promoted general of brigade. At the time of Napoleon's escape from Elba he had command of an infantry battalion in the north of France, and when it became clear he was preparing to take these troops over to the returned Emperor (as well as inciting the garrison at Lille to mutiny) the Bourbons ordered his arrest and imprisonment at Soissons. Napoleon soon had him out though – and leading the famed Chasseurs of the Guard; five squadrons: 1,267 of perhaps the best officers and men ever to ride into battle under the Tricolour. To these were attached several dozen of the Mameluks.

Like his fellow cavalry commanders Lefebvre-Desnoëttes and Colbert, he was wounded at Waterloo; and then rearrested by the Bourbon's police. However, he succeeded in escaping and at last made his way to Texas. (His brother Henri, in command of the Guard's artillery at Waterloo following the death of Desvaux de St.-Maurice, also collected a wound but afterwards got away to Hungary.)

In Texas Lallemand founded the Champ d'Asyle: a colony for fugitives from the second Restoration who trained together with the idea of sailing to free their old master off St.-Helena. They slept in their cloaks, woke to the sound of drums and named the paths through their camp after Austerlitz, Eylau and Wagram. Unfortunately, yellow fever and marauding cannibals (Indians) put an end to the scheme.

Later both Lallemands served under Louis Philippe – and benefitted under the terms of Napoleon's will.

LARREY, Jean Dominique, Baron (1766 – 1842)

Napoleon was always deeply concerned over the welfare of his troops and the care of the wounded. Consequently, Larrey's position as his chief

144

military surgeon was an important one.

He was born near Bagnères-de-Bigorres (Pyrénées), and had, first of all, entered the navy. At Toulouse he began to study surgery under his uncle Alexis Larrey. He then (in 1787) went to Paris and became an auxiliary surgeon with the Royal marines. He joined an expedition to South America; and once back in Paris finished his training under the great Sabatier. In 1792 he joined the Army of the Rhine and while in the field invented the 'flying ambulance'.

Following this he was placed in charge of the military hospitals at Toulon, Antibes and Nice and in the former founded his own school of surgery and anatomy. After several more campaigns he became professor at the School of Medicine (Military) at Val-de-Grâce in Paris. But then, almost immediately, was summoned by Napoleon to join the 1796 campaign in Italy. At Frioul he managed to stamp out a typhus epidemic and Napoleon decorated him for this. Also he began a study of the causes as well as the treatment of wounds: including his reaching the conclusion that a bayonet-charge might be frightening but was far less effective than well-directed powder and ball. In Egypt he superintended the wounded under Desgenettes and later was wounded himself at St.-Jean d'Acre. At Alexandria he had all his horses killed to make sure the hospitalised troops didn't go short of food, and on his return to Paris was promoted to Chief Surgeon of the Imperial Guard, with six other surgeons serving under him. Napoleon also awarded him the Legion of Honour.

On the later campaigns he was in charge of the hospitals at Austerlitz, Eylau, Essling, Wagram, on the Berezina and at Baützen. He also spent some time in Spain. At Eylau the appalling cold made it very difficult to operate properly, but he never left the table. In Spain he contracted typhus but treated himself and recovered. At Wagram he achieved wonders for the casualties, using *cuirasses* as soup kettles and, despite protests from the fighting generals, killing more horses to make a nourishing broth. He then supervised the removal of the 10,000 wounded to Vienna. After Wagram, for 'his bravery and devotion to the task' he was created a Baron and given a pension of 3,000 francs, later withdrawn by the restored Bourbons. In 1812 he was promoted Chief Surgeon of the Grand Army by special decree. Finally at Waterloo he was again in evidence, although eventually wounded and taken prisoner.

Napoleon always referred to 'my virtuous Larrey' or as 'the soldier's friend' and left him a sizeable bequest in his will: as due to a man he held 'in the highest esteem'. Eventually the Bourbons gave him back his pension and appointed him Chief Surgeon to the Royal Guard – but from this point on he devoted himself increasingly to writing and was one of the first members of the new Academy of Medicine. Much of his writing was about improving the treatment of wounds; but also included the medical section of the scientific results of the Egyptian expedition. (Whilst in Egypt he had become very interested in embalming.)

with surgery for its own sake. At his hospital for members of the Imperial Guard at Gros-Caillou, his superintendent Montessuy received two francs per man per day to feed the sick on 'white bread, Malaga and Burgundy wines, good fat chickens, fish and baked potatoes'. There had to be 'heat and light in the wards and clean linen, furnishings and utensils'. Every guardsman who died was placed in a coffin with a shroud to the value of seven and a half francs.

He died at Lyon. A statue of him now stands in front of the church of Val-de-Grâce in Paris.

The Emperor's final words on him: 'An honest man withal – in fact the greatest man I have ever known.'

LATOUR D'AUVERGNE, Théophile Malo Corret de (1743 – 1800)

Not an intimate of Napoleon's but honoured by him as 'the premier grenadier of France' – which was then turned into a brilliant public relations exercise.

Born at Carhaix in Brittany, he was the son of a lawyer descended from an illegitimate half-brother of the great Turenne. He first entered the army in 1767 by means of a certificate of nobility signed by his friends. In 1781 he served under the Duke of Crillon during the expedition to Minorca and for his bravery in action was promoted captain. But although an accepted aristocrat now, upon the outbreak of the Revolution he refused to join the *émigres*. Instead, as an avowed French patriot he fought with distinction as a volunteer on the new government's campaigns along the Rhine and in Switzerland. For two years he was a prisoner of the English: time he spent writing a book about the Celtic people of Brittany: *Origines Gauloises*. Back in France, although in poor health, he immediately volunteered again: this time to replace the conscripted son of an old friend, a generous act which at last brought him to the attention of Napoleon. He finally died in battle at Oberhausen on June 27, 1800.

Having been named by Napoleon 'the first grenadier of France' his reputation for bravery gained a powerful, almost mystical hold over France's ordinary soldiers. (So much so that any company marching by his grave near the Rhine always did so at attention.) Meanwhile his heart had been embalmed and eventually in 1883 – after once belonging to Garibaldi – became the treasured possession of the city of Paris.

Napoleon also ordered that 'the name of Latour D'Auvergne shall remain on the pay-list and roll of his company. It will be called out on all parades, when a non-commissioned officer will reply, *Mort au champ d'honneur*.'

LAURISTON, Jacques Alexandre Bernard Law, Marquis (1768 – 1828)

Such an elegant name; and it went with the man.

A brilliant artillery officer, sharing many of the new ideas about guns and gunners with Napoleon. Also a loyal supporter of Napoleon until the Hundred Days. He did not approve of the escape from Elba and adhered to the Bourbons: from whom he received a peerage and the command of the Royal Guard.

Born at Ponthierry, his father had been a general before him. He joined the artillery in 1786, was an enthusiast for the Revolution and became brigadier in 1795. The following year, and for a reason that remains a mystery, he resigned; but he had been friendly with Napoleon and re-enlisted in 1800 as his *aide-de-camp*. Soon after this the First Consul placed him in charge of the artillery school at La Fère.

Napoleon began to use him as a diplomat; first to Denmark; then in carrying the ratification of the Peace of Amiens to London, where the delighted populace unharnessed his horses and themselves pulled his carriage through the streets. For a time he was the Emperor's watchdog of the French navy, but in 1805 he was promoted general of division and took part in the main actions of that year against the Austrians. In 1808 he helped conduct the negotiations at Erfurt.

After a brief spell in Spain he was switched back to Central Europe in time for the Battle of Wagram, where his disposition of the artillery is considered to have been a major addition to the French victory.

In 1811 he was France's ambassador to St.-Petersburg, only to be recalled and given a command in the invasion and eventual retreat from Russia. At Lützen and Baützen he commanded the 5th Corps, but was captured after the Battle of Leipzig and the Allies then kept him a prisoner until the first abdication.

In 1817 Louis XVIII created him a marquis and in 1823 Charles X promoted him to marshal. During the subsequent Spanish War he captured Pamplona.

LEFEBVRE-DESNOËTTES, Charles, Count (1773 – 1822)

A cavalry general, and one of the bravest soldiers in the Grand Army, he was also a thoroughly convinced Bonapartist who later benefitted under the Emperor's will.

He had joined the Revolutionary armies in 1792, first serving along the Rhine. In 1798, promoted captain, he became one of Napoleon's ADCs and accompanied him to Italy, Egypt and then in 1800 to Italy again.

Napoleon had soon spotted the younger officer's potential as a cavalry leader and after Marengo always used him in this capacity, under the Empire generally with the chasseurs of the Imperial Guard. He fought with distinction at Austerlitz and was promoted colonel. After the 1806-7 campaign against Prussia and Russia the Emperor made him general of brigade and a count of the Empire.

Switched to the Iberian Peninsula, he took part in the Siege of Zaragosa, fought under Lannes at Tudela, but then had the bad luck to fall into English hands at Benevente. They shipped him back to Great Britain where he spent the next two years, most of the time living on parole near Cheltenham. However, he couldn't bear to remain away from the war in Europe indefinitely. In 1811 he escaped back to France and by the following year was commanding a division of the Old Guard cavalry in Russia. Wounded at Tarutino, he was one of the few who accompanied the Emperor by fast sleigh back to Paris. Napoleon then confirmed his promotion to general of division.

He fought at Lützen, Reichenbach, was defeated at Weimar by Platov's Cossacks and then in the battles of France was wounded at Brienne but recovered to fight at Arcis.

During the Waterloo campaign he was one of the fastest officers to put a foot in a stirrup – and consequently a marked man afterwards. In command of the Light Cavalry of the Guard, he charged at Fleurus, Quatre Bras and then went down, wounded, during the main charge at Waterloo itself. He announced his intention to stay in the battlefield and be killed, but Lallemand, also wounded, persuaded him to join the retreat. Although scarcely capable of riding he took up a position in front of 3,000 cavalry north of Paris – until the surrender of July 3, when he shaved off his moustache, posed as a commercial traveller and eventually made his way to America. The Bourbons sentenced him to death *absente reo*. Pardoned in 1822, in returning to France he was ship-wrecked and drowned off the coast of Ireland.

LETORT, Louis Michel, Count (1773 – 1815)

General, and Napoleon's ADC from the start of the Waterloo campaign. Also Colonel-in-Chief of Dragoons in the Imperial Guard.

He saw service in Spain as a lieutenant-colonel, where he was described as 'a daredevil of Lasalle's ilk; if his skin was as full of holes as a colander it was for the Emperor's sake, for France and for the uniform he wore.' (Commandant Henry Lachouque). At the close of this period he was decorated with the Order of the Three Golden Fleeces.

He next served in Russia as general of brigade, and in 1813 at Hanau after the Battle of the Nations he charged straight at Wrede's Bavarians and Cossacks with his dragoons, routing them and ensuring the French retreat continued in good order. In the battles for France he fought at Montmirail and Château-Thierry, after which he received the Legion of Honour.

He was killed during the late afternoon of June 16, 1813 at the stream and village of Gilly. Napoleon, furious that Pirch's Prussians seemed to be escaping him, sent Letort ahead with the duty squadrons. Two squares of Prussians were overrun, but Letort was mortally wounded in the pursuit of the rest.

His children received money under the terms of Napoleon's will, together with Duroc's daughter, Bessières' son and the children of Mouton-Duvernet and Chartrand who the Bourbons had shot after Waterloo.

LOISON, Louis Henry (1771 – 1816)

Governor of St.-Cloud, he came from Damvilliers where his father was a lawyer. He entered the army as a private in the Royal Guards and was one of the first to desert and join the Revolution. When the National Guard was formed he tried to obtain a commission from Lafayette, but was turned down because at this time he could neither read nor write properly. In revenge he accused Lafayette of anti-Revolutionary activities to the Jacobin Clubs.

Was a leader of the mob which attacked the Tuileries in August 1792; was wounded and then hospitalised for seven months, when he at last mastered reading and writing. Upon leaving the hospital Robespierre placed him in charge of a battalion with the Army of the Ardennes; and in 1793 he became a general of division. He served usefully under Masséna in Switzerland and in 1800 was sent to organise a division of the Army of the Reserve. He is said to have botched his involvement in the Napoleonic victory at Marengo, but he fought well in the campaign of 1805. He received the Legion of Honour, the governorship of St.-Cloud and the temporary governorship of Münster and Osnabrück, where he stayed for two years and – his character defects showing through again – became a rich man.

His other main defect – fortunately rare in the Grand Army – was an overt brutality. During the Portuguese campaigns of 1808 and 1810 the name of Loison came to be synonymous with pillage, burnings and the massacre of villagers. At Bussaço in 1810 he fought bravely under Marshal Ney, but otherwise the latter was appalled by his campaign conduct.

During the period of the first abdication he served the royalists (officially), but is thought to have been a party to the escape from Elba and he certainly supported Napoleon with the utmost energy during the Hundred Days. Afterwards he fled and spent the last year of his life in Liége where he had bought an estate.

MAISON, Nicholas Joseph, Marquis (1771 – 1840)

A sound and vigorous general who won a justified promotion during the Russian campaign of 1812.

Napoleon made him general of brigade in 1806, a baron in 1808 and finally general of division during the Smolensk-Borodino actions.

He was very active in the 1814 battles for France. In command of 1st Corps based on Antwerp, he faced (together with Molitor in Holland) a combined Russian and Prussian force which far outnumbered his own. Plus a dissatisfied and therefore disaffected local population. In all he had something like 15,000 men, including units of the Imperial Guard (mainly Roguet's and Barrois' Young Guard). The latter, strangely enough, were a disciplinary problem, (with deserters, and the fact that he had only 300 cavalry), nevertheless, he fought a skilful delaying action, and at the same

time Napoleon re-took Reims had temporarily confused and halted Bernadotte.

Eventually, although forced back upon Lille, he won a surprise victory on
March 31. Recrossing the Belgian border, at Schweghem, near Courtrai, he
routed a large force under Thielmann and the Prince of Saxe-Weimar,
taking 1,000 prisoners and some good cannon.

With reluctance he took service under the restored Bourbons and was
created a marquis in 1817. But his Bonapartist sympathies found their way
out during the Revolution of 1830 and only one year later he was promoted
to Marshal of France.

MARBOT, Jean Baptiste Antoine Marcellin, Baron (1782 – 1854)

French general and the author of the best military *Mémoires* I have ever
read on the period. He served as ADC to no less than six of the marshals as
well as to the Emperor himself, and so was uniquely placed to exploit his
great abilities as an observer and later *raconteur*.

Born at La Rivière (Corrèze), the son of General Jean Antoine de Marbot
who died of his wounds and typhus during the Siege of Genoa. He became a
volunteer cavalryman with the Republican armies, was commissioned and
under the Empire took part in the Austerlitz and Friedland campaigns
before fighting with distinction in the Iberian Peninsula. He served as ADC
to Napoleon in Russia and was then badly wounded at the Battle of the
Nations. He rejoined Napoleon during the Hundred Days and at Waterloo
was wounded again, this time standing very near to his leader.

Exiled under the restored Bourbons until 1819, he now concentrated upon
his writing – although the three volumes of his *Mémoires* were not published
in their entirety until 1891. He continued to serve as a general under Louis
Philippe and in 1845 became a member of the Chamber of Peers.

The following is no more than a summary of the *Mémoires*, plus a few
illustrative anecdotes about Napoleon.

They begin under the Terror; and Marbot (at military school) remembers
being instructed to address his superiors as 'Citizen' instead of 'Monsieur'... Then there is a humorous account of his first meeting with
Napoleon at Lyon. The young general had just returned from Egypt, and as
a new national hero had been given the rooms ordered a week before for
Marbot's own father. Napoleon offered to share the rooms, but had to chase
after the older general's carriage in order to make this proposition. Friendly
relations restored, Marbot then found himself being introduced to Lannes,
Murat and Berthier. 'Napoleon gently pinched my ear, the flattering caress
which he always employed to persons with whom he was pleased and,
addressing my father, said I would become a second General Marbot one
day.'

The Marbots decided to leave Lyon the next day, then found they couldn't
because all the *post-chaises* in the city had been commandeered by Napo-

leon. 'There is the beginning of omnipotence!' prophesied Marbot *père*.

Once out on campaign Marbot's many cameos of Napoleon turned Emperor are both intimate and revealing: of the Head of State taking out his little notebook to check the tally of men available for the different battle positions; and later arranging to have the Austrians' captured colours brought in at just the right moment to impress the Prussian ambassador – who promptly advised his king not to go to war.

Also there is Austerlitz: described more vividly than in any other account. One senses the fierce driving on towards victory which came from the French soldiers. The cavalry of the Imperial Guard hurled themselves upon the Noble Guard of Russia, consisting of the most high-born of the Tzar's aristocracy, shouting: 'We'll give the ladies of St.-Petersburg something to cry about!' as they sabred left and right. This while the enormous Mustapha, the Mameluk who had personally chased the Grand Duke Constantine, called out to the Emperor in his broken French: 'If me do catch up with Prince Constantine, me cut off his head and bring it to you, Sire—' But this was too much for Napoleon. 'Hold your tongue, you savage!', he barked.

There are numerous anecdotes revolving around Napoleon's meetings and dealings with other VIPs. The young and impressionable Tzar on the raft at Tilsit, for instance; and another with the beautiful, but Francophobe Queen Louise of Prussia. 'Their interview showed no traces of their mutual hatred. Napoleon was respectful and attentive, the Queen gracious and disposed to captivate her former enemy. She had all the need to do so, being well aware that the treaty of peace created, under the Kingdom of Westphalia, a new state whose territory was to be contributed by electoral Hesse and Prussia.' The unhappy Queen Louise couldn't get over the loss of the city of Magdeburg, which the Emperor was determined to add to the new state, of which he intended to make his brother Jerome, King. During dinner the Queen tried every kind of verbal play to get the city back. Napoleon then changed the subject, pointedly praising a rose she was wearing. The story goes that she said: 'Will Your Majesty have this rose in exchange for Magdeburg?' But the Emperor was not going to be caught. Practicality won over chivalry. He praised the rose again, and the beauty of the hand holding it, but he didn't take the flower. 'The Queen's eyes filled with tears, which the victor affected not to see.'

There is much about the quarrels between the unsupervised marshals in Spain, on the Russian campaign, the bloody Battle of Leipzig and about the devotion of the ordinary people of France to their Emperor's cause. Also we catch many glimpses of him off-duty before and after receptions and even at a masked ball, calling for iced water to cool his face and neck.

However, his charisma when with his troops is the most lasting impression. No other man could inspire them as he did – or alarm them. Marbot relates how during the attack on Ratisbon in 1809 the Emperor was standing in discussion with Jean Lannes when a bullet, thought to come from a Tyrolean sharpshooter, caught him on the right ankle. At first the pain was so intense that Napoleon had to lean on the marshal in order to remain standing. But then Chief Surgeon Larrey arrived, dressed the wound and declared it trifling. Meanwhile though, a rumour that he was seriously wounded passed through the regiments like wildfire: and within minutes he was surrounded by thousands of his men, despite the enemy's guns being concentrated on the area. In the end, to prove he wasn't badly hurt, he called for his horse and rode up and down in front of them. The soldiers cheered with relief.

MENOU, Jacques François, Baron (1750 – 1810)

General and a close friend of Napoleon's from before the Egyptian expedition, he was of noble birth and originally Deputy for Touraine at the Estates-General. He espoused the Revolutionary cause and was promoted general of brigade, but his noble background continued to be a problem. (Especially after he lost an engagement to the royalists in La Vendée.) He had applied for a post at the War Office, but his name was now struck off the list of candidates and his troops taken away from him. He was again in trouble following 13 Vendemiaire (1795) – the 'whiff of grapeshot' incident. Entrusted with defending the Convention, he was accused of not having defended it energetically enough and hauled up before a military tribunal. However, on this occasion Napoleon intervened to save him.

In Egypt he was in command of a division, and at last began to prove himself as a fighting general. He stormed the Triangular fort on the outskirts of Alexandria, was wounded, but saw the action through and was then appointed Governor of Rosetta.

While in the Middle East he was converted to the Islamic faith in order to marry an Egyptian woman. He also busied himself forming a regiment of Mameluks ('all authentic head-hunters') to serve the French Republic.

In 1800 he succeeded Kléber as overall commander in Egypt, in this capacity showing genuine talent as an administrator until forced to surrender to Hutchinson the following year. No blame was attached to him for the surrender for French supply-lines had been rendered non-existent by the activities of the English fleet.

Upon his return to Europe Napoleon created him Governor of Venice. He worked hard there, particularly in the planning and construction of the present Public Gardens.

MOLITOR, Gabrièl Jean Joseph, Count (1770 – 1849)

He appears to have been a steady, dependable and, above all, persevering general rather than an inspired one. However, armies have need of such men; and he did make marshal in the end – although under a vastly different regime.

Under the Revolutionary government he rose to be colonel and in 1799

152

general of brigade. In 1800 Napoleon created him general of division, then in 1808 a count.

His chief claim to fame on the battlefield stems from the Aspern-Essling-Wagram campaign of 1809. Before Aspern-Essling, commanding a division of Masséna's 4th Corps he was the first to cross to Lobau Island, which he occupied and then set up cover-fire for the passage of the Grand Army to the north bank of the Danube. On May 21, as the vanguard again, his were the first French troops to be attacked by the Archduke Charles. Taken by surprise, his outposts were driven in; but with great determination he regained the initiative. He put all four of his regiments into Aspern and through the afternoon several Austrian attacks were repulsed. At 5.00pm the Archduke ordered a general attack on three sides. (Meanwhile Napoleon was still having trouble getting his back-up units over the pontoon-bridges. The Austrians were floating hulks and even an old windmill down the river to smash into them.) In the next couple of hours parts of Aspern changed hands up to six times, but Molitor held on; and eventually was reinforced by the fresh troops of General Légrand and General Carra St.-Cyr. The overall battle, we know, proved a stalemate; but if Molitor had given way in this, the most hotly-contested sector, then the French faced an almost certain defeat.

In 1814 his tenacity was again proven during the battles for France. In command of what was termed the 'Corps of Holland' (in reality a mere 4,000 men), although retreating, he skilfully harried and delayed a force of 50,000 Russians and Prussians led by Bülow and Wintzingerode.

His final promotion to Marshal of France came in 1824 and seems to have been for political reasons. The Ultra[1], Charles X, alarmed at the restlessness throughout the country, tried to gain popularity by advancing men of honesty and true merit. Insofar as the Bourbons were concerned it was already too late.

MONTHOLON, Charles Tristan, Count (1783 – 1853)

A General, he was born in Paris. At age 10, whilst in Corsica, he took mathematics lessons from Napoleon and went to school with Lucien and Jerome Bonaparte. He later studied at Brienne before he entered the cavalry.

He was ADC in Italy to Macdonald and Berthier, and later fought in Prussia, Poland and Spain. He received no less than five wounds at Wagram. Napoleon promoted him general of brigade and in 1811 made him both a count and a chamberlain. In 1812 he was Minister Plenipotentiary to Würzburg, accompanied the Emperor in 1814 to Elba and served as his ADC at Waterloo. Afterwards he went with him to St.-Helena, taking his wife Albine and their children, and remaining on the island until Napoleon's death.

1 The Ultras were the total reactionaries among the restored Bourbons.

Back in France, in 1840 he was sentenced to 20 years' imprisonment for his part in the attempted *coup* by Louis Napoleon (later Napoleon III). He served seven of them, during which time he composed his *Mémoires de Napoleon à St.-Hélène* and the *Récits de la Captivité de Napoleon a St.-Hélène*. Napoleon had left him 2,000,000 francs in his will.

Some of the facts in the *Mémoires* are extremely doubtful, (for instance, that the throne of Mexico was offered to the ex-Emperor on St.-Helena). But Napoleon's thoughts and conversations ring true.

For instance: The French have two equally strong passions which seem mutually contradictory, but which nevertheless spring from the same sentiment: a love of equality and a love of distinction. A government cannot satisfy both at once except by exercising the most strict justice. The laws and actions of government must be equal for all; honours and rewards must be bestowed only on those most worthy of them in the eyes of all.

MOUTON-LOBAU, Georges, Count (1770 – 1838)

Already a general under the Revolution, he had commanded an infantry regiment at Montpellier, was *aide-de-camp* to Joubert at Novi and was promoted general of brigade by Napoleon in Italy. He was wounded during Ney's great charge at Friedland and created general of division in 1807.

He organised the grand review for the Tzar and the King of Prussia following the Peace of Tilsit; performed admirably during the Peninsular War and the 1809 war with Austria, following which he was made Count of Lobau in honour of his dramatic recapture of the village of Essling. He was taken prisoner in Saxony serving under Gouvion St.-Cyr and kept confined within Hungary until after the first abdication of Napoleon. He was considered too fanatically Bonapartist to be offered a commission by the restored Bourbons and at Waterloo he commanded Napoleon's 6th Corps.

He was wounded at Waterloo, taken prisoner and then escaped, not returning to France until 1819. Elected to the Chamber of Deputies in 1828 and promoted Commandant of the National Guard in Paris by Louis Philippe, he became Marshal of France just one year before his death.

Napoleon always thought very highly of Mouton-Lobau. He served as principal *aide-de-camp* at Smolensk and later accompanied the Emperor out of Russia.

ORNANO, Philippe Antoine, Count (1786 – 1863)

General, and later a marshal, he was promoted general of brigade in 1811, of division in 1812, (when he also became a count) and finally Marshal of France under the Second Empire in 1861.

Of Corsican descent, he was a distant cousin of the Emperor, (who left him a small amount in his will). Prior to this his family had served the French monarchy through several generations, the first of these being Alphonse d'Ornano, a colonel fanatically loyal to Henri III, who in 1588 played a 'key' role in the assassination of the Duke of Guise. (In 1980 there was another Ornano high in the service of the President of the French Republic.)

Although still very young, Napoleon's Ornano gained rapid promotion – and especially in connection with his responsibilities for the cavalry of the Imperial Guard. In 1813, when he took over command of all the dragoons of the Guard from General St.-Sulpice, he was still only twenty-eight, but had seen service as little more than a boy during the San Domingo expedition, then at Austerlitz and later in Portugal and Spain, where he was promoted general of brigade after the fighting at Fuentes de Oñoro. Later he charged at Borodino, Malo Yaroslavetz and was badly wounded at Krasny.

While still recovering, he fought with distinction at Lützen, Baützen, the Battle of the Nations at Dresden and then in many battles for France before being in command of the entire Guard in Paris during 1814 – until Marmont's surrender.

Adhering to Napoleon during the Hundred Days, he was arrested upon the second Restoration. However, he had taken no part in the Battle of Waterloo: having been critically wounded in a duel several weeks before.

PAJOL, Claude Pierre, Count (1772 – 1844)

One of France's best cavalry officers through the course of the Revolution and the Empire.

Unfortunately, in the Waterloo campaign, after performing brilliantly at Ligny, it was due to the mistakes of Grouchy that his considerable abilities were never brought into the final crucial stages at Waterloo itself.

Born at Besançon, Pajol was the son of an *avocat*. In 1791 he went with a volunteer battalion to join the Army of the Rhine, and during 1794-6 he served under Kléber, then in '97 and '99 with Hoche and Masséna in Germany and Switzerland. Promoted colonel by General Moreau, he then greatly impressed Napoleon at Austerlitz as a commander of light cavalry. Following the subsequent Friedland campaign the Emperor promoted him general of brigade and in 1808 a baron.

In 1809 he took part in the Danube operations and in the 1812 invasion of Russia he had command of a division, although in the retreat his health finally broke down and he didn't rejoin the Grand Army again until Dresden, where he fought, according to all witnesses, with the utmost valour.

It seems that his talents were destined to be wasted on more than just the occasion of Waterloo. In the 1814 battles for France, for instance, which were largely hit-and-run affairs by the French and therefore favoured by the cavalry, he spent most of his time shadowing the cautious Schwarzenberg when he could have been winning engagements elsewhere.

Despite this, he adhered to Napoleon during the Hundred Days; and he manoeuvred magnificently with his mixed cavalry and infantry to make the best of the Prussian rout at Ligny – and could have done equally well in the pursuit towards Wavre if Grouchy hadn't put the brakes on.

Following the bad news from Waterloo he then conducted a very skilful retreat upon Paris before fleeing the country; for he knew he was on the Bourbons' hit-list. But he had his revenge. In 1830 he helped overthrow the last Bourbon Charles X, after which Louis Philippe created him a peer of the realm.

PELET-CLOZEAU, Jean Jacques, Baron (1779 – 1853)

A general of brigade, he commanded the 2nd Regiment of *Chasseurs-à-Pied* of the Old Guard during the Waterloo campaign. He fought to the bitter end at Waterloo itself, stripped down to his shirt-sleeves, never ceasing to urge his men on 'in the cause of the Emperor and for France!'

He first came to Napoleon's notice as a colonel of infantry during the expedition to Russia. He was a 'key'-*aide* to Marshal Ney during the retreat from Moscow and at the crossing of the Berezina. Napoleon promoted him general of brigade after another distinguished performance at Krasny, where he was also wounded. With this rank he served with the Old Guard through 1813-14, eventually becoming its adjutant-general. He commanded the *chasseurs* of the Guard at Arcis and stayed close to Napoleon at Fontainebleau during the crisis of the first abdication, then making a personal selection of the volunteer Guardsmen to accompany their leader into exile. The ex-Emperor embraced him warmly at Montargis *en route* for Elba.

Adhering to the Bonapartist cause in the Hundred Days, he was to be one of the officers most in evidence at Waterloo: despite the fact that Napoleon had forgotten to promote him general of division. Nevertheless he performed on the day with great coolness as well as bravery. There is one cameo of him while waiting to advance, eating a meat sandwich and sipping a glass of Madeira. He was in the thick of it at Plancenoît, where the Young Guard took such a hammering, and he intervened personally to stop some of the enraged Frenchmen cutting the throats of their prisoners. Our last glimpse of him is in the evening of the battle, still galloping about on his mare Isabelle, rallying groups of his chasseurs to keep fighting even in their retreat.

For a time under the second Restoration he was forced to go into hiding.

QUIOT DU PASSAGE, Joachim Jerome, Baron (1775 – 1849)

No senior officer could possibly have done more than Quiot tried to do at Waterloo, and yet at the end of the day with so little to show for it.

His previous service in Russia, at Leipzig and then in the battles for

France had gained him promotion to general of brigade. He was a skilled leader of infantry and a keen Bonapartist, and when he returned to Napoleon during the Hundred Days was placed in command of the 54th and 55th Regiments of the Line in d'Erlon's 1st Corps. However, when General Allix failed to turn up in Belgium Quiot was promoted on the spot and took command of 1st Division within the corps.

Due largely to bad staff-work d'Erlon's troops had taken no real part in the Waterloo campaign until June 18 – but then they fought without respite.

Quiot led the first assault on the vital farm of La Haye Sainte in the middle of the battlefield, captured the orchard but failed to win the actual building from its German defenders. He then moved forward to join the main attack upon Wellington's lines: which was repulsed with heavy losses. He was next ordered to attack La Haye Sainte again – still without success. Finally, late in the afternoon Marshal Ney himself led an assault on the farm – with Quiot – and took it, which suddenly exposed the English centre to short-range artillery fire. As his gunners punched holes in Wellington's hard-pressed line everything seemed at last to be going France's way. But the reserves Ney demanded to finish the job came too late.

Quiot was proscribed upon the second Restoration, but later pardoned.

RAPP, Jean, Count (1772 – 1821)

Born at Colmar, he entered the army at age 18, first coming to Napoleon's notice as *aide-de-camp* to General Desaix. He fought with great bravery during the Italian campaign and was beside Desaix when the latter was mortally wounded at Marengo. Napoleon used him in Egypt and on a mission to Switzerland, and at Austerlitz he commanded a division of the Imperial Guard's cavalry, smashing several squadrons of Russia's mounted troops. The Emperor had watched this through his telescope and from now on Rapp's star was decidedly in the ascendant.

After Wagram he was created count and like his master only narrowly escaped death due to Cadoudal's bomb in 1801. He was much valued as an emissary by Josephine and in 1809 seized a would-be assassin of the Emperor. It was claimed he had the man secretly shot.

Following the horrors of the retreat from Moscow (during which he earned high praise from Marshal Ney) he was sent to defend Danzig, which he held on to through a year-long siege before its final capitulation. He took his troops over to Napoleon during the Hundred Days and was placed in command of the Army of the Rhine.

After Waterloo he became reconciled to Louis XVIII, was created chamberlain and in 1819 a peer of the realm. But he was still at heart Napoleon's man and only survived the Emperor by a number of months.

REILLE, Honoré Charles Michel Joseph (1775 – 1860)

A general under Napoleon, and later a Marshal of France. Promoted general of brigade in 1803 and of division in 1806, he fought with distinction during the Peninsular war and especially in the defeat at Vittoria in 1813, where he controlled a strong resistance to Wellington along the Bilbao-Vittoria road, probably the hardest-fought part of the battle. Having adhered to Napoleon during the Hundred Days he was placed in command of 2nd Corps at Valenciennes and Avesnes and later attacked the Allied centre at Waterloo.

He was included in the general amnesty by Louis XVIII, became a peer in 1819, a marshal under Louis Philippe in 1847 and a senator in 1852. By this time too he had purchased the château of Coudreaux from the ruined family of Marshal Ney. His descendants still live there.

At Waterloo he fought bravely and determinedly but without much success. But then at Quatre Bras and at Waterloo itself, not even Ney was able to crack the Iron Duke.

RICHEPANSE, Antoine (1770 – 1802)

General. Born at Metz, he first of all trained to be a cavalry officer, but as time went on and he gained promotion so he revealed his other great capability as a leader of infantry.

An early enthusiast for the Revolution, he was promoted general of brigade at Altenkirchen and served under Hoche. In Italy he took part in the action at Novi and was promoted general of division.

Posted back to Germany, he now came under General Moreau and proved himself a big success during the Hohenlinden campaign. At the Battle of Hohenlinden itself, while Ney and Grouchy held up the Austrian frontal-attacks Richepanse crept his men through the forest to the right. It was sleeting and at one point he was surprised by an Austrian column which nearly cut his own force in two. But all the time he was edging nearer the Austrian rearguard positions. Being December they could hardly have been expecting a battle of such mobility, and as the French opened fire so the carnage and confusion grew immense. When the fighting was over they had lost 8,000 dead on the two fronts, 12,000 prisoners and at least ninety guns. (Plus the will-power to take the offensive again in the immediate future.)

Hohenlinden was destined to be the summit of Richepanse's military career though. In 1802 Napoleon sent him to put down a revolt on the West Indian island of Guadeloupe. This he did; only to succumb himself to yellow fever.

Napoleon bestowed on his widow the title of Countess.

ROGUET, François, Count (1770 – 1840)

'Old Man Roguet' of the Imperial Guard: the arch-grumbler of the Grand Army, but a true Bonapartist and exceptionally tough.

He commanded a brigade of the Young Guard at Essling, then the 2nd Guard Division in Spain and Russia. He fought with great distinction at Borodino and Krasnoye, and we have a vivid description of him coping with the privations of the retreat: 'Neither the rigours of the climate nor the misfortune of war had shaken his confidence in the rising again of the good star,' Henry Lachouque writes. 'Wearing regulation uniform with a white stock and rags for boots, he marched on foot at the head of his orderly division, eating gruel and drinking melted snow, sleeping in camp, happy when he had a fire.' Apparently he never even caught a cold and arrived back in France without a sou in his pocket. A *cantinière* lent him 1,000 francs and Prince Eugène had given him a new *pelisse*.

Later he fought at Lützen, Baützen, was wounded at Dresden and distinguished himself again at Leipzig. In 1814 he fought his way out of Antwerp with the Young Guard and commanded an Old Guard division in the Waterloo campaign. He charged at Ligny and Waterloo and afterwards retreated with the foot of the Guard to the Loire, finally submitting there to Marshal Macdonald.

After 1830 he was recalled to the army by Louis Philippe.

SEBASTIANI, Horace François Bastien, Count (1772 – 1851)

General, and later a marshal under Louis Philippe. He was also a Corsican and regarded as a 'crony' by Napoleon, who often spoke to him very informally as well as using him as a diplomat in addition to his regular duties as a cavalry officer.

Originally destined for the church, he joined the army on the outbreak of the Revolution, fought with great bravery at Arcola and was promoted colonel in Verona. He became a convinced Bonapartist during the events of 18/19 Brumaire, and went with Napoleon on the Marengo campaign, (which led to his being created general of brigade and being sent to the Camp of Boulogne). He was wounded at Austerlitz and promoted general of division.

In 1806 Napoleon sent him on a mission to Turkey, where he was wildly successful. He managed to detach the Sultan, Selim III, from the European Coalition and when Constantinople was threatened by an English squadron under Sir John Duckworth it was Sebastiani's supervision of the artillery which forced the ships to retire.

In the Peninsular war he commanded 4th Corps, with which he became involved in several indecisive skirmishes with Wellington. But he covered himself in glory during the worst parts of the retreat from Moscow and survived to fight again at the Battle of the Nations, where he was wounded. However he quickly recovered; having a marvellous physique and good-looks as well. (His nickname to the troops was 'Cupid of the Empire'.)

He adhered to Napoleon during the Hundred Days, was put on half-pay after Waterloo and later selected as deputy for Corsica. But it was Louis Philippe who really restored his fortunes, creating him Minister for Marine and Foreign Affairs, sending him as a special envoy to London and Naples and creating him a marshal in 1840. The one dark shadow over these closing years was the mysterious murder of his daughter, the Duchess of Praslin.

He is buried at Les Invalides.

SÉGUR, Philippe Paul de, Count (1780 – 1873)

General and ADC to the Emperor, but better-known today as a writer: the author of the outstanding book on the Russian campaign of 1812, (although parts of it were disputed by Gourgaud who fought a duel with Ségur and wounded him).

The son of a general and grandson of a marshal of the French who was granted a special pension by Napoleon. He fought at Ülm and later in the Prussian campaign, where he witnessed Napoleon's first visit to the tomb of Frederick the Great. 'He walked rather hurriedly at first, but as he drew near the church he moderated his pace, which became slower and more measured as he approached the remains of the great king to whom he had come to pay homage. He remained there nearly ten minutes, motionless and silent.' Then he ordered Frederick's sword and other trophies to be sent back to Les Invalides.

As a lieutenant-colonel he was wounded at Somosierra when ordered by the Emperor to lead a renewed attack by the Polish Light Horse against the Spanish batteries. He served throughout the Russian campaign, and he was Colonel-in-Chief of the 3rd Guards of Honour in 1813. In 1815 he actively supported La Bédoyère's attempt in the House of Peers to have the King of Rome proclaimed 'Napoleon II'.

His *Histoire de Napoleon et de la Grande Armée pendant l'Année 1812* was published in two volumes in 1825 and immediately produced a reaction favourable to the earlier-executed Marshal Ney whose gallantry in command of the rearguard in Russia it praised. Even the Duchess of Angoulême expressed her regrets over his death after reading it.

SOURD, Jean Baptiste, Baron (1779 – 1849)

A colonel under Napoleon; later under Louis Philippe a general of division. He was a typical example of the way the genuinely dedicated Bonapartists in the army were prepared to fight for their beliefs in the Emperor and for France: and never moreso than during the Waterloo campaign.

Born at Signes. A cavalry officer, with service in Russia and the battles for Paris behind him, Sourd had command of the 2nd *Chevau-Légers-Lanciers* of the Imperial Guard when the revived Grand Army moved into Belgium.

Attached to Marshal Ney on the French left-wing, he fought at Quatre Bras on June 16, and on the 17th was with the vanguard of a cavalry pursuit of Wellington towards Mont St.-Jean. The Duke had left a few batteries and mounted squadrons to hold up the French 'pack' at the village of Genappe. In the ensuing action there Sourd received no less than six sword-cuts and when Surgeon General Larrey arrived he decided that the right arm had to be amputated. Ney, next on the scene, was about to scribble a note to HQ recommending Sourd's promotion to general of brigade. (Colbert, his superior officer, had been wounded at Quatre Bras the previous day). But the colonel pleaded with him not to send it, for it would have meant him giving up his present command, he declared. Larrey gave him a slug of brandy, a cartridge to bite on and operated by the side of the road. After which, with the stump sewn up he rode off to rejoin his men.

He took part in the main cavalry charge at Waterloo the following day.

VANDAMME, Dominique Réne, Count (1770 – 1830)

Born at Cassel (Nord), he entered the army in 1786 and served in most of the Revolutionary campaigns in the north. Promoted general of division in 1799.

A gifted and determined general, and one of Napoleon's most devoted officers. He loathed the Bourbons and would never afterwards take service under them.

At Austerlitz he led his division (Soult was his army commander) in the famed storming of the plateau where the Russians had thought themselves invincible – but only until Vandamme's arrival! He performed brilliantly, even though Napoleon could give him very little support. But the Emperor recognised his success and immediately after the battle invested him with the Grand Eagle of the Legion of Honour: generally reserved for the marshals and princes. In 1806-7 he again distinguished himself in Silesia and for this was created Count of Unselburg. At Wagram he commanded the Würtemburgers. Which seems ironic because in his later, serious reverse (he was captured at Kulm in 1813) it was at the hands of a Würtemburger general. Napoleon was taking up his positions for the Battle of Dresden and it was Vandamme's task to cut off the expected Allied retreat along the Pirna road. He ran into some beaten Russians who were then suddenly reinforced by a Prussian corps (and other Germans) and the French were trapped.

Vandamme performed with amazing dash and bravery, but could not avoid capture. His failure too, largely negated the otherwise successful action at Dresden...

Upon release he went back to his native Cassel, until the Hundred Days when he was in command of the 3rd Corps at Ligny, taking the village of St.-Amand. But at Waterloo itself Grouchy's non-appearance meant that his skills were wasted.

Not surprisingly he was exiled by the returning Bourbons – until 1824 – and he never served with the French army again.

161

VILLARET—JOYEUSE, Louis Thomas (1750 – 1812)

Admiral. Born in Gascony and avoided his family's intentions that he should make a career in the Church. He ran away from home to join the army, got involved in a duel when he killed his opponent and then ran away to sea.

He served in the Indian Ocean, was promoted to captain of a frigate, but soon afterwards was captured by the British navy and not released until 1789. An enthusiast for the Revolution, he next commanded the *Prudente* off San Domingo and in 1794 was promoted rear-admiral. He did very badly in the action of June 1, 1794 against Lord Howe; and equally badly against Nelson at Aboukir Bay. (Perhaps the sea was never really meant to be his destiny.) However he commanded the fleet transporting the French expeditionary force to San Domingo in 1801; happily, this time, with no mishaps. Then in the following year Napoleon appointed him Captain-General of Martinique, where he lived quietly and pleasantly for the next seven years – until forced to surrender the island to the English.

For the last year of his life he was Governor of Venice.

VILLENEUVE, Pierre Charles Jean Baptiste Silvestre de (1763 – 1806)

Admiral. Poor Villeneuve! He really was a much better sailor than given credit for, with several successes to his name before the disaster of Trafalgar. However, although promoted by Napoleon, he was then expected to do impossible things by a taskmaster who knew little or nothing about sea warfare and with a navy greatly inferior to England's. His final piece of bad luck came at Trafalgar: he faced an opponent of genius. Villeneuve has been criticised for his pessimism, but whoever did win a victory against Nelson? Not that this saved him from the Emperor's wrath. In the aftermath of the battle there had to be a scapegoat.

Born at Valensole (Basses Alpes), he entered the navy at fourteen. Having declared for the Revolution he was promoted captain in 1793 and rear-admiral in 1796. He took part in the unsuccessful expedition to Ireland then went on the Egyptian expedition. At the Battle of the Nile he commanded the back-up squadron and later got his ships away to Malta. In 1804 Napoleon appointed him the successor to Latouche-Tréville in command of the important Toulon squadron.

In this capacity his orders were to divert Nelson and his fleet away from the coasts of Europe in order to facilitate the invasion of England. Accordingly he sailed for the West Indies in July 1805. After many adventures, including the capture of fourteen British merchantmen and an inconclusive action off the Azores against Sir Robert Calder, he returned eventually to Coruña then moved to Cadiz and finally offered battle to Nelson off Cape Trafalgar on October 21, 1805. Prior to this his overriding concern had been to keep his fleet intact whatever happened – despite the Emperor's impatient missives. However, he had been stung by the Minister

162

of Marine (Decrès) hinting that he might be replaced and hoped to impress the Emperor with a spectacular victory. However several of the French and especially the Spanish ships were in poor condition; also the weather was playing tricks.

Nelson was just the sort of commander to take an inspired risk. He attacked in two columns and broke the French fleet into three parts. By engaging this closely even the acknowledged skill of the French gunners was rendered useless. The battle raged – increasingly in favour of the English. Nelson was mortally wounded; Villeneuve displayed the utmost personal courage; his deputy Admiral Magon was killed; the Spanish proved unreliable. When the closely-contested 'hand-to-hand' fighting died down, of their thirty-three ships of the line the French and Spanish had lost seventeen (captured) and one blown up. Among those captured was Villeneuve's dismasted flagship, the *Bucentaure* – with the admiral still on board . . .

Trafalgar effectively ended Napoleon's hopes of invading England from Boulogne. Now he would have to rely upon dominating Europe and imposing the Continental System (squeezing England economically by depriving her manufacturers of their traditional markets). Meanwhile the full force of his temper turned upon the luckless admiral.

Villeneuve was first of all taken to England and imprisoned at Reading; but he was allowed to return to France the following April, where he died under the most strange circumstances. At the time it was widely assumed that he committed suicide. He wrote a pathetic last letter to his wife from a hotel in Rennes: 'How will you receive this blow? I weep more for you than myself. The fact is, I have reached a point where life is a disgrace and death a duty. Here, denounced by the Emperor, rejected by his minister who was my friend, charged with an immense responsibility in a disaster for which I am blamed and to which I was led by fate, I have to die.'

Why then did the police suppress this letter? And refuse to tell his wife how he died? Naoleon afterwards stated he had killed himself with a hatpin rather than face a court-martial. Later certain officials put it about that he'd been found with six knife wounds. Assassination? But why? Napoleon, although terrible in his rages, was never a bloodthirsty man. Or did Decrès have anything to do with it? The conundrum remains.

One point I will make though. Villeneuve could have taken the easy way by joining the Bourbons and the *émigres*. It took guts and a sense of honour and also, I think, patriotism for him to go back to France at all.

WATHIER DE ST.-ALPHONSE, Pierre, Count (1770 – 1846)

General of division – and another out-and-out Bonapartist whom the Bourbons hunted (unsuccessfully) after Waterloo where he commanded the 13th Division of Milhaud's 4th Cavalry Corps.

A grizzled veteran of Wertigen (under Murat), Schliez, Friedland and the retreat from Moscow, he is best-known for his quick efficient action which put paid to the British cavalry charge at Waterloo. Wellington's horsemen had savaged d'Erlon's infantry, but then swept on to attack the French gun emplacements: where Wathier caught them with his *cuirassiers* under Dubois and Travers. (Delort's cavalry under General of Brigade Viscount Farine then attacked their other flank.) General Ponsonby was killed, two of the four colonels, and the British Dragoons suffered something like eight hundred casualties.

=6=
La Garde

As for their thirty-three-year-old chief, who had seized power in an atmosphere laden with the wreckage of the Revolution, he had just performed the initial act of his political life as sovereign in creating an elite corps, a symbol of obedience, heroism, and devotion to France and to the Emperor, whose memory is imperishable and whose glory is eternal: The Imperial Guard.
– Commandant Henri Lachouque

The idea of an Imperial Guard goes back to the heyday of Rome under Augustus: trained troops who were separate from the main army, and who the leader believed he could call upon when all else failed. (Although several later Caesars did die at their hands!)

As Commandant Henri Lachouque, in his definitive study of La Garde points out, the idea was then continued by most of the kings of France.

In the distant past the chief was served by a mayor, or *major*, who guarded his door and a constable who took charge of his stables, assisted by a marshal. In the Louvre, Philip Augustus was guarded by sergeants-at-arms renowned for their strength and bravery; hence the word *noble* derived from *nobilis*, meaning renowned or known. Soldiers wearing rich hauberks and carrying bows, swords and maces marched in the royal processions and accompanied the King to war.

Following the downfall of Robespierre there was a Directory Guard, then a Consular one (cobbled together by Murat) and finally Napoleon's Imperial Guard for which his friend Bessières had special responsibility until his death in 1813 when his duties then largely devolved upon Marshal Mortier.

But the Guard was not just for the leader's protection (Napoleon was extremely careless about his own personal safety anyway). He insisted that it was a fighting force – and the ultimate reserve in all his subsequent campaigns. By repute it came to be feared throughout Europe and except for the surrender of the marines of the Guard at Baylen in southern Spain in 1808 (on Dupont's orders) its members did not experience defeat until the final hour of the battle at Waterloo.

165

Membership of the Guard was regarded by those who obtained it as something sacred. They would rather forego promotion than be transferred to a line regiment; and the Emperor knew most of them by name – even down to the level of private. They grumbled all the time of course (about the wars, the wine, their barracks and having to sleep two to a bed), but their loyalty was absolute and unswerving.

In 1814 Marshal Ney advised Louis XVIII to form a new Royal Guard. Five hundred infantry, 120 cavalry and 120 gunners of the Imperial Guard had accompanied Napoleon to Elba. In 1815 all the original 'grumblers' rallied to his cause; and at Waterloo they showed they were prepared to die for him.

In addition to those already profiled for special Bonpartist or other reasons the following were the most important generals to serve within the Imperial Guard, together with a note of their best-known actions:

ARRIGHI DE CASANOVA, General, Duke of Padua.

Colonel-in-Chief of Dragoons of the Guard. Distinguished at Friedland, and in Spain. Commanded cuirassier division in 1809; cavalry corps, 1814. Arrested after Waterloo.

BARROIS, General, Count.

Commanded 2, and 4 Young Guard Division 1813-14. Was at Baützen, Dresden and Leipzig. Young Guard Division at Ligny, Waterloo.

BASTE, Vice-Admiral, Count.

Commander of the marines of the Guard. In Spain he was decorated with the Order of the Three Golden Fleeces. He fought at Wagram; later at Almazan. Commanded Young Guard Brigade, 1814. Killed at Brienne.

BELLIARD, General, Count.

Commanded cavalry corps at Château-Thierry, Laon, Fère-Champenoise and during defence of Paris. Brought the news of Marmont's surrender to Napoleon at Fonatainbleau.

BERTHEZÈNE, General, Baron.

Decorated with Legion of Honour after Wagram; then made Adjutant-General of the Guard. Commanded Young Guard in Russia. He was distinguished at Berezina, Lützen and Baützen. Colonel-General of the Guard in 1813. Prominent during Waterloo campaign in the fight for St.-Amand.

BOULART, General, Baron.

With the Guard artillery in Spain. Promoted colonel after Essling. Distinguished at Wagram, Smolensk, Leipzig, Montereau, Reims. Beneficiary in Napoleon's will.

BOYER DE REBEVAL, General, Baron.

Adjutant-General of the Guard. Decorated with Legion of Honour after Neugarten. Distinguished at Wagram. Commanded chasseurs of the Guard 1812. Wounded at Borodino, again at Dresden and Craonne. Commanded Guard Division during defence of Paris.

BRAYER, General, Baron.

Distinguished in Russia, Germany and the later battles for France. Took an entire division over to the returned Emperor at the start of the Hundred Days. Also a beneficiary in Napoleon's will.

CAFFARELLI DU FALGA, General, Count.

ADC to Consul/Emperor. Adjutant-General of the Consular Guard. Commanded division at Austerlitz; Northern army in Spain; and the Guard in Paris, 1813. Governor of palace to Marie Louise.

CHARPENTIER, General, Count.

Commander of Smolensk Garrison, 1812. Young Guard Division, 1814. Saw action at Craonne, Laon, Fère-Champenoise, and at the defence of Paris.

CHARTRAND, General.

Commanded Young Guard Brigade at Ligny, Waterloo. Shot under second Restoration.

CHASTEL, General, Baron.

Commanded grenadiers. Awarded bonus after Friedland. Fought in Spain and Russia.

CHRISTIANI, General, Baron.

Colonel in command of instructors' battalion at Fontainebleau. Commanded 2 Old Guard Division in the battles for France. Distinguished at Neuilly-St.-Front, Crouy, Fère-Champenoise, and the defence of Paris.

With 2 Grenadiers, 1815. Charged at Ligny, Waterloo. Arrested under second Restoration.

CLAPARÈDE, General, Count.

Commanded Polish division attached to Guard, 1812. At Smolensk, Borodino, Krasny. Distinguished at Tarutino. Wounded at crossing of the Berezina.

CORBINEAU, General, Count.

Commanded cavalry brigade at Berezina, and 2 Guard Cavalry Division at capture of Reims. ADC to Emperor. Put down rebellion in La Vendée 1815.

CURIAL, General, Count.

Promoted colonel at Eylau, general after Friedland. Commanded Old Guard Division and wounded at Essling. Commanded Young Guard at Wagram. Saw action at Lützen, Leipzig, Hanau; then Montmirail, Craonne, Fère-Champenoise, and the defence of Paris. Governor of Rambouillet in 1815. Beneficiary in Napoleon's will.

DAHLMANN, General, previously a Guide of Italy.

Major with *Chasseurs-à-Cheval* of the Consular Guard. Colonel of chasseurs with Imperial Guard. Charged at Austerlitz. Killed at Eylau (1807).

DAUMESNIL, General, Baron.

He was also a former guide of Italy and with the Consular Guard. Promoted captain at Marengo, and major at Austerlitz. Wounded at Madrid, then lost leg at Wagram. Governor of Vincennes from 1810.

DAUTANCOURT, General, Baron.

Captain in the *Gendarmerie d'Élite* under the Consulate. Colonel with Polish Light Horse of the Imperial Guard. Distinguished at the crossing of the Berezina, 1812. Promoted general at Hanau. Commanded Guard Cavalry Brigade at Brienne, Montmirail, Montereau, Berry-au-Bac, and in the defence of Paris. Commanded *Gendarmerie d'Élite* again in 1815. Beneficiary in Napoleon's will. Recalled to service under Louis Philippe.

DECOUZ, General, Baron.

He was awarded the Legion of Honour after Wagram. Commanded Young Guard Brigade, 1813 and division during retreat from Leipzig. Killed at Brienne.

DÉRIOT, General, Baron.

Colonel with Guides of Egypt; also Vice-Governor of palaces there. Chief of Staff of Horse Guard in Spain and received Order of the Three Golden Fleeces. He was Chief of Staff of Guard after the second abdication.

DESVAUX DE SAINT-MAURICE, General, Baron.

Commanded Old Guard horse artillery in 1812. He fought at Krasny, Lützen and Leipzig. Killed at Waterloo.

DORSENNE, General, Count.

Promoted colonel at Austerlitz; general, 1804. Granted bonus after Eylau. Commanded Old Guard at Essling; the Guard Corps in Spain. Appointed Governor of Northern Provinces. Died 1812.

DUMOUSTIER, General, Count.

Captain in the Consulate Guard; adjutant at the Tuileries. Commanded 2 Guard Division in Spain. Awarded bonus after campaign of 1812. He saw action at Lützen, Baützen, Dresden and Waterloo. Recalled to army by Louis Philippe.

DUROSNEL, General, Count.

ADC to the Emperor. He helped train Polish Light Horse; commanded right-wing at Benevente. Wounded at Essling. Governor of Vilna, 1812 and then in command of Moscow Garrison under Mortier. Governor of Dresden, 1813.

ÉMÉRY, Surgeon – with status of general.

Attached to Elba battalion, 2 Chasseurs. Accompanied the Emperor on his journey back to Paris in 1815; was present at Waterloo campaign. Beneficiary in Napoleon's will.

ESPAGNE, General, Count d'.

Commanded cuirassier division. Killed at Essling.

EVAIN, General, Baron.

Commanded Guard artillery during defence of Paris. Also commanded the artillery school at Douai.

FLAMAND, General, Baron.

Served with the Consulate Guard. Promoted captain at Marengo. Adjutant-major with grenadiers of the Guard at Jena; colonel with the chasseurs at Essling, and in Spain. Promoted general during Battle of Dresden. Commanded Young Guard at Leipzig. With Guard Reserve Brigade in 1815.

FRIANT, General, Count.

Commanded Line division at Austerlitz; colonel-in-chief of Grenadiers. Wounded at Borodino. Commanded Old Guard Division at Dresden, Leipzig, Hanau, Montmirail, Craonne, Reims and Arcis. Commander of *Grenadiers-à-Pied* of the Guard at Waterloo; and wounded again. Beneficiary in Napoleon's will.

GROS, General, Baron.

Colonel-commandant with the chasseurs of the Guard. Promoted to colonel at Austerlitz; to general at Friedland. Commanded Young Guard Brigade in 1809. Wounded at Essling. Commanded the chasseurs in Russia; the Young Guard again in 1813. Distinguished at Dresden. Retired under first Restoration.

GUYE, General, Baron.

Commanded Young Guard brigade in 1814. Wounded at Craonne, but recovered to take part in the defence of Paris. Commanded the Young Guard at Ligny. Recalled to service under Louis Philippe.

GUYOT, General, Count.

Captain with *Chasseurs-à-Cheval* of Consulate Guard. Distinguished at Austerlitz; promoted colonel after Eylau. Charged at Wagram. Promoted to general in 1809. Commanded Guard Heavy Cavalry, 1814; saw action at La Rothière, Montmirail, Vauchamps, Arcis. Colonel-in-Chief of Cuirassiers. Commanded Guard Heavy Cavalry again at Ligny, Waterloo. Beneficiary in Napoleon's will.

HAXO, General, Baron.

Commanded engineers of 1st Corps in Russia. With the Imperial Guard 1813-15. At Fleurus, Waterloo.

HENRION, General, Baron.

Colonel with the chasseurs and then the gendarmes in 1814. Commanded 2

Chasseurs at Montmirail, Craonne. With 4 Chasseurs at Waterloo as Colonel-in-Chief. Recalled to the army by Louis Philippe.

HULIN, General, Count.

Colonel commanding grenadiers of the Consulate Guard. Promoted general with the Imperial Guard. Distinguished at Jena. Governor of Berlin 1806. Awarded bonus after Eylau and Friedland. Governor of Paris during Malet conspiracy, also during later defence of the capital. Arrested under second Restoration.

JAMIN, General, Marquis of Bermuy.

Colonel with grenadiers. Distinguished at Arcis. Promoted general; and was also deputy commander of the Cuirassiers. Killed at Waterloo.

KRASINSKI, General, Count.

Commander of the Polish Light Horse. Was at Benevente and Wagram. Awarded Order of the Three Golden Fleeces; Legion of Honour. Switched to Lancers of the Guard, 1810. Wounded at Borodino. Commanded Young Guard Cavalry Brigade at La Rothière, Montmirail and Reims. Commanded all Polish units of the Grand Army in 1814. Present at Fontainebleau during abdication crisis, then returned to Poland.

LA FERRIÈRE, General, Count.

Deputy commander of grenadiers, 1813. Distinguished at Hanau. Commanded 3 Old Guard Division, 1814. Saw action at Reims; lost leg at Craonne. Commander of the cavalry school at Saumur from 1815. Beneficiary in Napoleon's will.

LANABERE, General, Baron.

Colonel-commandant of the chasseurs in Spain. Fought at Somosierra; was wounded at Essling. Adjutant-general of Imperial Guard, 1809. Adjutant-general of 2 Guard Division in Russia. Killed leading the charge at Borodino.

LANUSSE, General, Baron.

Commanded Young Guard brigade, Germany 1813-14. Distinguished at Lützen; wounded at Baützen. Promoted general of division, late 1813.

LARIBOISIÈRE, General, Count.

Commander of Guard artillery. Awarded Legion of Honour in 1808. Posted to Spain 1808-10. Commanded artillery of the Grand Army in Russia. Died of exhaustion, 1812.

LATOUR-MAUBOURG, General, Viscount, later Marquis.

Commanded cavalry corps in Russia; also at Krasny. Commanded 1 Cavalry Corps at Reichenbach, Leipzig. At Leipzig he lost a leg – and said to his batman that in future there'd only be one boot to polish!

LEPIC, General, Count.

Colonel of grenadiers with the Grand Army. Charged, and was wounded, at Eylau. Awarded bonus at Tilsit. Commanded Guard detachment in Spain. Decorated with Legion of Honour after Wagram. Then, Spain again and later Russia. Colonel-in-Chief 2 Guards of Honour in 1813.

MEUNIER, General, Baron.

Major in the chasseurs of the Consulate Guard. Colonel of the Line in 1804. General commanding 1 Young Guard Division at Brienne, La Rothière, Craonne and Laon. Commander of 14 Military District, 1814; and 2 Young Guard Division, 1815, until disbanded south of the Loire.

MICHEL, General, Count.

Colonel with 1 Grenadiers at Eylau. Awarded bonus after Friedland. Commanded Old Guard unit in Spain. Made general in 1811; commanded grenadiers in 1812; Old Guard Brigade, 1813; 2 Old Guard Division, 1814. At Var; and wounded at Montmirail, but recovered to take part in defence of Paris. Rejoined Napoleon in 1815. Commanded Old Guard Division at Ligny. Killed leading the final charge of the Guard at Waterloo.

MORAND, General, Count.

Commanded 1 Corps in 1812. Wounded at Borodino. Commanded 4 Corps, 1814. Besieged in Mayence (Mainz). Colonel-in-Chief of Chasseurs-à-Pied at Waterloo. Commanded the remainder of the foot Guard after the battle.

MOUTON-DUVERNET, General, Baron.

Colonel-commandant of 2 Conscript Chasseurs in Spain. Adjutant-general of the Guard chasseurs, 1811. Awarded bonus for Russian campaign. Commanded fusilier brigade at Baützen. Promoted general, 1813. Rejoined Napoleon after his return from Elba. Was shot under second Restoration.

NANSOUTY, General, Count.

With cavalry reserve at Wagram. Commanded horse of the Guard, 1813. Present at Dresden, Leipzig, Hanau, La Rothière, Champaubert and Berry-au-Bac. Taken ill at Soissons, March, 1814 and relieved by Sebastiani. On April 2, 1814 he agreed to serve the restored Bourbons.

PAC, General, Count.

ADC to the Emperor. Decorated with the Legion of Honour at Wagram. Awarded bonus after Russian campaign. Commanded Polish lancer regiment attached to Imperial Guard in 1814. Distinguished at Berry-au-Bac and Craonne. Also Laon, Epernay.

PETIT, General, Baron.

Commandant 1 Grenadiers, 1814. Distinguished at Château-Thierry, Reims. Embraced by the Emperor during farewell ceremony at Fontainebleau. Was commandant of Grenadiers of France. Rejoined Napoleon, 1815. Commander of 1 and 2 Grenadiers. Charged at Ligny. Commanded last reserve of the Guard at Waterloo: 1,200 grenadiers, sappers and marines. Proscribed under second Restoration. Recalled to the army by Louis Philippe. Beneficiary in Napoleon's will.

PORET DE MORVAN, General, Baron.

Lieutenant with Grenadiers of the Consulate Guard. Major with 1 *Tirailleur*-grenadiers in Spain. Was general commanding Young Guard Brigade, 1813. Saw action with Young Guard Division at Craonne; wounded at Laon. Deputy Commandant with Chasseurs of France after first abdication. Rejoined Napoleon in 1815. Commander of 3 Grenadiers of the Guard. Charged at Waterloo; wounded. Proscribed afterwards. Recalled to the army by Louis Philippe.

ROTTEMBOURG, General, Baron.

Promoted Colonel of the Line at Jena, 1806. Wounded at Wagram. Adjutant-general of the Guard for the grenadiers. Commanded Young Guard Division, 1813. Distinguished at Baützen. Commanded 5 Young Guard Division, 1814. Present at Brienne, La Rothière and Arcis.

ROUSSEAU, General, Baron.

Major in Fusilier-Chasseurs; wounded at Essling. Colonel-commandant 6 Voltigeurs (Chasseurs), 1813. General commanding brigade of 1 Young

Guard Division, 1814. Captured Epinal, then forced to retire wounded. Saw action at La Rothière.

SAINT-SULPICE, General, Count.

Commanded 2 Cuirassier Division at Wagram. Colonel-in-Chief of Dragoons of the Guard, 1809; then Master of the Horses. Commanded Guard Cavalry Division in Russia; and at Bezovka. Colonel-in-Chief of 4 Guards of Honour, 1813. At Lützen, Baützen.

SORBIER, General, Count.

Commanded Guard artillery reserve in Russia. Distinguished at Borodino. Was present at Gorodnia and the crossing of the Berezina. Very active in re-organising the artillery for the campaign in Germany.

SOULES, General, Count.

Major with grenadier section of the Consulate Guard. Distinguished at Marengo. General, 1804. Colonel-in-Chief of the chasseurs of the Imperial Guard. Bonus after Friedland. Later agreed to serve the Bourbons and voted for the execution of Marshal Ney.

TINDAL, General, Baron.

Commandant 2 Dutch Grenadier; and 3 Grenadiers in Russia. Distinguished at Krasny and at the crossing of the Berezina. Adjutant-general of the Guard and in command of Young Guard Brigade, 1813. Became ill with fever. Charged and was wounded at Dresden.

WALTHER, General, Count.

Captain of Grenadiers at Austerlitz; Colonel-in-Chief afterwards. Then made chamberlain to the Emperor. Made a count, 1808. Commanded Guard in Paris and Spain; and again at Wagram. Served throughout Russian campaign. Distinguished at Lützen. Commanded 3 Guard Cavalry Division at Leipzig. Died at Küsel, December 1813.

It is worth noting here that when Walther died, (mainly due to the wounds he received at Dresden), the Emperor wrote to his wife, 'I share your grief most profoundly. In your husband I have lost one of my bravest and most trusted generals. I am asking my Grand Marshal (Bertrand) to go and see you and arrange what is best for you and your daughters...'

This is fairly typical of the personal concern which Napoleon showed for the families of officers who had served the Empire through the years of glory and those of its downfall.

=7=
The Administration

Napoleon created the Empire with the help of friends, and with the help of friends he ruled it, not just a few intimates, but very many friends of every class and many skills. He was able to win these friends and keep their loyalty because he himself was a good friend to them.
– Vincent Cronin

There were fewer ministries in those days, of course: an obvious advantage. Bureaucracy too, was much more primitive. The sophistication of government flowed from Napoleon's own office, and if the directives were carried out efficiently then the country functioned accordingly. Extra-governmental intrigue there most certainly was (Talleyrand, Fouché), but this was political not departmental. There was sometimes corruption (Bourrienne *et al*); but not unduly so, because Napoleon was ever alert to root it out, and a number of potential culprits simply didn't indulge themselves, knowing that a proven case brought instant dismissal.

At city and district level (with good prefects) the administration was probably the best France had experienced since the all-powerful years of Richelieu. These prefects owed their appointments entirely to Napoleon and were promoted on merit. If they failed then they had only themselves to blame.

At the highest level there was an obvious emphasis on the War Ministry linked to the Treasury on account of France being in an almost permanently embattled state. But French industry and agriculture both prospered during the period, and during the Peace of Amiens the nation's exporters put the whole of the rest of Europe in the shade: so much so that England's government with full mercantile backing broke the peace.

Napoleon hated paperwork but was brilliant at it. His mind worked like lightning, and in a few short, sharp sentences of dictation he could determine French efforts for years to come. Once his policy was clear in his own mind he moved straight to its implementation. There was very little fuss and no ambiguity. The *Code Civile* is a masterpiece not only of logic and humanity; it is, in addition, brilliantly written and superbly clear.

175

In drafting the *Code Civil* Cambacérès and Napoleon had had to recognise that there were two distinct systems running through old French law: 'Customary' law as practised in the North and Roman law in the South.

Eventually the *code* of 1800-04 would run to 2,281 articles and set out to combine what the First Consul regarded as the true 'rights of man' with the best of the old law. To develop it along these lines, but also to see that justice was real, he therefore appointed two lawyers from the North: François Tronchet and Felix Bigot de Préamenou; and two from the South: Jean Portalis and Malleville. Tronchet was the best-known of the four, as the former defender of Louis XVI on trial for his life.

The lawyers didn't always agree about the *code*, (Portalis, a devout Catholic, found it hard to go along with Napoleon's more liberal views on divorce), but by and large they got on; and the system worked well.

They functioned as a special part of the official council of State: alongside such distinguished advisers as Nicholas Mollien, Plancy, La Chaise, the eloquent Jean Baptiste Treilhard, Stanislas de Giradin and the writer and prefect Antoine Claire Thibaudeau.

There is nothing wrong with the increased centralisation of government provided that the government is good; and there is nothing wrong with a dictatorship if the dictator is benevolent and has the nation's good as his ideal. Unfortunately this doesn't happen often enough, but on those occasions when it does the nation involved is likely to prosper. It says much for Napoleon's France that it remained on a war-footing and still managed to be prosperous, and that for over a decade it succeeded in being more efficient than the Allies, despite their money and greater resources of manpower.

Napoleon made few mistakes in his selection of ministers and civil servants; he also worked them extremely hard. The rewards were there too, but they were commensurate with the results achieved. Moreover each member of the administration was aware that the leader was quite capable of doing the job himself. Montalivet, Napoleon's last Minister of the Interior, complained that *le patron* knew what he was going to say almost before he'd opened his mouth. Even Talleyrand had to admit that the ruler he came to detest was still a man of genius.

ANDRÉOSSY, Antoine François, Count (1761 – 1828)

Diplomat. Although of Italian descent, he was actually born in the Languedoc. (One of his ancestors had been associated, around the 1660s, with the construction of the Languedoc Canal, and Andréossy himself always took a great interest in waterworks, canals, lakes and the like.)

He had attended the School of Artillery at Metz, where he obtained a commission in 1781. He then became an enthusiast for the Revolution and served along the Rhine in 1794 and in Italy the following year, mainly as an engineering officer. He was made general of brigade in 1798 when he accompanied Napoleon to Egypt. The future Emperor was much impressed by him in the Middle East and even more so when he found he had his support during the events of 18/19 Brumaire.

In 1800 he was promoted general of division and during the Peace of Amiens appointed ambassador to Great Britain. In this last capacity, being generally well-disposed towards the English, he worked hard to maintain the fragile peace, although eventually coming round to the view that the government in London, ever vote-conscious, would do exactly what its merchants wanted: which meant war again. The rows over the possession of Malta were a mere excuse. Andréossy noted sadly: 'It is not such and such a fact but the totality of facts comprising the First Consul's *gloire* and the greatness of France that frightens the English.'

When Napoleon became Emperor he created his former ambassador Inspector General of Artillery and a count of the Empire. But he was soon using him again as a diplomat. In 1808 he was ambassador to Vienna, in 1809 the governor of Vienna during the French occupation and in 1812 he was sent as ambassador to the Ottoman Empire.

Having adhered to Napoleon during the Hundred Days, he was banished from public life by the Bourbons and devoted himself to writing: works on artillery tactics, military history and, of course, on irrigation. But in the last year of his life he re-emerged as elected Member for the Aude.

BOISSY D'ANGLAIS, François Antoine de (1756 – 1828)

Statesman; recalled from exile and much favoured by Napoleon. He had intended to make a career in literature, but was then elected a member of the States-General and in the earlier years of the Revolution proved a gifted orator and committee-man. However, he was a moderate (which in turn caused him to be accused of monarchist sympathies). On the 18 Fructidor he was banished to England; lucky, perhaps, to escape with his life.

Napoleon recalled him upon becoming First Consul. He created him a member of the Tribunate and in 1805 a senator; following which he proved one of the most vocal and best speakers of that body. He also held some special responsibilities for assessing the output of the press.

He went along with the first abdication; believing the Emperor had made the right decision. But he adhered to Napoleon during the Hundred Days and was proscribed on the second Restoration. Afterwards he devoted himself to the literary work he had started in his youth: the most notable being his study of the life and thoughts of Malesherbes.

BOULAY DE LA MEURTHE, Antoine Jacques, Count (1761 – 1840)

Politician and civil servant. Originally a lawyer, in 1795 he became a member of the Council of Five Hundred. In 1797 he and a more extremist Revolutionary friend, Bailleul, put forward the idea of expelling from government and the administration all ex-nobles and persons who had held jobs under the monarchy. It caused a great outcry and was rejected by the Directory, which in turn caused Boulay to throw in his lot with Napoleon and the *coup* of 18/19 Brumaire.

The First Consul created him a councillor of state and Superintendent 'of the national domain': a sort of Minister of the Environment and Local Government. In this capacity he was directed 'to deal as indulgently as possible with regard to individuals and as sternly as possible with property'. He was created count in 1808, but was forced to flee to Germany after the Hundred Days when he adhered to the Emperor's cause.

In 1820 he was permitted to return to France on condition that he lived quietly and did not seek public office. However, he surfaced again – briefly – in 1830 when he edited a 700-page book attacking Bourrienne's *Mémoires*, rightly, for being a travesty of Napoleon's life and mere window-dressing for the Bourbons. No Parisian publisher would handle the book, so Boulay had it printed in Brussels.

BOURRIENNE, Louis Antoine Fauvelet de (1769 – 1834)

Napoleon's secretary before Méneval. Also a bad friend, whose basic dishonesty made him the tool of Fouché and later the Bourbons, and whose *Mémoires*, although racily written, are unreliable to say the least.

Born at Sens, he became an intimate of Napoleon's in the military school at Brienne and then managed to remain attached to him, on and off, until 1802 when he was dismissed over a fraudulent bankruptcy and posted off as Minister to Hamburg. Further frauds followed (including the sale of illegal passports), until in 1810 he was investigated and then compelled to pay back most of nearly one million francs that he'd embezzled. After this he became an agent for the Bourbons and from 1815 sat in their Chamber of Representatives as Member for the Yonne.

He died insane at Caen.

It has been claimed that his *Mémoires* were actually written by a hack journalist, Maxime de Villemarest. However, if read with caution (in parts they are no more than clumsy fantasy) they do provide cross-references useful to our knowledge of the early Italian campaigns, the expedition to Egypt and the first years of the Consulate. In addition his descriptive portrait of his former master has a ring of truth to it. 'His finely-shaped head, superb forehead and pale, elongated visage and meditative looks', he writes, 'have been painted many times. But the quickness of his glance and the rapidity of his expression were beyond imitation. It may be truly said that he had a particular look for every thought that arose in his mind – an appropriate face for every impulse that touched his soul.'

Despite being in the pay of Fouché he states that Napoleon had 'the weakness to fear' his Minister of Police, 'but at the same time he considered him necessary.'

He is reasonably accurate about the scenes of 18/19 Brumaire, which he witnessed in close-up, and, in their aftermath, about the drawing up of the new Constitution. But his account of 'the violent quarrel between Jean Lannes and Napoleon' over the 400,000 francs involved in 'doing up' the former's Paris house sounds far-fetched and is probably, at least in part, the author's own invention. It would have been untypical of Napoleon to tell Lannes to take the money from the funds of the Imperial Guard. And certainly untypical of the marshal to accuse his best friend of betraying him. That Lannes got into debt is true, but the First Consul/Emperor was extremely generous to him with pensions and annuities.

CAMBACÉRÈS, Jean Jacques Régis de, Duke of Parma (1753 – 1824)

Statesman. Despite disagreements over a variety of things he remained Napoleon's trusted and valued adviser throughout the Consulate and the Empire; as well as being co-author of the *Code Civile*. Also – and another mark of his high esteem – he was one of the few homosexuals Napoleon would tolerate near his person. (A second, one must suspect, was the painter Isabey.)

Born at Montpellier, of the legal nobility, he first of all became a councillor in the Court of Finance at Toulouse. However, on the outbreak of the Revolution he immediately espoused the cause of the Girondins. He was elected Deputy for Montpellier to the States-General and later sat for Herault in the National Convention. At this time he was less an adept politician and more interested in reform of the judiciary. He dithered over the trial and execution of Louis XVI. He doubted whether the Republic had the right to impose the supreme penalty. (Which seems somewhat pedantic: the Republic had the power to do exactly what it liked.) In the end though, he voted for the execution and was forever dubbed a regicide.

In 1793 he became a member of the Committee of General Defence, which then became the Committee of Public Safety. He was not chosen as one of the later directors, although his experience and brilliant oratory resulted in his being a prominent member of the Five Hundred. Largely due to the influence of Sieyès, in July 1799 he became Minister of Justice.

He was certainly a party to the *coup* of 18/19 Brumaire, which as much as anything led to his being retained by Napoleon as Second Consul. After this he had to prove himself – and did. Upon the switch to Empire Napoleon had no hesitation in creating him Arch-Chancellor and President of the Senate for life. (Outside the Bonaparte family these were the highest civil positions in France.) 'You have succeeded', he addressed the new Emperor in his turn, 'in teaching a people whom civil effervescence had rendered impatient of all restraint and inimical to all authority, to cherish and respect a power exercised uniquely for its glory and repose.'

In the words of a contemporary, Cambacérès 'was a typical man of the South. Cautious, subtle, a good member of the Convention, an eminent lawyer. He justified the confidence which Bonaparte placed in him and proved to be a skilful, cool-headed adviser. If he did nothing to prevent Bonaparte becoming a despot, then he often succeeded in tempering the eccentricities and harshness of his master, at least in matters of detail.'

Cambacérès provided the necessary legal expertise in drafting the *Code Civile*. It was presented in Napoleon's brilliant language, but inside it were 'the dry bones of law' which made it practical. And he was never afraid to speak his mind. As, for instance, in his opposition to the execution of the Duke of Enghien; and again over the disastrous involvements in Spain and Russia. But he accepted office again during the Hundred Days: which led to his being exiled until 1818, mostly in the Netherlands. Upon his return to France he lived quietly in retirement, a man amnestied but still a regicide...

In the day-to-day running of his office he had a fine grasp of realities. Just one example: although not a military man, in 1806 we find him intervening on behalf of the dragoons of the Imperial Guard to get them better overcoats for their march on Berlin. *He knew it would be colder there than Paris*. Again, he would spend hours over a single sentence of the *Code Civile* to get it right.

He was a big man, good-looking in his way, and with a typical pederast's concern for appearance. (He insisted his wig should have three rows of curls and he used a *lorgnette*.) He was a considerable gourmet. He often said 'A country is governed by good dinner parties.' And when he deputised for Napoleon at Council meetings, he invariably broke off the proceedings in time for lunch. He would serve truffled pâté, partridges roasted on one side and grilled on the other and elaborate soufflés. Napoleon, who allowed himself only twenty minutes to eat a meal, once quipped: 'To eat quickly, dine with me. To eat well, with the Second Consul. But leave yourself two hours. And don't expect to talk!' (The last remark referred to Cambacérès' belief that gastronomy was a serious business. However, the Emperor regarded his top legal brain with genuine affection and often, out on a campaign, would pause to send Cambacérès truffles and German hams by a fast stage. It was, he considered, a small recompense for loyalty and sound advice.)

CARNOT, Lazare Nicholas Margeurite, Count (1753 – 1823)

Politician and minister – and still today one of the great heroes of Republican France with a street named after him in every major city.

In fact it was his deeply-held Republican convictions which precipitated his quitting office under Napoleon – even though the latter recognised his immense abilities and was desperately anxious to retain him. As Minister for War and a member of the Committee of Public Safety, his brilliant organisation of the new Revolutionary armies had undoubtedly saved the nation in the face of the Allies' confident invasions; and he accepted the same portfolio under the Consulate. However, he refused to countenance the idea of France becoming an empire with yet another hereditary monarchy and would not return to office again until the dark days of 1814 when fresh invasions threatened.

Born at Nolay, in Burgundy, he was the son of a lawyer. Placed with the engineers at Mézières, he became an officer at twenty and in 1783 a captain, while his essays, *Sur les machines en général* and one on balloon warfare gained him admittance to several societies in Paris. Yet another essay, in praise of Marshal Vauban, won first prize at the Academy in Dijon.

However, it was following the outbreak of the Revolution that his activities became significant, not only for France, but also to the general advancement of Napoleon Bonaparte. Elected a deputy for the Pas de Calais to the National Assembly and then the Convention, he immediately devoted himself to army affairs. Later, after the French had suffered several severe reverses, he was nominated to the Committee of Public Safety and organised the *levée en masse*: the thirteen armies comprising three-quarters of a million men which saved France from the invading Allies. The speed and efficiency of his administration work proved crucial to these operations, and he was frequently on the battlefield himself, checking up on details of supply.

He was probably the first man in high places to recognise the abilities of the younger Napoleon – and the first to promote him. Upon receipt of a plan from the general to improve things on the Italian front he promptly placed him in command there, with – as we know – remarkable results. But by this time, having to cope with the intrigues of Revolutionary politics was getting Carnot into very great difficulties. Already, back in 1795, he had survived one attempted arrest. (In the Convention there was an indignant outcry: 'Will you dare to lay hands on the organiser of victory?') He could not survive Paul Barras' *coup* of 18 Fructidor however, and fled to Switzerland, only returning upon Napoleon's invitation in 1799.

Back at the War Ministry over the next two years he was the principal of French successes in Italy and under General Moreau along the Rhine. Again, his administrative work was brilliant: keeping the armies at a peak of efficiency and rooting out corruption (gifts from local suppliers, etc.) wherever he found it. Needless to say his own honesty and integrity were above suspicion.

By this time, however, his period in office was limited by his totally inflexible Republican principles. He voted against Napoleon becoming Consul for Life and in 1801 resigned. (Later he would deliver a rousing speech in the Tribunate against the change to Empire.) At first Napoleon refused to accept his resignation; then realised he couldn't compel him to continue. Instead, he awarded the departing minister a substantial pension and commissioned him to write a treatise on fortifications for the Military College of Metz...

In 1814, with the French falling back on all sides, Carnot at last agreed to return to public service. Napoleon immediately promoted him general of division and as such he conducted a remarkable defence of Antwerp. Also, he alone at the Council of State opposed Napoleon's first abdication: because he realised it would bring back the Bourbons. Yes, he was opposed to the Empire, he argued, but surely the alternative was so much worse.

He joined Napoleon again during the Hundred Days and was made Minister of the Interior; which led, not surprisingly, to his being proscribed under the second Restoration. Under a sentence of death if he returned to France, he switched to writing and to Science and lived out the remaining years of his life at Magdeburg.

CAULAINCOURT, Armand Augustin Louis, Marquis (1772 – 1827)

The French general who never really proved himself as a general, but who became one of Napoleon's greatest diplomats as well as a close personal friend of the Emperor.

Born of a genuinely *Ancien Régime* noble family in Picardy, he wanted to be a soldier and entered the local military college at the age of fifteen. In 1792, commissioned captain, he was imprisoned because his Revolutionary views were considered too moderate and was only released on the understanding that he re-enlisted as a private (grenadier). In which capacity he served for three years before being promoted back to his former rank.

He campaigned in Italy where he was promoted colonel and became Napoleon's *aide-de-camp*. He was a good-looking man with immaculate manners and Napoleon recognised his future potential as a diplomat. When Alexander became Tzar Caulaincourt was promptly packed off to St.-Petersburg, and, seemingly, did a good job there.

In 1804 he was promoted general of division, honorary Master of Horse, awarded the Grand Cross of the Legion of Honour and awarded pensions on the dukedom of Vicenza. He was tainted with having been implicated in the kidnapping of the Duke of Enghien – which he always afterwards denied, claiming his promotions were due simply to his loyal service to the Emperor.

He became France's official ambassador to Russia in 1807, where he evidently worked very hard in the cause of peace. However, he later failed to secure the Tzar's sister Anna as a second wife for his master. He then asked to be recalled in 1811, realising that the English had the Tzar's ear and commercial trust – although Alexander and he had become personally close. He advised Napoleon against the expedition into Russia, but still accompanied it. (His brother was killed during the Battle of Borodino.) In the retreat from Moscow he shared the Emperor's sleighs for the fourteen days and nights it took to leave the country ahead of the Grand Army. 'I've never experienced such cold', he wrote. 'The thermometer showed 25°C of frost. Breath froze on the lips and around the eyelids. The carriage was also frozen hard and white.' One can imagine what it was like for those left on foot with the rearguard.

Napoleon next used Caulaincourt to try to negotiate with the Allies: a thankless task, for they were sniffing victory and gave him short shrift. He helped negotiate the humiliating Treaty of Paris. However, although Talleyrand wanted him in the new French government, he refused to desert his fallen chief. During the Hundred Days he was Minister for Foreign Affairs – although by this time he had grown convinced that Napoleon's reign was doomed.

Following the second Restoration he went into permanent retirement on his estate in Aisne.

Except for Marshal Ney (in his moments of temper) no-one was allowed to speak to or about the Emperor as Caulaincourt did. He was a truthful man and Napoleon knew it. On one occasion he told his master that unless the wars were ended even the French would desert him. Unfortunately the Allies were not so easily convinced.

During the last years of the Empire he was largely controlling France's diplomacy.

Upon the first abdication Napoleon entrusted almost all of Marie Louise's letters to Caulaincourt. 'They are going to take my Empress and my son from me. Give me your hand. Embrace me. I want you to be happy, my dear Caulaincourt. You deserve it.' The Emperor was in the middle of his suicide attempt. And it was the diplomat who broke his grip and dashed out to find help.

Eventually – like Napoleon – he died of a stomach cancer.

CHAMPAGNY, Jean Baptiste Nompère de, Duke of Cadora (1756 – 1834)

Minister; and an underrated one. Born at Roanne-le-Forez of a noble family and originally educated for a naval career. However: in 1789 he was returned as Deputy for Roanne to the States-General. While a member he worked hard to improve French marine affairs and upon the Assembly being terminated in 1791 he returned to private life. In 1799 Napoleon made him a councillor of state for the navy and then sent him to Vienna as France's ambassador.

In 1804 Champagny became Minister of the Interior and in the next three years revealed a great capacity for dealing with tricky administrative problems. He had his enemies, of course, and was accused of greed and injustice. Nevertheless in 1807 Napoleon appointed him to succeed Talleyrand as Minister for Foreign Affairs, and in this position he was the principal person involved in the enforcement of the Continental System: the policy of isolating Great Britain and then denying her manufacturers anywhere to sell their goods. He was also much involved in army recruitment, helped to organise the great industrial exhibition of 1808 and was entrusted with seeing through the public works programme. Meanwhile from the Foreign Office he set in motion the annexation of the Papal States and the abdication of Charles IV of Spain.

In 1808 Champagny became a member of the new Napoleonic nobility with the title of Duke. He helped negotiate the Peace of Vienna (1809) and Napoleon's second marriage to Marie Louise. There then came an unexplained disagreement with the Emperor and he left office in 1811...

On the first abdication in 1814 he first of all agreed to serve the Bourbons and was made a peer of the realm; but he is thought to have been involved in the escape from Elba. Certainly during the Hundred Days he worked for Napoleon – although in the position of 'Surveyor of Public Buildings'. (Probably the minor title covered other things: like fortifications.) In any case, upon the 1815 restoration of the Bourbons he lost his peerage, which he only regained after the general amnesty of 1819.

Not exactly a fanatical Bonapartist; but one of the Emperor's most brilliant appointments. Napoleon liked him also because, after the devious, lazy Talleyrand, he had something of his own lightning rapidity in forming decisions.

CHAPTAL, Jean, Count of Chanteloup (1756 – 1832)

Born at Nogaret, and trained as a chemist. Later, as a member of the Senate, he introduced the metric system of weights and measures. Napoleon's invariably harassed Minister of the Interior and Public Works (until his surprising and altogether bizarre resignation), he was, nevertheless, good at the job. The First Consul, and later the Emperor, kept his own firm grip on what was happening architecturally, but the overworked and often then much-criticised Chaptal had to see that the new drains went in on time; that the novelty gas street-lamps worked; together with a thousand and one other things throughout France.

He built the great new storehouses for food in the capital which became known as Les Halles: the stomach of Paris. And he brought in the improved water supply. Napoleon had said: 'In ten years' time Paris should house three million people.' But, Chaptal replied, you can't improvise population. 'What about drinking-water, for instance?

'Well,' Napoeon then said, 'you must find another water-supply.'

The minister offered him the alternatives: either artesian wells or they bring in water from the River Ourcq. 'We'll adopt the latter plan,' Napoleon decided. 'Go home and tomorrow morning order five hundred men to start work at once near La Villette to dig the necessary canal.'

Later Chaptal would state in his *Mémoires* that Napoleon liked men who could 'transmit the law and government orders to the extremities of society with the speed of an electric current'.

Having taken office in 1800, he served until 1804: resigning allegedly because Napoleon had supplanted him in the eyes of a Comedie Française actress, Mlle Bourgain. But in his period of office he literally moved mountains (of builders' rubble apart from anything else!) His particular speciality was improving the Paris hospitals, but also he was the first person to experiment.with adding sugar to wine to help its maturing qualities.

Despite his resignation Napoleon made him a senator and a count, and in December 1813 he accepted the position of special commissioner to Lyon, France's second city. During the Hundred Days he served as Director of Trade and Industry.

He died a peer of France in 1832.

CLARKE, Henri Jacques Guillaume, Duke of Feltre (1765 – 1818)

Not one of Napoleon's most inspired promotions; and ultimately he would prove a bad friend. He was a poor soldier, and not much better as an administrator – although the full extent of his incompetence didn't become apparent until he served under the restored Bourbons. Under Napoleon he was merely carrying out his master's very precise orders.

According to his contemporaries he was 'pompous, vain and narrow-minded'. And a man who took advantage of his English name to make the preposterous claim of descent from the Plantagenets! On the other hand he seems to have possessed a glib tongue and been an adept flatterer.

Although born in France, his family were actually of Irish extraction. He received a good education in Paris and then became a supernumenary captain in the service of the Duke of Orléans. He held various appointments under the Revolution and Robespierre's Committee of Public Safety.

He evidently next made himself useful to the Directory, because Barras gave him the sinecure of running the topographical department and then sent him off to Italy to keep an eye on Napoleon: where he changed his allegiance. He could clearly see who the future 'star' was...

After 18/19 Brumaire Napoleon made him a councillor of state, gave him apartments in the Louvre and raised his salary at the topographical office to 80,000 francs per annum. After Austerlitz he made him Governor of Vienna; then later Governor of Berlin.

Following the peace with Russia at Tilsit, Clarke replaced Berthier at the War Office and was created a duke, although his work consisted of little more than rubber-stamping the Emperor's own directives.

However it was during the Malet conspiracy that the real truth about Clarke showed through. With his master away in Russia he just didn't know what to do. Instead of being firm he panicked, leaving Savary to clear up the mess – although he later signed some of the execution orders.

Not surprisingly he went over to the Bourbons in 1814. His reward was full control at the War Office, where again, left to his own devices, he proved a total failure. In the end Louis XVIII had to get rid of him, by way of compensation making him the ludicrous gift of a field-marshal's baton.

CONSALVI, Ercole, Cardinal (1757 – 1824)

Italian churchman and diplomat. He was hardly a member of the *élite*, but one might be forgiven for having thought so at the time. He was much in evidence at the Tuileries and at official receptions and took a very active part in the Empire's religious affairs.

Born in Rome and educated at the Cardinal York College at Frascati, his promotion through the ranks of the Catholic Church was rapid and in 1800 Pope Pius VII created him cardinal and a secretary of state.

Politically he was a royalist; but he was also a flexible man who believed in the temporal as well as the spiritual powers of Rome and pursued his diplomacy accordingly. It was he, who in July 1801, concluded the Concordat between Paris and Rome and then stayed on in France as the Vatican's special representative. There were some celebrated exchanges between the First Consul/Emperor and the subtle legate. At one stage of haggling over the Concordat Napoleon threw the eighth draft of it in the fire. Later at a Bastille Day dinner he exclaimed, 'I don't need the Pope. Henry VIII didn't have a twentieth of my power and yet he managed to change his country's religion. I can do the same. When are you leaving?'

'After dinner', the Cardinal replied and reached for the next side dish.

In the end though, Consalvi's common-sense prevailed and France was officially reconciled to the Catholic faith, 'the religion of the great majority of French people', to quote Napoleon. The Emperor had enormous respect for the Cardinal's intellectual and diplomatic skills and by and large they got on well together socially. There was another big blow-up between them over papal matters in 1807 and Consalvi resigned. But it was Napoleon who then apologised.

In his later years Consalvi returned to the Vatican and became the pontiff's right-hand man in the administration of the Papal States.

DARU, Antoine Noël Bruno, Count (1767 – 1829)

A soldier turned statesman, Daru was eventually destined to become Napoleon's highly efficient Secretary of State.

Born at Montpellier, he entered the artillery as a teenager, although he had a parallel interest in literature. During the Revolution he was a commissary to the troops protecting the coasts of Brittany against English raiders. But then, in the confusion of the times, he was thrown into prison as a suspected royalist. However, following the downfall of Robespierre, he returned to the army and his promotion was swift. By 1799 he was Chief Commissary to Masséna's army in Switzerland, where he revealed the most amazing and conscientious organisational abilities. Meanwhile, for relaxation he wrote poetry.

After the rise to power of Napoleon he was appointed to the reserve army intended for the Italian campaign, in which capacity he signed the 1800 armistice with the Austrians. Still anxious to write, he then returned to private life, but entered the Tribunate as a democrat when the English broke the Peace of Amiens.

In 1805 he was promoted Commissary to the Grand Army which marched into Central Europe against Austria and the Russians. After Austerlitz he helped draw up the Peace of Schönbrunn and was in turn appointed Intendant-General. He accompanied the Emperor on the Prussian campaign and against the Russians, and, after the Battle of Friedland in 1807, largely drafted the Treaty of Tilsit. At the same time he was the unofficial governor of Prussia, a task he carried out admirably: sound in finance; meticulous in administration. Also, Napoleon respected him because he spoke his mind. He was, for instance, strongly opposed to the Emperor's marrying Marie Louise of Austria, believing he should select a Frenchwoman. And he refused to play the courtier. 'No matter', Napoleon stated. 'I want an enlightened and vigilant administrator and Daru is precisely that. He has judgement, intellect, the power to be decisive and a body and mind of iron.'

In 1811 he appointed him Secretary of State and in 1812 took him on the Russian campaign, when he suffered the full horrors of the retreat from Moscow, but never once deviated from his task of feeding and clothing the army with what was available. At the crossing of the Berezina he suggested getting Napoleon over the ice-swollen river by balloon. And later he figured in the dramatic confrontation between the general staff and Murat when the latter was about to desert his command.

Finally, back in France, he worked near-miracles to raise a new army for the Emperor and in 1813 became Minister for War.

He adhered to Napoleon during the Hundred Days; but was so generally esteemed for his honesty and integrity that upon the second Restoration he was created a peer. He insisted on being regarded as a democrat though and denounced the activities of the Ultras on every possible occasion.

In the closing years of his life, he returned to his other love: literature. He wrote a 7-volume history of Venice, a history of Brittany, translated the poems of Horace and composed a 6-canto poem of his own about astronomy.

He died at Meulan.

DECRÈS, Denis, Count, later Duke of St.-Germain (1761 – 1820)

Admiral and minister. He was also the one naval man who seems to have occupied a place among Napoleon's intimates, although ultimately deserting him for the Bourbons. He first qualified for the army as an officer-cadet, switching to the navy at age 18. He was serving along the Indian coasts when the Revolution occurred, then advanced rapidly and in 1797 was promoted rear-admiral.

In 1801 he sailed for Egypt where he blew up his ship rather than surrender to the English. As a result, he was later awarded a sabre-of-honour. Under Napoleon he was promoted vice-admiral, a grand officer of the Legion of Honour and, upon his marriage to Mme Saligny he became the Duke of St.-Germain. Although suspicious of sailors, Napoleon genuinely liked him and created him his Minister of Marine. For this reason Decrès escaped the action at Trafalgar which stigmatised most of France's other senior naval officers. After this, with Napoleon's reluctance to tackle the English again at sea, the minister's energies were generally taken up with deploying his large force of marines on land. (They were often used for garrison duties.) He also had a big say in the affairs of the so-called 'Baby Guard': formed with the sons of guardsmen who had died previously in the service of the Empire. They were groomed to become a future *élite* corps and attached to King Louis Bonaparte of Holland. Upon his abdication they then returned to France and were incorporated into the main forces.

After 1814 and his siding with the Bourbons, Decrès was often publicly reviled and in 1820 was assassinated, apparently by his valet who placed a small keg of gunpowder underneath his bed.

DUBOIS, Louis Nicholas Pierre Joseph, Count (1758 – 1845)

Prefect of Police from 1799. It is claimed that he owed his long occupancy of the office to the fact that Napoleon – although disliking him – found him extremely useful as a spy on the activities of Fouché, his bitter enemy. He was made a count of the Empire in 1808 and then a member of the Council of State.

He remained loyal to the Emperor during the Hundred Days and upon the return of the Bourbons retired to Vitry-sur-Seine. Pasquier, who succeeded him, was warned against 'the abominable state' in which he would find the department.

DUMAS, Guillaume Matthieu, Count (1753 – 1837)

A French general who was, nevertheless, frequently used within the administration for political and diplomatic duties.

Dumas first joined the army in 1774 and fought in the American War of Independence as ADC to Rochambeau. From 1783-6 he explored the coasts of Turkey, and during the Revolution he assisted Lafayette. The Legislative Assembly then entrusted him with bringing back Louis XVI after the flight to Varennes. In 1792 he was elected President of the Assembly; but then accused by the Jacobins of being a monarchist. He escaped to London.

Recalled under the Consulate, Napoleon first charged him with reorganising the Army of the Reserve at Dijon. He became a councillor of state in 1801 and as such argued with Napoleon that the Legion of Honour should go only to the military. 'No!' came the reply. 'If we distinguish between military and civil honours, then we must institute two orders, whereas the French nation is one.'

188

Dumas served as commissary-general at Austerlitz and in 1806 at Naples as Minister for War attached to Joseph Bonaparte. He served briefly in the Peninsular War and then in Germany, which included negotiating the armistice after the Battle of Wagram. In 1810 he became a count and during the Russian campaign head of the army's administrative office; a post he held until captured at Dresden.

Louis XVIII retained him as a military adviser, but during the Hundred Days Joseph Bonaparte persuaded him to return to the Emperor: who immediately appointed him Commander of the National Guard. Under the second Restoration he devoted himself to writing – 19 volumes of his *Précis des Evénements Militaires* before blindness forced him to give up. But he was active again as an anti-Bourbon agitator during the Revolution of 1830; after which Louis Philippe created him a peer and reappointed him councillor of state.

FAIN, Agathon, Baron (d.1837)

Napoleon's military secretary and archivist. He served on every campaign from 1806 to Waterloo – and his three volumes of *Mémoires*, published between 1823 and 1827, are essential to our knowledge of the final years of the Empire.

He gives us, for instance, the most pictorial account of the expedition to Russia – and then as one of the chosen few to accompany the Emperor by fast-sleigh back to France. It is the evening of December 5, 1812. Marshal Mortier says to General Delaborde: 'A most unexpected event is about to occur, but in my opinion a necessary one. We must not be discouraged. As Emperor in Paris he will be ten times more valuable than by marching with an army in disorder. His job here is finished.' By 8.00pm, the thermometer in Surgeon-Larrey's buttonhole registers -22°F. Thirty chasseurs selected by the wounded Lefebvre-Desnoëttes are already in the saddle, huddled inside their dark-green capes, their heavy moustaches rimmed with ice. Count Wonsowicz takes up the reins of a sleigh drawn by six horses, assisted by the grooms Fagald and Amodru, which are pulling the sleeping-box containing Napoleon and Caulaincourt with the Mameluk Roustam-Raza, the Emperor's orderly, freezing in the seat behind. Another six horses set off pulling the second box containing Duroc, Mouton-Lobau, Fain himself and Lefebvre-Desnoëttes. The valets occupy a third...

He writes of the night Napoleon spent crying over Duroc's death at Markersdorff after the Battle of Baützen (1813). The Emperor had twice ordered his staff to disperse because their large group of horses surrounding him was drawing the Russians' fire. A cannonball came over, bounced off a tree, cut General Kirgener (the Guard's engineer commander and Jean Lannes' brother-in-law) in two and then struck and mortally wounded Duroc. 'The turn of the wheel of Fortune has ravaged these souls of iron', Fain adds.

189

At Fontainebleau the next year he remarks sarcastically: 'This abdication actually suits many people's purposes.'

He was on good terms with Méneval, the Emperor's former private secretary now serving Marie Louise, and warned him that Metternich would do everything in his power to prevent the second Empress rejoining her husband.

Fain recalls the scene on April 19, 1814 in the courtyard of the Cheval Blanc at Fontainebleau where he bids 'goodbye' to his master *en route* for Elba. Standing beside him are the Duke of Bassano (Maret), Generals Petit, Belliard and Ornano, the Count of Turenne and several others. General Lefebvre-Desnoëttes ordered the present-arms by 1500 veterans of the Guard. 'But not one marshal of the Empire and not a single member of his family', he records. Napoleon embraced General Petit as a gesture to all of them; and then commanded that an eagle be brought forward. This he kissed three times, saying: 'Dear Eagle, let my embrace echo in the hearts of these brave men! Farewell my children!'

Although loyal and discreet, the baron was never in awe of Napoleon – and on more than one occasion complained that his dictation was too fast. 'It makes me keep blotting the paper – and then I have to interrupt you, Sire, and ask you to repeat things!' Nevertheless, as a secretary he was intelligent and accurate and both Berthier and he grew to be adept at interpreting their master's meaning.

Fain worked tirelessly thoghout the Waterloo campaign. But he couldn't cope with everything – and so sometimes the Emperor either dictated or gave orders verbally to his staff officers. It has often been conjectured that a substitution of marshals and generals on the French side would have made all the difference to the battle. Well, two Fains would certainly have made a difference. The orders he took down from Napoleon were clear and made sense. Which is a lot more than can be said for a number of those issued by Soult or carried by Flahaut and La Bédoyère.

FESCH, Joseph, Cardinal (1763 – 1839)

Archbishop of Lyon, Grand Almoner of France, and the most prominent and active religious figure in the country immediately before and under the Empire. Which is hardly surprising since he was Napoleon's uncle – or rather part-uncle – being half-brother to Madame Mère. He was tall, commanding and above all a skilled negotiator; but at the same time, according to those who knew him well, an easy, agreeable and extremely good-humoured man who frequently defused his nephew's black moods. As Lucien Bonaparte once remarked, he was 'ever fresh, not as a rose, but like a good radish!'

Born at Ajaccio, he was often the playmate of the spirited and unruly little Napoleon, to whom he taught the alphabet. He was always destined for the church though and at fifteen was sent to the seminary at Aix-en-Provençe.

(Later it was he who administered the last sacraments to Napoleon's father at Montpellier.) He was also something of a literary man and eventually would be the recipient of the Emperor's private papers.

At the time of the Revolution he was arch-deacon of Ajaccio and like most Corsicans anti-French: although also because of the witch-hunting of priests going on in Paris and elsewhere. However, he was gradually converted to the ambitions of the Bonapartes and in 1793 went with the family to Toulon. For a while, due to 'the Terror', he was compelled to hide the fact of his being a priest and even worked as a storekeeper. When Napoleon commanded the Army of Italy he became one of its contractors. But when his nephew became First Consul he was able to take up religious duties again and his promotion was rapid. Napoleon showed himself determined to return France to the Roman Catholic faith – with certain in-built national safeguards – and he entrusted Fesch with the complex negotiations which led to the Concordat of 1801. Afterwards he was created an archbishop and in 1802 a cardinal.

In 1804 he was France's ambassador to Rome (with Chateaubriand as First Secretary). His objective: to secure Pius VII's presence at Napoleon's coronation. He needed to proceed with the utmost tact but eventually managed the task, accompanying His Holiness to Paris and then assisting at the ceremony in Notre Dame. On December 1, the night before the coronation, he married Napoleon and Josephine in a private religious ceremony with Talleyrand and Berthier as witnesses. This was to overcome the Pope's complaint that their previous marriage had been only civil. In the following year he was created Grand Almoner and a senator as well as being invested with the Legion of Honour.

Through the remaining years of the Empire Fesch devoted most of his time to smoothing over the quarrels which arose between Paris and the Vatican; and also trying to patch up the various differences between members of the Bonaparte family. (Murat and Caroline were a never-ending problem, as becomes clear from the 'Uncle'/Cardinal's letters.)

On a number of occasions he incurred Napoleon's wrath. There was the crisis of 1809, for instance when France annexed the Papal States. The Cardinal was accused of being too lenient towards Rome when in reality he was trying to make a peace. Then there was the subject of the Pope's detention at Fontainebleau in 1812. Fesch strongly resisted this as bad policy, in consequence of which Napoleon banished him to his diocese and cut off his stipend. However, the Cardinal continued to work for a reconciliation between church and state, and after 1812 this was largely achieved.

Following the first abdication he settled in Rome, but returned to Lyon during the Hundred Days. Upon the second Restoration he again took up residence in Italy – and from there ignored repeated Bourbon demands that he should resign his archbishopric. He too could be a determined fighter if he felt strongly about something.

One of his last actions on Napoleon's behalf came in 1819 when he procured the controversial Corsican doctor Antommarchi to replace the dismissed O'Meara on St.-Helena.

In his earlier years he had something of a reputation for gambling and enjoying the theatre. But he developed into an exemplary cardinal, greatly interested in the education and clean living of France's priesthood. His personal kindness is perhaps best illustrated by his final years in Rome, where more than anyone he was responsible for the care and comfort of the now nearly-blind Madame Mère.

FOUCHÉ, Joseph, Duke of Otranto (1763 – 1820)

Politician and minister. He was – with Talleyrand – one of the two arch-plotters under the Consulate and during the Empire. (Bourrienne, and one or two more of Napoleon's promotions and later dismissals, although equally corrupt, weren't even in the same league when it came to intrigue.) At times he appeared to be something quite superior to a mere Minister of Police: nearer to a very sinister Minister of the Interior – with a foreign spy network as well. He was also a survivor. Napoleon dismissed him on several occasions, then felt compelled to make use of him again – until by the end, under Louis XVIII, the minister's career had completed its full circle: from regicide to the Bourbon's committed instrument.

While witnessing Fouché go forward to make his hypocritical submission – kissing the hands of a king who loathed him – with Talleyrand limping along beside him and leaning on his arm, Chateaubriand couldn't resist one of his celebrated comments: 'Just look at those two,' he said. 'Vice supported by Crime!'

And yet – even the hypocrite is capable of some surprises. He offered to provide false passports to allow Ney to escape his inevitable fate after the disaster at Waterloo (which characteristically the marshal refused). Also he was a model family man; devoted to a notably ugly wife and a lot of children. (However, so was Hitler; and so are most of today's Mafia bosses.) Perhaps the truth lies somewhere closer to the events of his first years in politics – grafted on to the basic character of the man. Once involved in the machinations and double-think/double-talk of nearly all high government he just couldn't resist going on with it. As in 'live' Greek theatre one senses a natural master trying on the various possible masks, then having the paintwork retouched or ordering something new. Occasionally he will step back to admire the cleverness of his selection...

Fouché was born at Nantes, the son of a sea-captain. Because he showed aptitude in science and literature he was sent to finish his studies in Paris, after which he became a tutor. Part of this time was spent at Arras, where he met Robespierre and, apparently, lent him money to support himself as a deputy to the States-General. Soon he would become a deputy himself; to the Convention: from the Loire. He voted for the death of Louis XVI and

192

then served as a commissioner – allegedly a moderate one – in various parts of France for the next seven years. (Moderate? Perhaps only by the standards of 'The Terror'. He sent one hundred priests to be drowned in the Loire at Nantes...) Eventually he fell out with Robespierre, but survived – and survived a further indictment in the Convention, when Boissy d'Anglais described him as 'a thief and a terrorist whose crimes would cast eternal disgrace on any assembly of which he was a member'.

Protected by Barras, much of his later period as a Revolutionary commissioner was involved with espionage – until, on August 1, 1799 he became Minister of Police: a position for which he seems to have been ideally suited.

Dark and swarthy, with a pinched face, a whining voice and a callous disregard for others, he set about making his newly-acquired position impregnable. He writes that during those last days of the Directory he found 'the treasury empty: therefore no money, no police '. So he set up a system of gambling halls connected with brothels and taxed them accordingly. He banned public political discussions and clamped down on the press.

Over the events of 18/19 Brumaire he first ditched Barras and next Sieyès, seeking to make himself indispensable to Napoleon. The latter never liked him, but recognised that someone had to do the job. Though not as Fouché was doing it. He even spied on Josephine – and he recruited Bourrienne to spy on the First Consul himself. Abroad he had three penniless princes of the *Ancien Régime* working for him as well as several of the exiled Jacobins, keeping a foot in both camps. When Napoleon tried, in 1804, to abolish his office altogether it coincided with the Cadoudal conspiracy. By which time Fouché had convinced the other members of the Bonaparte family that they needed him and with their help gained reinstatement; together with a dukedom, about which he concluded: 'A pretty good prize in the Imperial lottery'.

He continued to plot; often with Talleyrand, and on other occasions with the Murats. And when Napoleon became exasperated again and packed him off to Italy he flattered Eliza Bonaparte into negotiating a reconciliation with the Emperor. After which he conspired for the return of the Bourbons.

After the first abdication, as 'head' of the provisional government he received the Count of Artois (the future Charles X) back into France. But he returned to Napoleon during the Hundred Days and was reappointed Minister of Police. (When, it is claimed, he sent the plans for the Emperor's Waterloo campaign to the Duke of Wellington, in cipher, via a Flemish postmistress – then had her arrested on the Belgian frontier, just in case the battle went the wrong way!) I doubt the story, but with Fouché one never can tell...

Following the second Restoration the Bourbons at last felt equal to dealing with the former regicide. He was kept on as a minister for three months, then posted as ambassador to Saxony. While there, in January 1916 he was denounced as a regicide in both chambers and condemned to death if he ever returned to France.

He settled for an Austrian passport and a house in Trieste. Evidently a large proportion of his ministerial fundings had accompanied him into exile.

FRÉRON, Louis Marie Stanislas (1754 – 1802)

Politician, editor, later Commissioner on San Domingo. Everything suggests he would have risen higher under the Empire. Had he lived longer that is; and not blotted his copybook a second time. Certainly Napoleon had come to recognise his talents – and by 1800 appeared not only to forgive and forget the 'cleansing' of Toulon, but even appeared eager to promote him.

Born in Paris, he was the son of a famous editor who had attacked Voltaire (and in consequence been satirised in the latter's fiction). With King Stanislas of Poland as his godfather, and his obvious natural talents as a writer, plus in 1776 inheriting his father's journal *L'Année Litteraire*, a brilliant career was predicted for him. However, he had been at school with Robespierre and Camille Desmoulins and grew up to become an ardent (and sometimes violent) revolutionary. He turned the editorial side of *L'Année Litteraire* over to Royon and Geoffroy and founded a new, outspoken, anti-government political journal *L'Orateur du Peuple*.

Under the Revolution proper he was almost immediately influential. In 1793 together with Paul Barras, the Convention charged him with 'purging and purifying' Marseille and Toulon: where he first met Napoleon. At the time he gained a reputation for the utmost severity – but in fact he came to oppose the worst excesses of 'the Terror' and consquently conspired with Barras to bring about the downfall of Robespierre. (He personally brought the accusation against Fouquier-Tinville, 'the Terror's' odious Public Prosecutor; and he then purged the Convention of its remaining fanatics.)

He was now not only associated with moderation but actively urging it. Together with a European peace. In 1796 he published his *Mémoire Historique sur la Reaction Royale et sur les Malheurs du Midi*; and in the same year was again appointed Commissioner for Marseille. Here he met and fell in love with the 16-year-old and already beautiful Pauline Bonaparte. It was evidently a passionate affair on both sides; the letters between them are quite something. But Madame Mère disapproved. And so too did Napoleon, not yet aware of Fréron's changing tack and no doubt remembering the atrocities of Toulon.

Exactly what brought about the reconciliation between them isn't certain. Only that Fréron was suddenly appointed Napoleon's Commissioner for San Domingo. This despite the fact that Pauline was also accompanying the expedition there as General Leclerc's wife.

Back in favour with Napoleon he now seemed set for big things. Unfortunately though, the disease-ridden climate finished him off. He died there in the same year as Leclerc and General Richepanse on Guadeloupe.

194

GAUDIN, Michel, Duke of Gaëta (1756 – 1841)

Financier. A man of great importance under both the Consulate and the Empire, although of lesser consequence politically than Lebrun. He was more the hard worker at the Treasury; Lebrun the inspired speculator.

He had served at the Treasury under the Directory, and it was only on Sieyès' advice that Napoleon first of all retained him. But he was so pleased with the man's shrewd judgement and good book-keeping that he left him with the finance portfolio through until the abdication of 1814 – and then again during the Hundred Days. He created him a duke in 1809.

Gaudin's quiet, but natural abilities had been frustrated under the Directory, whose monetary dealings were lazy and corrupt. Under the vigorous, and above all honest Napoleon, he was suddenly transformed into one of the country's best civil servants. He founded the Bank of France, overhauled the financial administration in both and capital and the provinces and even produced a genuine register of land and properties.

He was dismissed from office on the second Restoration, much to France's loss.

GIRARDIN, Stanislas, Count (1762 – 1827)

Statesman. Came from a family of the old nobility. King Stanislas (ex-Poland) was his godfather and Jean Jaques Rousseau his tutor. Although a convinced Revolutionary, and an elected member of the National Assembly, his background proved to be dangerous. During The Terror he escaped to England, thanks to a note mistakenly signed by Marat. He then ventured back into France in 1794, only to be thrown into prison by Robespierre: when he was lucky to escape with his life.

Under the Consulate and the Empire he owed his rise to a developing friendship with Joseph Bonaparte. He accompanied the latter to Naples and Spain and in 1810 was promoted general of brigade and made a count. After this the Emperor entrusted him with many delicate diplomatic missions.

He seems to have escaped the Bourbons' hit-list and in 1819 was elected to the Chamber of Deputies. His *Journal et Souvenirs* was published a year after his death and is generally favourable to his erstwhile master.

GRIMALDI, Honoré Gabriel, Prince of Monaco (1778 – 1841)

The Empress Josephine's principal equerry; also Prince of Monaco (as Honoré V) from 1790.

The small principality set within Provençe in the South of France has been ruled by the Grimaldi family since the 13th century. However, Prince Honoré fought with the Revolutionary armies, including alongside Moreau, Ney and Richepanse at the decisive Battle of Hohenlinden in 1800, where he was wounded. Later he served under Murat in Germany (1806) and then in

Spain for most of 1808.

He became greatly attached to Josephine, as most of her attendants and intimates did, and he kept the post of equerry to her after the divorce, despite being offered a similar position with Marie Louise.

Following the first abdication there was a very real danger that Monaco might be abolished as a principality. However, Talleyrand managed to keep it intact by planting a special clause in the Treaty of Paris.

The British occupied it during the Hundred Days, so there was no chance of the prince taking part in the events of the Waterloo campaign.

LANJUINAIS, Jacques, Count (1753 – 1827)

Liberal politician and President of the Lower House of Representatives which Napoleon gave to France on his return from Elba in 1815. A democrat of known honesty and integrity, who, although a Republican, had voted against the death of Louis XVI. 'I am a legislator, not a judge', he said at the time.

However, as result of Waterloo this Parliament of Napoleon's was a short-lived experiment. Upon the second Restoration Lanjuinais was made a peer of the realm.

LAS CASES, Emmanuel August Dieudonné, Marquis (1776 – 1842)

Chamberlain, and, for a time on St.-Helena, Napoleon's secretary.

Born at the château of Las Cases, Revel, in the Languedoc, he was educated in Paris, and at sixteen he joined the navy and became a lieutenant in 1789. He spent several years stationed at San Domingo, but on the outbreak of the Revolution, being by birth an aristocract, he took refuge in London, giving language lessons and pubishing in 1799 his *Atlas Historiques et Généalogique*: a popular success.

He returned to France under the Consulate, although he didn't come to Napoleon's personal attention until 1809. The Emperor then made him Chamberlain, a count of the Empire and used him on many errands of state.

Having adhered to the revived Bonapartist cause during the Hundred Days, after Waterloo he decided to accompany his master to Rochefort and later served as his mouthpiece in negotiations aboard the *Bellerophon* (Napoleon's English being practically non-existent). His period at St.-Helena lasted little more than a year though. In November 1816 he was arrested as the result of a letter he'd written criticising the English governor's treatment of his famous prisoner. First of all deported to South Africa, he was then exiled in Germany and didn't return to France until 1831 when he became Deputy for St.-Denis.

His *Mémoires* of St.-Helena are considerably biased in favour of Napoleon but make fascinating reading nevertheless.

'Circumstances, the most extraordinary,' he writes, 'have kept me near the most extraordinary man that ever existed. I collected day by day all that I saw of Napoleon and all that I heard him say during the period of eighteen months in which I was constantly about his person.'

He goes on:

'Contrary to the general opinion, the Emperor is far from possessing a strong constitution. His limbs are large but his fibres [muscles? – RH] are relaxed. With a very expanded chest he is constantly labouring under the effects of cold. His body is subject to the influence of the slightest accidents. The smell of paint is sufficient to make him ill; certain dishes too. All his strength is in his mind . . .'

Napoleon loved to describe the characters of his marshals and generals, he recalls:

'In this way he spoke of Lannes, Masséna, Duroc, in fact of practically every officer he'd ever promoted. Upon learning of the execution of Marshal Ney he referred to him as a martyr . . .'

'Talleyrand, was always in a state of treason, but it was in partnership with Fortune! His circumspection was extreme; he treated his friends as if they might in future become his enemies, and he behaved to his enemies as if they might at some time or other become his friends. Also he was the principal instrument and the active cause of the death of the Duke of Enghien.

Napoleon continued:

Fouché was the Talleyrand of the clubs just as Talleyrand was the Fouché of the drawing rooms. Intrigue was to Fouché as necessary as life itself: intrigue at all times, in all places and with all persons. Nothing ever came to light but he was found to have a hand in it . . .'

Of his own family Napoleon said:

'Pauline was too careless and extravagant. She should have been immensely rich considering all that I gave her, but she used to give nearly everything away. Madame Mère in contrast carried parsimony to its most ridiculous extremes. She was very willing to receive money provided she could hoard it!

Joseph's qualities are only suited to private life. In the discharge of the high duties which I confided in him he did the best he could. His intentions were good, and therefore the principal fault lay not so much with him as with me for raising him above his natural sphere . . .'

Speaking of the Waterloo campaign after breakfast one day, Napoleon said:

'The situation of France was critical but not desperate after the battle. Every preparatory measure had been taken on the supposition of a failure in the attack on Belgium. Paris had twenty-five days to prepare itself for defence, and the mass of the Russian and

Austrian armies was not ready to take the field. Neither arms, nor ammunition, nor officers were wanting in the capital; the number of sharpshooters could easily have been augmented to 80,000 and the field-artillery to 600 pieces.'

But, as Las Cases records him adding:

'Treason began to penetrate our ranks. Great numbers of troops sank under the effects of fatigue and discouragement. My lieutenants became dispirited and therefore unfortunate. They were no longer the same men who figured at the beginning of the Revolution or who distingished themselves under the Empire.'

LAVALETTE, Antoine Marie Chamans, Count (1769 – 1830)

Napoleon's Director-General of Posts, and one of the cleverest as well as most resourceful of his friends and supporters.

Born in Paris and educated at the Duke of Harcourt's College, he first of all thought of making his career as an academic and became a librarian at St.-Geneviève. However, he was soon swept away from this by his enthusiasm for the Revolution, and by the time he met Napoleon – at Arcola with the Army of Italy – he was already a lieutenant. The general found that in addition to his courage the young man 'possessed solid information, a scrutinising mind, wonderful sagacity, prudence and perfect good-breeding'. From now on he began to entrust Lavalette with some of the most important and delicate (because secretive) of his missions.

This included sending him to Paris to observe what Barras and the other members of the Directory were up to; and again to spy on their representatives in Switzerland where they were negotiating with the Germans. Soon after this he married Emilie de Beauharnais, a niece of Josephine's.

He was one of Napoleon's closest companions during the Egyptian expedition, proved perhaps the most useful of his couriers and go-betweens during the events of 18/19 Brumaire and then served as postmaster-general throughout the Consulate and the Empire. (Not an easy task when there were war-zones in various parts of Europe and the most important lines of communication were often the longest.) He was also councillor of state and the Emperor made him a count and decorated him with the Legion of Honour. At one stage in 1814 Napoleon regarded his as 'nothing less than my eyes and ears in Paris'. 'The Emperor's presence is imperative,' Lavalette's encoded reply ran, 'if he wishes to prevent his capital from being handed over to the enemy.'

During the Hundred Days Napoleon offered him the Ministry of Home Affairs, but he insisted on returning to the control of France's posts – a job he considered of greater importance until (hopefully) the nation's enemies had been defeated in Belgium.

He had certainly conspired to help his master escape from Elba and after Waterloo the Bourbons marked him down as their next intended victim after

Marshal Ney. Sentenced to death, in December 1815 he escaped from the Conciergerie by swapping clothes with his wife and then hiding with three British officers, Sir Robert Wilson, John Hely-Hutchinson and Michael Bruce, who later smuggled him out of France to Bavaria disguised as an English colonel.

Pardoned in 1822 he returned to find that his wife didn't recognise him; events had caused her to lose her reason. However, after his patient nursing this was eventually restored and their remaining years together were particularly happy ones.

His *Mémoires*, published a year after his death, are entertaining in addition to their plentiful supply of information. He comes over as a warm and agreeable personality who is nevertheless highly intelligent – and sharply intuitive. About Marmont, for instance, he writes: 'His education had been particularly well-attended to, and he had entered the army while still quite young. The principal features of his character were...an unbounded passion for glory and ambition.' Also of Napoleon in the aftermath to the disastrous Russian campaign of 1812: 'He admitted everybody; showed severity towards some – intrepidity in the presence of all. He explained the causes of the misfortunes of the campaign, and without seeking to dissemble the fault that had been committed, he boldly claimed the support he wanted to begin the war again, repel the enemy and conclude a peace, of which he, more than anyone, felt the absolute necessity. His noble courage in wrestling with misfortune electrified the whole country.'

Lavalette was also particularly close to Josephine; cntinuing to visit her at Malmaison after the divorce. He goes on to describe how in 1814 she completely charmed the Tzar Alexander. The Russian monarch declared that she greatly resembled the Empress Catherine, offered protection to her daughter Hortense and wanted to find a German principality for Eugène de Beauharnais. Later, when he heard the ex-Empress was seriously ill he immediately sent his personal physician...

Finally there are the excitements of the Hundred Days, beginning with Napoleon's arrival in Paris. 'I flew to the Elysée to see him. He ordered me into his private-room and came to greet me with a frightful epileptic laugh. 'Oh, my God!' he said, raising his eyes to heaven and walking two or three times up and down the room. This appearance of depression was very short however: he soon recovered his coolness and asked me what was going on in the Chamber of Representatives.'

LEBRUN, Charles François, Duke of Piacenze (1739 – 1824)

A statesman, and even more importantly, a financier. For much of the Empire's course he was the equivalent, for Napoleon, of a Chancellor of the Exchequer.

Born at St.-Sauveur Lendelin (Manche). Although not rich, his father gave him a good education and then sent him to several other European

199

countries to study civil law. Returning to France and settling in Paris, he became secretary and adviser to Louis XVI's minister Maupeau, which led to his sharing the latter's downfall in 1774. Lebrun returned to the country. He translated Homer and Tasso and in 1789 published his *Voix du Citoyen*, an objective prediction of the course of the Revolution and suggesting a liberal constitution as the sole remedy. He was then elected Deputy for Dourdan in the Constituent Assembly, where he opposed the issue of paper money, of state lotteries and other financial measures. Later he narrowly escaped execution under the 'Terror'.

In 1799 he was appointed Third Consul by Napoleon, partly it is claimed on the strength of the clear, crisp prose-style of his books. Anyway, this big, unwieldy man quickly proved himself something of a financial genius. Napoleon used to visit him late at night, sit at the foot of his bed and question him about bank-rates, bills of exchange and the national debt. Fairly soon he was trusting him with the entire financial strategy of France. He also assisted with the drafting of the *Code Civile*. He served as one of the four pages carrying Napoleon's train at the 1804 coronation and was named Arch-Treasurer of the Empire. But he was greatly opposed to Napoleon's re-establishment of the nobility and tried hard to refuse the dukedom of Piacenza.

Later he went as the Emperor's special governor to Genoa where the city's finances had become chaotic. And from 1811 to 1814 he served as Governor-General of the Dutch, who nicknamed him 'the good Stadtholder'. Louis XVIII on his restoration also wanted to enlist Lebrun's financial expertise and made him a peer of the realm. But he returned to Napoleon's side during the Hundred Days and was appointed Grand Master of the University. At the second Restoration he was excluded from the peerage, then reinstated in 1819. Five years later, in his eighty-fifth year, he died on his estate at St.-Mesmes, still indulging his literary pursuits.

He was often accused of being parsimonious and calculating. However, as he pointed out, that is how you put the nation's finances in order. More significantly, from Napoleon's point of view he was honest, a firm bureaucrat and not overly ambitious. He understood how to pay for the Grand Army's campaigns whilst keeping the country prosperous – and yet still retain some money in the Treasury.

His son served as one of the Emperor's ADC's: another mark of favour.

MARET, Hugues Bernard, Duke of Bassano (1763 – 1839)

Statesman as well as Foreign Minister, Maret was also a journalist much concerned with the *Moniteur*, which eventually became Napoleon's official 'mouthpiece'.

Born at Dijon, the son of a doctor, he originally studied law but, fired by the ideas of the Revolution, he began to take down the debates in the National Assembly and to publish them in what he called *Bulletin de l'Assemblée*, (later incorporated into the *Moniteur*). Politically he remained a moderate though, and in 1792 he entered the French Foreign Office. Later that same year he was posted to London with the idea of obtaining peace with Britain. However the execution of Louis XVI in Paris dashed these hopes and Maret was then sent to Naples as France's official ambassador. On the way he was captured by the Austrians and held a prisoner for over two years until exchanged for Louis XVI's daughter, the future Duchess of Angoulême. Upon returning to France he again devoted himself to journalism – and received an indemnity of 150,000 francs for his imprisonment.

When Napoleon came back from Egypt in 1799 Maret became one of his secretaries and soon a secretary of state. He was a hard worker, discreet but determined, and unswerving in his loyalty, including at times making excuses for the First Consul's harsher decisions. After appointing him to the Foreign Office (where eventually he succeeded Talleyrand as Minister) Napoleon came to rely on him greatly; and, of course, adopted the *Moniteur* as France's only reliable government newspaper. As Fouché once put it: 'Maret sees only with the eyes and hears only with the ears of his master'. Even so, he discharged all of the Consul/Emperor's wishes with immense skill, even accompanying Napoleon to the various battlefields, where the latter quipped that not a shot could be fired without Maret having something to do with it!

He largely drafted the constitutions for the Italian and Swiss republics; also the one intended for Spain, had the situation there not developed into the Peninsular War.

He favoured a permanent alliance with Austria (and hoped the marriage to Marie Louise, which he'd negotiated, would bring this about). He concluded peace treaties with both Austria and Prussia before Napoleon's invason of Russia, only to see his work in ruins when the Grand Army failed there. Also by this time he was facing continuous problems in Italy due to the rebellious behaviour of Murat and Caroline Bonaparte in their kingdom of Naples.

After 1812 his influence over foreign affairs was often superceded by Caulaincourt, but he remained one of Napoleon's secretaries of state right through until the departure for St.-Helena. And he continued controlling the *Moniteur*. A cautious man by nature, nevertheless he had plotted for the return from Elba and worked tirelessly on his master's behalf during the Hundred Days. Under the restored Bourbons he was exiled to Grätz, not returning to France until 1820. In 1830 Louis Philippe made him a peer of the realm.

MÉHÉE DE LA TOUCHE, (1760 – 1826)

Probably the most sinister individual to function and prosper under the Empire. Certainly not of the true *élite*, even if he aspired to be (his kind were anathema to Napoleon), however, as Fouché's 'creature' and payrolled

201

agent provocateur he seldom strayed far from the central affairs of government and from contact with the Emperor.

He was the son of a doctor at Meaux and originally intended to follow that profession. However, he fell into criminal ways and was imprisoned. Released upon his father's petition, he was soon in trouble again, was sent to Brest but managed to elude the navy's intake. He next pops up after the Revolution and in the role he was to pursue for most of the rest of his life. To begin with the French government sent him to St.-Petersburg, with a false passport describing him as the 'Chevalier de la Touche'. But almost immediately the Russians unmasked him as a spy and put him outside their borders. In Poland he established the *Warsaw Gazette*, but was again discovered and banished. Then he started dabbling in the home politics of the Revolution itself: first as a member of the Jacobin clubs, next as assistant-secretary to various departmental communes and eventually as one of the most prominent regicides. Though he later denied it, he was one of the assassins during the September massacres. (Like Tallien, his name is on a note for the payment of the killer squads.) Later he became Tallien's secretary and at one stage was even proposed as a member of the Directory.

He worked against Napoleon over the events of 18/19 Brumaire, but this didn't discourage the wily Fouché from employing him as a spy. The First Consul had had him banished to England, but Fouché made contact with him in London and recruited him as a double agent: a man who pretended to hold royalist sympathies in order to gain the confidence and secrets of the *emigrés*; even offering his services as an intermediary with various disillusioned Republican figures in Paris. In this way Fouché from a distance was able to wreck all of the main royalist plotting. In Paris General Moreau was disgraced, General Pichegru captured and then found strangled in his cell, Georges Cadoudal was captured, tried and executed and the Duke of Enghien kidnapped and shot. Moreover proof was uncovered that members of the British cabinet were implicated. Méhée had become one of the spymaster's most spectacular successes. An Eric Ambler or John le Carré type figure at least a century ahead of his time.

Apart from a lack of conscience, his best assets were his knowledge of public affairs, a suave and insinuating manner and an ability to cope with most of the European languages. Also, like Fouché, he made a lot of money from his activities and survived even the restoration of the Bourbons. Having betrayed the royalists, he spent his last years living like one.

MÉNEVAL, Claude François de, Baron (1780 – 1842)

Napoleon's long-serving and long-suffering principal private and Cabinet secretary. Also one of the best of his biographers. (*Mémoires pour servir a l'histoire de Napoleon 1, 1802 – 1815*, 3 Vols. Also, *Napoleon et Marie Louise*.) Although staunchly Bonapartist he was an acute observer and, of course, in a unique position to observe. Formerly a soldier (a junior officer) he continued to serve Marie Louise after the first abdication and then accompanied her out of France to Aix. He returned to the Emperor again during the Hundred Days and was bequeathed 100,000 francs in his will.

His initial meeting with his new employer reads characteristically. He was just 24 and was shown into a room full of writing tables and musical instruments: leftovers from the reign of Louis XVI. Napoleon quizzed him about his health and previous experience. He stated that he was feeling very unsure of himself but would do all in his power to meet the First Consul's needs. Napoleon then pulled his ear and told him to start at seven the following morning. After a worried and therefore sleepless night he arrived on time only to discover the Consul was busy with his ministers. However, two hours' later he walked in and commenced dictation as if Méneval had been with him for years...

'Napoleon was at that time moderately stout,' he records; and puts forward the (unlikely) diagnosis that this was brought on by the Consul's frequently taking baths at irregular hours. He goes on:

> The size of his chest bespoke a robust constitution; his forehead was high and broad, his eyes grey, penetrating and wonderfully alert. His nose was straight and well shaped; and his teeth were fairly good and the mouth perfectly modelled, the upper lip slightly drawn down towards the corners and the chin a little prominent. His skin was smooth, and his complexion pale but of a pallor which denoted a good circulation of the blood. His very fine chestnut hair, which until the time of the expedition to Egypt he had worn long, cut square and covering his ears, was clipped short. The hair was thin on the upper part of the head and left bare his forehead, the seat of such lofty thoughts.

However:
> ...when excited by any violent passion his face assumed an awful expression. A kind of rotary movement appeared on his forehead and between his eyebrows; his eyes flashed fire; his nostrils dilated, swollen with the inner storm. But these transient movements, whatever their cause may have been, in no way brought disorder to his mind. He seemed to be able to control at will these explosions, which as time went on became less frequent. His mind remained cool.

(One exception he agrees was the celebrated half-hour haranguing of Talleyrand, when Napoleon lost his temper totally and referred to his Vice-Grand Elector as so much dung wrapped up in a silk stocking.)

Méneval found Napoleon very simple in his domestic habits. Usually the

Consul dined with Josephine and the family, except on Wednesday when the ministers came. He lunched alone on simple food, Chambertin mixed with water and then a cup of coffee.

Afterwards he received men of letters or artists whose conversation he greatly enjoyed. And he had an absolute contempt for conspiracy, and had no fear that unprincipled persons might reach his apartments. Indeed, he had a conviction of the impotence of conspirators [he should have watched Talleyrand and Fouché much more closely, much sooner – RH] and listened with ill-concealed impatience to various reports brought to him by the police.

He insists that his master was:
...Indulgent, easy to please, merry with a merriment that was often noisy and familiar in a manner which did not awaken a corresponding familiarity. He played with men without mixing with them.

But he admits to a terrible working schedule; especially as the fighting on different battlefronts increased. He'd be woken up at all hours of the night to take dictation, when Napoleon:
Would appear in a white dressing-gown with a Madras handkerchief around his head...walking up and down with his hands behind his back or helping himself from his snuff-box. His ideas developed as he dictated and with an abundance and clearness which showed that his attention was firmly fixed on the subject he was dealing with....

At least though he was sympathetic to what Méneval was having to cope with; and would send out for sherbet or ices for him. On other occasions he deliberately wouldn't waken him, but in the morning the secretary would find his desk covered with annotated papers and reports.

Just occasionally, he adds, his master might lapse into complete idleness, or what appeared to be idleness on the surface, although in reality this covered an increase in mental activity. At such times he seemed at a loss for something to do. He would visit Josephine for an hour, then return, sleep for a few minutes, sit on the edge of Méneval's desk, speak on all sorts of disconnected subjects and finally, quite suddenly, come out with some new and ambitious plan and start dictating again. He had, obviously, the most enormous capacity for work.

Also in the *Mémoires* there is the sadder portrait of Napoleon after the return from Elba. Méneval felt he had lost his nerve and sensed an approaching doom. 'All his words were stamped with a calm sadness and a resignation which made a great impression on me.' Nevertheless, given the opportunity, the secretary would have accompanied him to St.-Helena.

MIOT DE MELITO, André François, Count (1762 – 1841)

Diplomat and intimate of Napoleon, who seems always to have dealt with him in an informal and friendly way as well as trusting him with several important missions. He was Minister Plenipotentiary to Tuscany, ambassador to Sardinia and later France's administrator on Corsica. In 1806 he went with Joseph Bonaparte to Naples, and in 1809 was again attached to him in Spain: it was claimed to make sure that the Emperor's eldest brother did all that was expected of him in France's interests.

After the second abdication he retired and devoted himself to writing his *Mémoires sur le Consulat, et le roi Joseph*.

MOLLIEN, Nicholas, Count of the Empire (1758 – 1850)

Paymaster-General. Also Councillor of State.

A somewhat foxy-faced man; but honest for all that. One evening at the Tuileries Napoleon asked the Countess Mollien why she had no diamonds about her person. 'Sire,' she replied, 'my husband's fortune belongs to the country. People suppose us to have unlimited wealth, but it isn't ours!' The Emperor took the point and soon afterwards presented her with a box containing several valuable jewels.

On the other hand, Mollien could be irritatingly orthodox in getting his sums right. Also harsh. There was the occasion after her divorce when Josephine had got her finances into a muddle. Several members of her staff had been cheating; while she herself as usual had been overgenerous to her friends. At Malmaison Mollien went over the books and reduced her to tears. Which he proudly reported to his master. 'But you did not have to make her cry!' Napoleon shouted at him; and then sat down to write a consoling note.

He tended to be cautious in matters of public expenditure. Often Napoleon would ignore his advice if he required money for a scheme he believed in: such as the endeavours of Gros d'Avillers and François Richard (Richard-Lenoir) to boost France's industrial and manufacturing capability. Mollien was also profoundly against state speculations. But Lebrun was brilliant in this area and had Napoleon's backing.

Otherwise the Paymaster-General was sound and kept his job even as late as 1815 when the returned Emperor said to him: 'My friend, the time for complaints is past. France must now choose between me or the Bourbons.' Mollien dutifully went off to put together some more money.

NARBONNE–LARA, Louis Marie Jacques, Count (1755 – 1813)

General turned diplomat. Born at Colorno (Parma), his mother being a lady-in-waiting to Elizabeth, the Duchess, while his father was a Spanish nobleman. (Although there are some claims that his real father was Louis

XV – which might account for the fact that he was largely brought up at Versailles with the royal princesses.)

Entering the army he became a colonel at twenty-nine, and in 1791 – through the influence of Madame de Staël – achieved the extraordinary promotion to Minister for War. In this position he was accused of being incapable and wasteful and forced to resign, and these same accusations followed him back into the army.

After 1792 he left France, travelling to Switzerland, Germany and England, where he met up with Madame de Staël again and is thought to have been her lover. He obviously had considerable charm, because on his return to France in 1801 he made use of Josephine to gain the much coveted position of *aide-de-camp* to Napoleon. It was the latter as Emperor who turned him into a diplomat, first sending him as Minister Plentipotentiary to Bavaria and then as French ambassador to Vienna. It was in this last capacity that he truly shone. There were several hard-fought diplomatic duels with Metternich, especially when Austria deserted France for the Allies. But Metternich retained a healthy respect for France's ambassador.

He died at Torgeau in Saxony.

PONS DE L'HÉRAULT, André (1772 – 1858)

Industrialist, historian and friend of Napoleon. A latecomer to the *élite*, but vital to our overall knowledge of the Emperor on Elba.

Born at Sète, into a middle-class family, he first served in the merchant navy, then joined the Revolutionary armies and met Napoleon as a captain of artillery during the siege of Toulon. However, in 1809 he was appointed administrator of the important iron-ore mines on Elba, and as such was one of the officials who received Napoleon at the start of his exile (May, 1814). He was also present when the contingent of the Imperial Guard arrived, and recalls that 'Cambronne was in the seventh heaven' and 'the homely mugs of the soldiers were wet with tears'. They formed a square on the Place d'Armes to listen to the Emperor's welcome. 'I thank you for sharing my fate. I find you noble representatives of the Grand Army. We shall make wishes together for our dear France, the mother country, and rejoice in her happiness...'

Outside his working hours Pons then became an almost constant companion of Napoleon's and was eventually charged with writing his 'Elba story'. (*Souvenirs et Anecdotes de l'Ile d'Elba*, (1897), and *Mémoires aux Puissances Allies*, (1899).) The two men sometimes disagreed about things. Pons was a staunch Republican. Also, he had to give up his house at Rio to the Emperor and move to a cramped *châlet* in the grounds. But he was the Emperor's regular guest at dinner and therefore had the opportunity to examine him closely:

He was tortured with the idea that he was being belittled, so he leaned even more upon his Imperial glory than upon his military achievements. Perhaps he was right. His military successes were immortal, an accomplished fact. It was not the same with his Imperial grandeur. However immense that might have been, fate had broken it, and he alone, the man, the great man, remained superior to events. It was, after all, the man one most respected in the Emperor.

In 1815 Pons was the first person to learn of Napoleon's escape plans; and responded by lending him and preparing a number of the ships. On the evening of February 26, together with General Drouot, Colonel Malet and Colonel Jerzmanowski of the Polish Lancers, he accompanied the Emperor's carriage from the Mulini Palace to the quay, where he was warmly thanked for his efforts. The 'grumblers' were already on board.

During the Hundred Days Napoleon made Pons a councillor of state.

RÉAL, Pierre François, Count of the Empire (1757 – 1834)

Councillor of State, but sometimes used by Napoleon for other purposes – until it was discovered that his main allegiance was to Talleyrand rather than France's ruler.

He certainly had a hand in the kidnapping of Enghien – as Murat did – and this was Talleyrand's idea.

But the most spectacular event involving Réal was the capture of the *émigres*' would-be assassin Georges Cadoudal (1771 – 1804), the British-backed agent who had returned to France to organise yet another attempt on Napoleon's life. Pichegru had crossed the Channel with him, the councillor declared, and was endeavouring to persuade General Moreau to join the plot. The police had arrested one Bouvet de Lozier, Cadoudal's lieutenant, who had talked.

Ever since the failed attempt to blow up his carriage in the Rue St.-Niçaise, Napoleon had been hoping to catch Cadoudal, and Réal was now put in charge of the hunt. The squat, bull-necked Breton (only just over five feet tall), with red hair and a scarred, broken nose, had been running the royalists' guerilla training-camp at Romsey – which Pitt had agreed to finance. But at last he was back in Paris and Réal set every policeman in the capital looking for him.

Cadoudal had been hiding in a fruit-shop, masquerading as a porter, but the police spotted him. There then followed a remarkable cab-chase, during which the terrorist shot one policeman dead and wounded another before being overpowered. He was put on trial and condemned to death. Pichegru had been found dead in his cell, it was thought by his own hand; Moreau, also put on trial, was found not guilty, but banished.

REGNAULT, (de St.-Jean d'Angély), Michel Louis Étienne, Count (1761 – 1819)

First prominent in public life as an elected member for the Constituent Assembly, where he was considered a moderate reformer. He wrote for the *Journal de Paris* founded by André Chenier and in the *Ami des Patriotes*, subsidised by the government. Under the Revolution he was first of all imprisoned, then appointed administrator of the army's hospitals in Italy. Whilst there (in 1796) he became friendly with Napoleon who found him 'an excellent comrade, obliging almost to a fault'. Règnault later started out with him for Egypt, but a sudden illness forced him to return to Malta, then France.

Over the next seven years his advance under Napoleon was steady but sure; to the Council of State, the *Institut* and also as secretary of state and a count of the Empire. He was probably his master's most reliable voice at the Council of State meetings, but far from being a sycophant. However, he had an important say in the transformation from First Consul to Emperor. Following the British and royalist assassination attempts he urged: 'They want to kill Bonaparte; very well, we must defend him and make him immortal.' Although, as he pointed out: 'It is important to establish that it is the people, not God, who give crowns.' And he succeeded in having a National Referendum on whether or not the imperial title should be hereditary. Three and a half million voted that it should be; less than three thousand against.

In 1815 he accompanied the Empress Marie Louise to Blois and was returned from there as Deputy. But during the Hundred Days he resumed his position on the Council of State and was proscribed by the Bourbons. With the help of Fouché he escaped to America, only returning to France (via Liège) under the amnesty of 1819. Unfortunately he died the same evening of his arrival back in Paris.

ROEDERER, Pierre Louis, Count (1754 – 1820)

A very close friend of Napoleon's, who often used him as someone akin to a minister-without-portfolio.

Born at Metz. Originally trained as a lawyer, he began to dabble in politics from the late 1780s. He had Revolutionary leanings, but of a moderate nature. By 1792 he had become a spokesman for those opposed to Danton and the extremists and as such was trusted by the beleaguered Louis XVI. He urged Louis to deal directly with the new Legislative Assembly and so isolate the extremists; which the King agreed to do, but who then gave a miserable performance. 'A weak character,' Roederer said later to Napoleon, 'his quiet during anger appeared to be patience, but his apparent courage in misfortune was merely resignation.'

He played a significant role in the events of 18/19 Brumaire (he was brought into them by Talleyrand). By this time he had become one of France's leading political journalists. And he put together the official notice which was printed and pasted up all over Paris explaining the need for a change from the directors to a consulate. 'They have acted in such a way that there is no longer a Constitution.' He also drafted Paul Barras' letter of resignation – which was accompanied by a large sum of money. (Barras duly signed, relieved to be let off so lightly: he who had sent so many of his political enemies to their deaths.)

Having come to power, Napoleon not only sought Roederer's advice on all matters to do with the press, he also frequently got him to work on public relations exercises: if there was anything which had to be said effectively to the nation as a whole. The First Consul was easy-going with those he trusted, but demanded three qualities in return: honesty, integrity and efficiency. 'I want my ten years of office to pass without dismissing a single minister, general or councillor of state,' he told his friend at the beginning of the Consulate. He would listen to argument, and criticism, but at the end of the debate still impose his will if he believed himself right.

Angular, hook-nosed and prickly, nevertheless Napoleon enjoyed the journalist's company; and the two men remained intimates despite disagreements between them – which occurred frequently. When they first met – over dinner at Talleyrand's – Napoleon said: 'I'm delighted to meet you. I've admired your talent ever since I read your article attacking me!'

On another occasion, when Roederer had advised Joseph Bonaparte not to accept the title of 'Prince of the Empire', Napoleon slapped his face. 'I thought you were my friend,' he shouted, 'instead of which you're nothing but a trouble-maker!' Roederer weathered the rebuke and Napoleon later apologised. He was also a gifted economist and agreed to go to Naples with Joseph as his financial adviser. Having helped him clean up that particular Augean stable, Napoleon then rewarded him with the Legion of Honour – and money: the *sénatorerie* of Caen, worth an annual income of 25,000 francs.

SAVARY, Anne Jean Marie René, Duke of Rovigo (1774 – 1833)

French general; but more often utilised by Napoleon for other purposes.

Born at Marcq-et-Chevrières (Ardennes) and educated at the College of St.-Louis in Metz, he joined the Army of the Rhine in 1792, and was promoted captain the following year. He went with Napoleon on the Egyptian expedition and became his ADC; and it was in this capacity the future First Consul spotted his latent administrative and diplomatic abilities. In time Savary would become one of the busiest of his public servants. And one who, given Napoleon's outbursts of impatience, had to take a lot of stick.

In 1802 he became chief of the secret police and the following year was promoted general of brigade. In 1804, while in command of the troops at Vincennes, he was deeply involved in the plot to kidnap the Duke of Enghien. Later he vehemently denied this, but neither his contemporaries nor subsequent historians have been prepared to believe him.

After Napoleon's coronation he reorganised the Paris police as well as an *élite gendarmerie* within the Imperial Guard. In 1805 he was sent on a mission to Russia, but returned in time for the Austerlitz and Friedland campaigns; following which he was created Duke of Rovigo and sent off to Spain to persuade Prince Ferdinand to accept the Emperor's 'protection'. During the earlier part of the Peninsular War he commanded the garrison in Madrid and saw action at Somosierra, Benavente and – back in Central Europe – at Essling, where he was a member of the Emperor's inner council.

In 1810 he replaced Fouché as Minister of Police.

It was in this capacity, in 1812, and with Napoleon away in Russia, that he was taken by surprise by the Malet Conspiracy. (Malet was an ex-Revolutionary officer, who plotted to spread the word that Napoleon had been killed in Russia and that he, Malet, had been appointed Governor of Paris. He had also forged a decree of the Senate which abolished the remaining Napoleonic apparatus of government.) The plot misfired, due to a subordinate of Savary's recognising Malet and promptly arresting him. But not before Savary himself and Pasquier, the prefect of police, had spent several hours locked up in La Force jail. The following day Malet, the generals Guidal and Lahorie and eleven others were shot. (Shades of the speedy dispatch of the Duke of Enghien?)

In 1814 he was a member of the Regency Council and advised Napoleon to accept the Allies' peace terms. This annoyed the Emperor, who exclaimed: 'Peace! Of course I want peace. War is not my job in life, and no-one values peace more than I do. But peace must be a solemn agreement. It must be lasting; and it must be related to circumstances within my Empire as a whole.' Just before this he had been lambasting Savary over the contents of the French newspapers. 'Such pompous phrases! They are making France look ridiculous!'

But Savary was no turncoat; and certainly not the instrument of the Allies. He was doing his best to expel Talleyrand from Paris, realising that the arch-intriguer was endeavouring to be recognised as the official spokesman for France at the coming Congress of Vienna...

During the Hundred Days he gave immediate support to the returned Emperor's cause, became Inspector of the *Gendarmerie*, sat in the Chamber of Peers and then tried to accompany his master to St.-Helena. Arrested on the *Bellerophon*, he was imprisoned (briefly) on Malta, but then escaped to Smyrna. For a while he lived in London, then returned to France where he was tried and acquitted. In 1828 he published his *Mémoires*: a considerably courageous thing to do, considering there was still a Bourbon king and his supporters had never forgiven Savary the death of the Duke of Enghien.

210

However, his fortunes were restored under Louis Philippe. In 1831 he was appointed Commander-in-Chief in Algeria, a post he held for two years until his health broke down.

SIEYÈS, Emmanuel Joseph, Abbé (1748 – 1836)

Although instrumental in Napoleon's coming to power he was then quickly relegated to a fine estate at Crosne – and obscurity. He had hoped to be 'the head' of France with Napoleon as its 'sword'. But the Corsican artillery-officer had had other ideas.

In the aftermath of the political writings of Voltaire, Montesquieu and Rousseau, Sieyès became the great living theorist of the French Revolution. His famous pamphlet: *What is The Third Estate?* had captured the nation's imagination. 'What has it been in the political order up to now? Nothing. What does it ask? To become something.' With Mirabeau as his voice he worked indefatigably to give the French a new and lasting constitution. Tall and balding, a lifelong bachelor, he recognised that he lacked the charisma to be a popular head of state, but he had every confidence in his ability to lead with the help of others. Having survived 'the Terror', he actively plotted the downfall of the Directory; first with the aid of General Joubert (who, unfortunately for him, was killed at Novi), then with Napoleon. Which led to the *coup* of 18/19 Brumaire.

Following the *coup* Napoleon allowed Sieyès more or less a free hand in choosing the members of a new Senate, but clashed with him over the planned constitution. Sieyès had wanted 'confidence coming from below, power from above'. He proposed a Grand Elector based at Versailles and 'meditating policy', plus two working consuls, one for home, the other for foreign affairs. Napoleon snorted with disgust at the very idea of Versailles: tainted as it was with the corruption of the old monarchy. A Grand Elector there would be like a 'fatted pig' he said. It was a time of decision and a contest between two finely-honed minds; but after ten days of argument Napoleon emerged the victor and Sieyès was gently eclipsed.

During the two Restorations the Abbé (a former regicide) was forced to leave France, not returning until 1830.

TALLEYRAND-PÉRIGORD, Charles Maurice de' Vice-Grand Elector (1754 – 1838)

Iago to Napoleon's Othello...
– Vincent Cronin

The little lame intriguer. Brilliant but blighted, he was a man unique in the history of France; perhaps in the history of any nation. That his lifelines coincided with the genius of Napoleon is perhaps one of the most fascinating

211

features of the period. It was generally accepted that the Consul/Emperor's appointment and subsequent alienation of him were both major mistakes. But if Napoleon had not taken part in the *coup* of Brumaire would it have stopped Talleyrand's plotting?

He was born in Paris, the son of General Charles de Talleyrand-Périgord and descended on both sides from the ancient nobility of France. When climbing on a chest of drawers as a child he fell and damaged a foot permanently. He received a good education at the Duke of Harcourt's College, but otherwise was totally neglected by his parents: which seems to have had much bearing on the later development of his character. Because of his lameness it was decided that he should enter the Church – a move he was against, because already he'd been thinking as a Revolutionary, albeit a moderate one. Nevertheless he was forced to submit to holy orders and in 1789 was appointed Bishop of Autun.

One of the first things he did as a bishop was to issue a manifesto proclaiming the necessity for a new democratic government and the abolition of class privilege. He also proposed the confiscation of church lands.

In January, 1791 he resigned his bishopric and was elected to the National Assembly – where he began to concern himself with diplomacy and went to London as adviser to Chauvelin. Meanwhile the increasing violence of the Revolution horrified him. Expelled from England, he obtained a passport from Danton and took a ship to the United States where he remained for the next two and a half years...

Returning to France in 1795, he began to write on colonisation and international affairs for the *Institut*; papers which were so impressive that in 1797 Paul Barras decided to make him Foreign Minister. (Madame de Stäel is also thought to have influenced the appointment.) However, although it was precisely the position he had been seeking he cleverly resigned two years later. This was because he could see the Directory heading into trouble and it left him free to conspire with Sieyès, Roederer and the others who made possible the events of 18/19 Brumaire and the shift of power to Napoleon. The latter immediately reappointed him Foreign Minister.

Talleyrand was lazy and vain (satin breeches, powdered hair), while his table manners, for one otherwise so cultivated, were abominable. He would take a fork and stuff his mouth to capacity with all manner of delicacies before beginning to chew: which he then did with his mouth still wide open; and very noisily. Also he was thoroughly corrupt. He had accepted huge bribes under the Directory, frequently diverted public funds into the receptive hands of his beautiful but feather-brained mistress, Catherine 'Madame' Grand – and even endeavoured to blackmail the American government. Of his best friend, Casimir de Montrond, he said he liked him because he wasn't overburdened with scruples.

At the same time though he was highly intelligent and an astute negotiator

212

who could be as subtle as he was skilful. Napoleon recognised his abilities and for a long time persevered with him as a minister despite the bad side.

The trouble came when Talleyrand's foreign policy differed from Napoleon's. He wanted peace with Great Britain at almost any price, whereas after the breakdown of the Peace of Amiens the First Consul, soon to be Emperor, regarded Pitt and the Tories as his continuing enemies – and all of his European intentions now hinged upon this belief. But the greatest ability of the Foreign Minister was in getting himself liked (and therefore thought of as a secret friend) by a majority of the Continent's hereditary rulers: a strategy which would become of the utmost importance to his ultimate intrigue. While he considered himself superior to most of the people he had to deal with he always knew how and when to charm.

Having helped in preparing France's Concordat with the Vatican, in 1802 the former excommunication on him was lifted and in the following year he married Madame Grand. (Apparently at Napoleon's express wish, for the Consul/Emperor was always very concerned about the marital status of those at court.)

Talleyrand had urged, and undoubtedly played a part, in the kidnapping and execution of the Duke of Enghien (how big a part is still being argued about). In 1806 Napoleon created him Prince of Benevento (a small part of Naples) and continued to use him very actively until the Treaty of Tilsit a year later. Did the minister betray the secret provisions of this treaty to London, as has been claimed?

But then Talleyrand resigned. He was totally opposed to France's involvement in Spain (and even moreso when Napoleon sent the set-aside Bourbons to lodge at the minister's château at Valençay). He remained a councillor of state, with the empty-sounding title of Vice-Grand Elector. And he began to plot with his old enemy Fouché as well as with the secret representatives of the Allies. When Napoleon first got wind of their scheming (which included a plan to replace him with Murat) he dashed back from Spain by *post-chaise*, then lost his temper completely and in the language of the barrack-room called Talleyrand a thief, a coward and a traitor. The ex-minister remained cool throughout this terrible scene and afterwards commented to an acquaintance: 'What a pity that such a great man is so ill-bred!'

However, Napoleon did not banish him from the court. He probably wanted him where he could keep an eye on him. As for Talleyrand, he continued with his intrigues against the Emperor; only now more determinedly and with improved secrecy. The Countess of Kielmannsegge gives this most remarkable picture of him as he went about his natural vocation in the drawing-rooms of the great:

When he approached me with his limping gait, his heavy body, his flashing eyes, his snake-like mouth and jaw, his paralysing smile

213

and his affected flatteries, I thought: *Nature gave you the choice between snake and tiger, and you chose to be an anaconda!* This first impression remained with me. Before I knew him better I avoided being alone with him owing to a certain feeling of discomfort. When I did come to know him I found him easy in disposition and from laziness, weak from habit and inclination, powerful in intellect and eloquence, clever and tireless in ensnaring those who easily gave in, who could be of use to him and whose minds allowed themselves to be enslaved.

In 1814 during the first abdication crisis he was without doubt in touch with Marmont over the surrender of Paris. And afterwards it was he who convinced the Tzar Alexander that the Bourbons should be restored. He then represented France throughout the Congress of Vienna; which included keeping the Allies' representatives at loggerheads and concluding a secret treaty between France, Austria and Great Britain against the growing strength of Prussia and the Russians.

The Bourbons were not particularly grateful for the help received from the former Revolutionary. Talleyrand was retained in office for less than a year; although they gave him the honorary post of Grand Chamberlain. By 1829 – aged seventy-seven – we find him still engaged in plotting: this time financing the *National*, a journal started by Thiers and Carrel which opposed the Ultra-Royalist measures of Charles X and played an important part in the Revolution of 1830. It was then Talleyrand who advised the eager, but hesitant Duke of Orléans to accept the crown as Louis Philippe.

Friendship with England was now a first priority of French foreign policy – and the new king could think of no-one better qualified than Talleyrand to serve as ambassador at the Court of St.-James. There were certain objections on the grounds of his advanced age. ('His face resembles that of a dead lion,' Guizot said.) But the King's idea prevailed and so the doyen of French politics set sail for Dover: together with his niece-by-marriage Dorothea of Dino, the beautiful young companion of his final years.

In London he chiefly concerned himself with the question of Belgium's independence. But the embassy wasn't an easy one. Lord Grey, England's Prime Minister, had privately described Talleyrand as 'one of the three greatest rascals in the world'; while the Foreign Secretary, the ebullient Palmerston who like Fox had admired Napoleon, called him 'Old Tally' and took delight in keeping him waiting for hours in his outer-office.

TALLIEN, Jean Lambert (1767 – 1820)

Mainly famous (or notorious) as a politician of the Revolution. Even so, he did influence certain events of the Napoleonic period and always remained on friendly terms with the Consul/Emperor. As for the latter, although never entrusting the ex-regicide with high office, he felt sufficiently well-disposed towards him to keep finding things he could do within the administration.

Tallien was of humble birth, but received an excellent education due to the generosity of the Marquis of Bercy, with whom his father held the position of maître d'hôtel. However, far from feeling gratitude towards his former benefactor, the young man soon became one of the firebrands of the Revolution. While working as a journalist with the *Moniteur* his widely-circulated broadsheet, *L'Ami des Citoyens* confirmed him as one of the more extreme Jacobins. And once elected to the Convention his name grew to be synonymous with terror and intimidation.

The then dramatic change in his behaviour resulted from a mission to Bordeaux. As Commissioner of the Republic it was his task to interrogate the beautiful young aristocrat Thérèse de Fontenay, née Cabarrus (1773 – 1835).That he became infatuated with the raven-haired prisoner – and then her lover – is undoubtedly true. But it wasn't quite the grand passion certain romantic writers would have us believe. Tallien could also see how her looks, wit and private fortune might help his continuing political ambitions. As for Thérèse, well, she was buying back her life.

Recalled to Paris, he took Thérèse with him, where she was immediately imprisoned, again on the orders of the Committee of Public Safety, while Tallien himself began to be accused of moderation and even non-Revolutionary activities. We now have conflicting stories. One is that from her cell Thérèse sent her lover a dagger, and a message saying: 'Coward, I die tomorrow!' The other is that she hid a note in the heart of a cabbage and threw it to him from her cell window. 'If you feel for me as much as you say you do,' she is alleged to have written, 'then save France, and you will save me too.'

Whichever is true (perhaps neither is), Tallien hurriedly gathered together the opposition to Robespierre which led to the events of 9 Thermidor (July 27, 1794) when he denounced the 'tyrant' and gained the support of the Convention. Robespierre was arrested, shot in the jaw and then guillotined along with twenty-one of his principal aides including St.-Just, Couthon, Dumas and Henriot. Fouquier-Tinville, the dreaded Public Prosecutor soon followed them. The Terror was declared officially over...

Under the Directory Tallien (having married Thérèse) remained an influential member of the Council of Five Hundred until May 1798. On March 6, 1796 he had been (with Paul Barras) a principal witness at the marriage between Napoleon and Josephine – and he actively supported the general's being given command of the Army of Italy. Their friendship continued when Napoleon invited him to join the expedition to Egypt – where he edited the official journal, the *Décade Egyptienne*. At one point during their stay in Cairo there were signs of the earlier 'blood-letter' being revived in him. Religious fanatics had killed several of the French garrison. 'Burn their mosques – and kill all the priests!' Tallien urged. However, Napoleon temporised, limiting the executions to the ringleaders.

Meanwhile, in Paris, Thérèse Tallien had already embarked upon the life of scandalous infidelity which had linked her name forever with the Directory at its most corrupt. Wearing see-through dresses, or sometimes even topless ones, she attended every party that mattered and generally considered herself the arch-priestess of fashion and liberty: an elevation she swiftly lost when Napoleon became First Consul. He not only banned her from the Tuileries but insisted that Josephine had nothing more to do with her. She also produced two illegitimate children (thought to be the Swedish Count Ribbing's) which Tallien repudiated.

He had been captured by the British on his voyage back from Egypt and taken to London where he found himself treated as a hero by Charles James Fox and the pro-Revolutionary Whig party. He returned to France in 1802, divorced Thérèse, and then became reliant on whatever secondary jobs Napoleon could arrange for him. He was even reduced at one stage to taking his meals with Thérèse and her new lover, the banker Ouvrard.

Eventually Napoleon placed him in the Consular Service; and during several years at Alicante he produced his two books about the Revolution and one on the French in Egypt.

THIBAUDEAU, Antoine Claire, Count, (1765 – 1854)

Councillor of State and favoured historian.

Perhaps the most accurate of all the memoirists as regards Napoleon's habit of thinking aloud and about his day-to-day behaviour while in power. He was also a close friend of Josephine's, sharing her fears that the change to the Empire would only make the regime increasingly despotic. He remained loyal though; and the ten volumes of his history of the Consulate and the Empire (published in Louis Philippe's reign) are not only well-written but very factual and totally without bias.

Originally a *député-syndic* at Poitiers, in September 1792 he was elected the deputy for Vienne to the National Convention and quickly established himself as one of that body's leading orators. Although he voted for the death of the King he was regarded as being a man of firm principles rather than extreme violence. He earned the nickname: 'Bar of Iron', but at the same time gained great respect for the logic and balance of his arguments.

A member of the Committee of Public Safety himself, after the fall of Robespierre – whom he descibes as being 'half-Mahomet, half-Cromwell' – he did much to place public affairs in France on a more moderate basis. And in 1796 he became President of the Council of Five Hundred.

In the end it was the shiftiness and corruption of Paul Barras and his cronies at the Directory which made him support Napoleon, to whom he wrote: 'The men of the Revolution, no longer able to oppose the counter-revolution, will help you carry it out, because from now on you are their only guarantee.' The new First Consul responded by appointing him a councillor of state and later a *préfet*: positions he held through until 1815, when as a former regicide he had to flee the country.

Of the Consular 'court' at the Tuileries, he writes that it was 'small, select, strictly decent and respectable'. But also very formal. He noted Napoleon's frequent acts of kindness, but it was only usually with his army officers that he became familiar in an informal way. 'He had,' he says, 'a special art of bringing tall men down to his own height or of raising himself to theirs.'

He ranges over a tremendous number of subjects insofar as they apply to his main source of observation. For instance, Napoleon's anger with Great Britain following the breakdown of the Peace of Amiens. 'Sir,' the First Consul told the English ambassador, 'you may kill Frenchmen, but you cannot intimidate them'. The Concordat with the Vatican makes fairly hilarious reading – while the functioning of the *Code Civile* is described in masterly fashion. Likewise the reform of the constitution:

> The English system might be the right one for them; they have a House of Lords. In France the raw materials out of which such a house could be formed are no longer with us. Do you think it a good idea to create them? If we made such a chamber out of the men of the Revolution we should have to place in their hands a large proportion of the landed property of France, which would be impracticable!

=8=
Arts And Science

The more I read Voltaire the more I like him: he is always reasonable, never a charlatan: he is made for mature minds. Until sixteen years ago I would have fought for Rousseau against all the supporters of Voltaire. Now it's exactly the opposite. I have been especially disgusted with Rousseau since I went to the East. Savage man is a dog!
– Napoleon, 1803

Architects

Napoleon's two chief architects for his restoration and further embellishment of Paris were Pierre François Fontaine and Charles Percier, with the latter considered to be the greater expert of the two on matters related to the fine arts.

Napoleon worked them hard. As First Consul he announced his intention to make Paris 'the most beautiful city in the world, the capital of capitals and with the largest concentration of people.' And on St.-Helena he would sigh and regret not having had another twenty years of personal rule to finish off the job.

He kept a very tight rein on their expenditure too, and not a single franc of public money was to be seen to be wasted. For himself he built only a small private theatre in the Tuileries and another at St.-Cloud.

However, the two men worked well under him – and appeared to share his penchant for long hours. Fontaine, the son and grandson of architects from Pontoise, concentrated on the size, shapes and positioning of buildings; Percier, the son of a keeper at the Tuileries, on making them look handsome. Napoleon liked architecture to be impressive rather than merely decorative and they willingly went along with this view.

Many of their plans and proposals never did come to fruition. (For instance, their intended Palais de Chaillot, the final extensions to the Louvre, and two of the four triumphal arches their master had demanded. Also boating-lakes along the Champs Elysées and a Palais des Archives designed for the Quai d'Orsay.) Nevertheless, the list of completed achievements is a source of wonder – and what gives the centre of Paris today its essential layout and appearance.

It all began with a new drainage system costing thirty million francs, and the compulsory purchase and pulling down of scores of dirty, overcrowded streets immediately west of the Louvre and the Tuileries. In addition Napoleon agreed to the installation of gas street-lighting (and himself devised a new numbering system for houses: the now-familiar odd numbers down one side of a street, even numbers on the other). Meanwhile the grandiose schemes were at the drawing-boards and, following the site clearances, work began in earnest.

The Madeleine (originally called the Temple of Victory); the Arc de Triomphe and the roads which spread out from it like bicycle-spokes at Etoile (now the Place Charles de Gaulle); the tall, maypole-like Colonne Vendôme; the white-columned Bourse and wide-stepped Chambre des Députés; the long, magnificently arcaded Rue de Rivoli (where Napoleon ordered there to be 'no shop signs, hammering, bakers or sausage-and-meat purveyors') with the elegant Rue de Castiglione just to the north; the bridges of Austerlitz, Jena and the Arts; the careful clearing of the area around Concorde to make it the finest assembly point in Europe; the remodelling of the high north face of the Louvre and the wing joining it to the Tuileries; the new layout of the gardens in the Tuileries and the siting of a second, smaller arch there: the Triomphe du Carrousel, which for a time carried the four bronze horses looted from St.-Marks in Venice; and the stone *quais* which at present line the Seine. All of this was accompanied by a vast rehousing programme. Not many architects can claim to have made such a decisive impact on a capital city.

Only once do they appear to have incurred their master's wrath. Whilst working on their alterations and additions to the Louvre they installed a fountain representing a group of naiads spouting water from their breasts. 'Get rid of those wet-nurses!' the Emperor barked. 'Don't you know the naiads were supposed to be virgins?'

ARNAULT, Antoine Vincent (1766 – 1834)

Playwright and poet. A good friend as well as a favourite author of Napoleon's. He sometimes accompanied the troops into battle and was present during the negotiations which led to the Treaty of Campo Formio (October, 1797). A somewhat spiky character – someone once inscribed his bust: 'Watch out – he bites!' – nevertheless he genuinely admired his patron. Of Napoleon the diplomat, he writes: 'He shows no haughtiness...but he had the poise of someone who knows his own worth and feels himself in the right place.'

He received over a million francs in royalties for his play *Oscar*, but that was in the super-inflated days of the Directory. The work was based on the stories of Ossian, who Napoleon is said to have regarded as a finer poet than Homer, except for *The Iliad*. He promoted Arnault to be *Secrétaire Général de l'Universite* and even had a say in the final part of his five-act tragedy *The*

Venetians. 'The hero must die', he told him. So Arnault changed the plot: to what was considered by many to be the best part of the play.

BERTHOLLET, Claude Louis, Count (1748 – 1822)

Chemist. Born at Talloires (Savoie), he went on to study at Chambéry and Turin. Then settled in Paris where he became a leading member of the Académie des Sciences. In 1794 the government made him responsible for the supervision of all chemistry taught in the Paris schools and he was one of the scientists selected the following year to 'acquire' useful items from the great collections of Italy and bring them back to France.

As a young man in Revolutionary Paris, Napoleon had attended Berthollet's public lectures. Consequently he was the obvious person to be invited to join the scientific side of the Egyptian expedition. Whilst there he played a prominent role in founding the Institute of Egypt; and also took some part in the administration of the government: for instance, in overhauling the hopelessly outdated tax-system and in confiscating Mameluk property for the benefit of the *fellahin*. He was interested too in irrigation, and supervised the construction of a number of French-style windmills.

But his real passion, beneath a somewhat cold and forbidding exterior, was chemical physics and analysis. He spent weeks studying the Egyptian methods for producing indigo, and then, more importanly, he travelled to the Libyan nacron lakes to study the formation of carbonate of soda through the contact of sodium with carbonate of lime on the beds of the lakes. Eventually his studies there would lead to the publication of his famous *Essai de Statique Chimique*, showing how chemical reactions depend on the masses of the reacting substances and not on elective affinities. This is still the basis for much modern chemical theory and practice.

Berthollet was one of the few selected to accompany Napoleon back to France in 1799. Upon the latter's becoming First Consul he was given a seat in the Senate and later created a Grand Officer of the Legion of Honour. Under the Empire he became a count.

He was something of a fair-weather friend outside his scientific dedication. He deserted the Emperor for the Bourbons when the Empire's fortunes declined, and for this act was rewarded a place in the House of Peers. He died at Arcueil, widely regarded as the foremost French scientist of his day.

BEYLE, Henri, alias STENDHAL (1783 – 1842)

Despite Napoleon's interest in, and patronage of, a wide variety of writers, in fact French literature under the Consulate and the Empire can hardly be regarded as anything other than a transitional stage between the classic period and the romantics and modernists to come. Chateaubriand's stately stylishness and acute observation; Madame de Staël's witty and poisoned pen; Constant's *Adolphe*, an early example of the psychological novel: all these stand out in a time that witnessed much output – but most of it devoid of great talent. Moreover even these three gave no lead and certainly less indication of the distinguished century about to begin. A slalom of literary riches which began with Stendhal, Balzac and Mérimée, continued via Victor Hugo, Lamartine, Gérard de Nerval, Baudelaire, Flaubert, Isidore Ducasse, Renan, the Goncourts, Dumas (*père et fils*) and went on to include Maupassant, Rimbaud, Villiers de l'Isle-Adam, Laforgue, J.K. Huysmans, the rarefied Mallarmé and finally Jarry and the young Paul Valéry. Not since the Greek playwrights and the heyday of Imperial Rome's poets, has any one nation produced such an array of literary talent in so short a space of time – and a body of work which caused the surrounding European writing of the day to appear positively 'old hat'.

However, although Beyle's greatest works (under the pseudonym Stendhal) were published long after the fall of Napoleon, nevertheless he belongs with the *élite* for two very special reasons. Firstly, because he was actually a member of it as a young man, and secondly, because he remained a convinced Bonapartist for all of his life . . .

Born in Grenoble, the son of a lawyer (whom he despised), he was first cousin to the Daru brothers and therefore the nephew of Napoleon's future Secretary of State. He'd intended to go to Paris and study mathematics, however Napoleon's coming to power in 1799 altered his sights and the following year he joined up with the French army in Italy. Here he discovered what were to be his longstanding loves: music, painting, great landscapes, passionate affairs. But he was also more than impressed by Napoleon and followed him back to Paris.

Beyle never became a fighting soldier. As a result of his family ties with the Darus he remained on the commissariat side. Even so, he went with the army on the Prussian campaign of 1806; was in Vienna in 1809 to attend Haydn's funeral and in 1810 was appointed Auditor to the Council of State. Unlike so many, he then survived the horrors of the retreat from Moscow. 'We have not seen a woman since the postmistresses of Poland, but by way of compensation we are great connoisseurs of fires', he wrote to his patroness, the Countess Daru. And again to Félix Faure: 'To have or not have boots and a *pelisse*, ah, that is an important matter!'

He served in Austria in 1813 and when the Allies invaded France he was busy helping organise the defences along the south-east frontier.

Napoleon's downfall automatically meant the sack for him. He began to write in earnest and to move in intellectual society – albeit as one of its poorer members. He wrote about music (lives of Haydn, Mozart and Rossini), travelling in Italy (*Rome, Naples and Florence*), love (*De l'Amour*, 1822), pamphlets on Racine and Shakespeare, and more importantly a series of novels, at least two of which are undoubted masterpieces. Upon the fall of the Bourbons in 1830 he sought and obtained another official appointment, this time as a consul in Italy, first at Trieste and then for a much longer period at Civita-Vecchia. Ennui reigned in both places for him but at least it gave him a base and an income to support his writing. He used repeatedly to speculate about the date when he hoped to be, not merely read, but fully appreciated: '1835, 1860, 1900, 1935...' But he could hardly have realised just how important he would become to later generations of writers: not least to Tolstoy, who gained from the clarity of his prose; and to Marcel Proust, inspired by his powerful psychological insights. He even managed to be prophetic about his own death, from apoplexy: 'There is nothing ridiculous about dying in the street, provided one does not do it on purpose!'

Of the two major books, in *Le Rouge et Le Noir* (1830), the anti-hero Julien Sorel is a Bonapartist through and through. In fact at the very outset he is knocked off a beam in the sawmill by his brute of a father, where he has been reading the *Mémorial de St.-Hélène*. Too young to have joined the Grand Army (the scarlet), he is compelled to study for holy orders (the black) and to become a tutor. His resentment over this is a prime cause for the tragedy of his subsequent adventures. The author also quotes Danton in his attacks upon the Bourbons' censorship: 'Truth – Truth in all her rugged harshness...'

Stendhal's other masterpiece, the *Chartreuse de Parme*, which Balzac so admired: ('*The* book of the Literature of Ideas!') includes the justly celebrated Chapters Three to Five entitled 'War' which made such a dramatic impact on Tolstoy. We encounter the disjointedness and disorganisation of the Battle of Waterloo through the eyes of a private person; and Marshal Ney appears in it as his real self, firm and courageous despite the incoming tide of misfortune. Later a corporal shouts at a general: 'Go and f*** yourself. You and all of the generals. You've all of you betrayed the Emperor today!'

Balzac's study and analysis of the *Chartreuse* is the finest piece of literary criticism I have ever read; and certain of his words would form a suitable epitaph for Stendhal:

> M. Beyle was naturally in the Emperor's service; 1815 tore him, necessarily,from his career, he passed from Berlin to Milan and it is to the contrast between the life of the north and that of the south, which so impressed him, that we are indebted to this writer. M. Beyle is one of the superior men of our time. It is difficult to explain how this observer of the first order, this profound diplomat who, whether in his writings or in his speech, has furnished so many proofs of the loftiness of his ideas and the extent of his practical knowledge, should find himself nothing more than Consul at Civita-Vecchia. No-one could be better qualified to represent France at Rome. .

On the other hand, Stendhal had already composed his own epitaph in a letter to his sister Pauline; and it is this that can be read on his tomb: *Qui giace Arrigo Beyle Milanese. Visse scrisse amo.*

Here lies
Henri Beyle of Milan
He lived, he wrote, he loved!

CAMPAN, Jeanne Louise Henriette *Née* Genest.(1752 – 1822)

A teacher, and also the grand arbiter of feminine behaviour and *étiquette* under the Consulate and the Empire.

Her father was Chief Clerk at the Foreign Office during most of Louis XV's reign and although not rich he provided her, his only daughter, with an excellent education: especially in classical literature; English (which she spoke fluently); Italian, with Goldoni as her teacher; and music under Albanesi. Being bright and attractive as well as cultured, at age 15 she was appointed reader and *gouvernante* to the King's three daughters – and soon became a great favourite of the court. When she married Monsieur Campan, son of the Cabinet Secretary, Louis XV gave her as a dowry an annuity of 5000 livres. Later she would become First Lady of the Bedchamber to Marie Antoinette and the Queen's loyal companion until her execution. She displayed great personal courage during the sacking of the Tuileries on June 20, 1792. After which she only just escaped with her life.

However, the Revolution reducd her to poverty, and then her husband became ill; so after the events of 9 Thermidor she supported herself by establishing a special school at St.-Germain, which she called (cheekily perhaps), the *Institution Nationale*. It immediately became *the* place for the daughters of those who prospered under the Directory, and then the Consulate, to be sent. The first house she took proved too small for all who wished to attend. She possessed the niceties of the *Ancien Régime*, but in other ways she was extremely modern and therefore set the tone and style for the more elegant of the ladies at Napoleon's court. (Even Lefebvre's wife, the amazing 'Madame Sans Gêne' considered seeking her advice at one point!) Among her better-known pupils were Hortense de Beauharnais, Emilie de Beauharnais (who later married Lavalette), Stéphanie de Beauharnais who became the Princess of Baden, Aglaé Auguié (who married Marshal Ney) and Nievés d'Almenara who married Duroc.

Napoleon doted on her. Having visited her establishment and witnessed her teaching his stepdaughter Hortense, he announced that she was 'the best teacher of the domestic sciences in France' and that he would send his 'ignorant' sister Caroline to her. Later still he sent Pauline there to be 'sorted out' – even though she was already married to Leclerc. And when he founded the Academy at Écouen for the daughters of members of the Legion of Honour he appointed Madame Campan Superintendent, a post she held until the second Restoration, when she was hounded out by the Bourbons, and then retired to Nantes.

During her last years she devoted herself to writing her *Mémoires sur la*

Vie Privée de Marie Antoinette, published the year after her death.

While she concentrated the attention of her pupils on the social arts and turned out the kind of young lady she boasted could go anywhere and be perfectly behaved, she nevertheless included in the curriculum the handling of household accounts, planning dinner-parties, being able to discuss politics and philosophy and also the production of theatrical entertainments.

CANOVA, Antonio (1757 – 1822)

Sculptor. Born at Passagno, a small village in the Asolo hills, his grandfather, who cut the stones for and carved burial monuments, noted and encouraged his creative talent. Later, when he had become famous throughout Italy, Napoleon persuaded him to travel to Paris and work on statues of Marie Louise and himself.

Once in the French capital he met and seems to have been partly influenced by Jacques Louis David. Certainly in his greatest single work, the nude figure of Pauline Bonaparte as Venus, there is an admixture of David's noble austerity with the softer contours of Hellenic art.

While working on the piece he apparently had the temerity to criticise the visiting Emperor for removing works of art from Italy's museums and also the famous bronze horses from Venice. However, he kept his job.

For the statue of Napoleon himself he persuaded the latter not to pose in uniform but to wear a suitably ancient-world apparel. The resulting piece, twelve feet in height, and carved out of stone from St.-Cloud, was then given a prominent position in the Louvre. Until the arrival of the all-conquering Wellington. Taking a leaf from the Emperor's own book he immediately ordered the figure to be shipped off to London.

CATEL, Charles Simon (1773 – 1830)

Composer. Born at L'Aigle (Orne), he studied at the École Royale de Chant (later to become the Conservatoire). From 1790 to 1802, he served as chief accompanist at the Paris Opera. He was also apointed (jointly with Gosser) musical director of the band of the National Guard, and he wrote much military music including the *Hymn of Victory* after the Battle of Fleurus in 1794. Meanwhile, too, he was writing the book (finally published in 1802) which replaced Rameau's as the standard French work on harmony.

But he became best-known, at the time, for his operas, of which there were ten. And especially for *Les Bayaderes*, which ran for no less than 140 performances. Napoleon took such a keen interest in this piece that he once made the bizarre request for it to be played 'with all the instruments muted and with every mark of expression suppressed!'

In 1810 he was appointed an inspector at the Conservatoire: a post he lost upon the return of the Bourbons. In 1815 he was elected a member of the Institute and in 1824 awarded the Legion of Honour.

CHAMPOLLION, Jean François (1790 – 1832)

Linguist and translator. An expert in no less than nine Oriental languages, however Champollion is best-known today as the unraveller of the secrets of the Rosetta Stone leading to our knowledge of Ancient Egyptian hieroglyphics.

The stone, a lump of black basalt three feet nine inches long and two feet four and a half inches wide, had been discovered by the French in 1799 and was inscribed with three scripts: in the hitherto totally baffling hieroglyphics, demotic Egyptian and Greek. In fact hierogrlyphics combine symbols representing ideas with others relating to sounds, but it was only by painstakingly deciphering these in relation to names in other languages that Champollion finally managed to clear up the mystery. It could be said, therefore, that he opened up the whole area of Egyptian history to us.

CHAPTAL, Jean Antoine (1756 – 1832)

Born at Nogaret. Trained as a chemist. Later as a member of the Senate he introduced the metric system of weights and measures.

CHATEAUBRIAND, François Réne, Viscount (1768 – 1846)

Author and diplomat; of whom I have never been able to turn up a satisfactory explanation as to why he should have a popular and expensive steak dish named after him. Perhaps he once left behind an unusually generous *pourboire* and the grateful inventor/chef decided to call the thickly-cut piece of beef after him. Anyway, he was one person Napoleon definitely wanted to join the *élite*, but who ultimately rejected the Empire's style and values. A temporary fascination became a dislike and finally led to a reactionary attitude. Of his writing abilities on the other hand there can be little reason for disapproval. He was a superb stylist and a brilliant memoirist, and if he lacked the overall imagination of Stendhal or Balzac, then he was their equal in his use of words and their near-equal as regards observation.

He was the youngest son of the Comte de Combourg, born at St.-Malo in Brittany, an area where the inhabitants, it has been said, are 'proverbially of cultured if not aesthetic temperament'. His parents wanted him to enter the Church and he studied at the College of Dinan, but he deliberately 'dropped out' in favour of an army commission. When the Revolution occurred, however, as a royalist he was forced to flee to America. He returned to France in 1791 and married Céleste Buisson de Lavigne, with whom he wandered about Europe; living in Belgium, Guernsey and then in England where he began to discover his true vocation as a writer. In 1797 he published the *Essai Historique, Politique et Moral sur Les Révolutions*; and in 1800, (when he decided it was again safe to return to France) he published

La Génie du Christianisme: a work considered to be generally favourable towards Napoleon's government. In fact, Hortense de Beauharnais used to read long passages from it to her stepfather, and the latter was so delighted that he appointed Chateaubriand his *attaché* to the French legation in Rome. Whilst there, however, he managed to get into some sort of scrape described as 'insubordination'. Following this Napoleon – still enamoured of his abilities – found him a position as envoy to one of the Swiss cantons (Valais). Eventually this led to a period of leave-cum-diplomacy in Palestine, resulting in his book *Itinéraire de Paris à Jérusalem*.

However, by this time Chateaubriand had reverted in his thinking to being a supporter of the Bourbons. When he became part-owner of the *Mercure de France*, in 1807 he published in it an article comparing Napoleon to Nero. The scandal was considerable. Napoleon couldn't bring himself to proscribe this writer he so admired, but when Chateaubriand was elected to the Académie Française in 1811 he was prevented from reading his *essai du reception* because it included further criticism of the regime. He never did take up his seat at the Académie officially.

In 1814, now in the *élite* of the restored Bourbons, he published his *De Bonaparte, des Bourbons, et de la Nécessité de se Rallier à nos Princes Lègitimes*. Naturally it pleased Louis XVIII immensely, who declared it 'as valuable a help to the Royal cause as one hundred thousand soldiers'. Chateaubriand was appointed ambassador to Berlin, then as Plenipotentiary to the later stages of the Congress of Vienna. His last post as a diplomat was in Rome during 1827.

After this he devoted himself to his various volumes of memoirs, his only regular visitor and confidante being the formerly exiled Madame Récamier. As his one intellectual diversion from the autobiographies and La Récamier he set about translating into French Milton's *Paradise Lost*.

A devout Catholic he doesn't appear to have let this inhibit his love life. But there is a kind of severity about his writing which in a way typifies Napoleonic art. There is a moral tone because a moral tone was thought to be right. As a result, though, one is left feeling that he never quite comes clean in the content; but what a marvellous master of prose!

Perhaps here though the Emperor himself might be allowed the last word on Chateaubriand. Catching sight of the author's long, sallow face and wild hair as protrayed by Girodet in the Salon of 1809, he remarked to Lemercier: 'A great writer surely. But he does look like a conspirator who has just come down the chimney.'

CHÉNIER, Marie Joseph Blaise (1764 – 1811)

French poet and a popular dramatist. Originally he was very much in favour with Napoleon, but then there was a sudden fall from grace – and later only a partial rehabilitation.

He was born at Constantinople where his father was serving as France's consul-general. At sixteen he received a commission into a dragoon regiment, but in 1789 threw up the army life and went to Paris where his much-acclaimed play *Charles IX* was produced at the Théâtre Française on November 4. He became an avowed Revolutionary, gaining election to the Convention in 1792, voting for the death of the King and pronouncing himself in favour of the official violence of the Terror. At this time he as writing the celebrated *Chant du Depart* and many patriotic poems. He was accused of being an accomplice to the trial and execution of his brother André, but succeeded in clearing himself of this charge, if not the one of cowardice in the face of what was obviously an unjust condemnation. He then became a Thermidorian, and in 1795 was admitted to the *Institut* and elected a member of the Council of Five Hundred. He first found favour with Napoleon when he joined in the *coup d'état* of Brumaire, after which the First Consul appointed him to the Tribunate.

But he began to voice his criticisms of the government and in 1802 was ousted from his position by the Senate. By way of compensation Napoleon found him a job in the education department. What really angered his benefactor though was the production of his tragedy *Cyrus*. This expressed grave doubts about the desirability of empire almost immediately before the great event of the coronation in Notre Dame. As a result, all of his plays were prohibited from performance and he was reduced to teaching in a boys' school. Later on the Emperor relented and awarded him a pension of 8000 francs. But he was never again received at the Tuileries.

CHERUBINI, Maria Luigi Carlo Zenobio Salvatore (1760 – 1842)

An Italian composer in France who, during the Revolution, Consulate and the Empire was both prolific and influential.

Born at Florence; by the time he was sixteen he had composed three masses, two dixits, a *Magnificat*, a *Miséréré* and a *Te Deum*. From 1777 he was in Venice for four years studying under Sarti and with the Grand Duke of Tuscany as his patron. Then in 1784 he was invited to London: where he wrote four operas for the King's Theatre. But from 1788 he settled permanently in France, having been appointed musical director of the newly-founded Italian opera company in Paris. Operas (and operettas) by him were now produced with biannual regularity, and apart from their success with the public they made a big impact upon musical thinking at the Paris Conservatoire.

Cherubini was a 'Gluckist' in that he believed simplicity of form, melodic beauty and the music being a real reflection of the drama, made for good opera. Also, though, he was one of the great masters of counterpoint, while his unusual harmonic combinations and instrumental effects excited those contemporaries and students struggling to throw off the static ornateness of music under the Bourbons. In 1799 both his productions of that year were runaway successes: *La Punition* and *La Prisonière*; and in 1800 anyone who was anyone in the capital attended the opening of his *Les Deux Journées*. Later successes included *Anacréon* and in 1804 *Achille a Scyros*.

Napoleon sometimes affected not to like his work and even quarrelled with him about its style and direction. But there was evidently an element of love-hate about their relationship. Perhaps exacerbated by Cherubini's announced intention of deserting the Emperor's *soirées* and the writing of 'entertainments' in order to re-concentrate on religious music.

However, during the Hundred Days he was made a Chevalier of the Legion of Honour and upon the second Restoration a member of the *Institut*.

CONSTANT, Henri Benjamin de Rebecue (1767 – 1830)

Politician, but better-known as the author of *Adolphe*, which has been called the first psychological novel. A tall, stooping, red-haired man, who was at first very popular with Napoleon, but then fell out with him as a result of his intimacy with Germaine de Staël.

Constant was born at Lausanne, but educated in Brussels, Oxford and Edinburgh. His relations with Madame de Staël date from 1794. In 1796 he entered politics with a written defence of the Directory; and not long afterwards he became a member of the Tribunate. With Mme de Staël banished from Paris under the Empire Constant also went into exile: first in Weimar, where he got to know Goethe and Schiller; later in Hanover.

He returned to France in 1814, was befriended by the Tzar Alexander and seems to have fallen in love with Mme Récamier, although she gave him little encouragement. *Adolphe*, his successful novel, was pblished in London in 1815. Then in 1825, his longest work: *De La Religion Considerée dans sa Source, ses Formes and ses Developpements* was published in Paris. His highly-regarded *Journal Intimé* did not appear in its entirety until after his death.

CORVISART DES MARETS, Jean Nicholas, Baron (1755 – 1821)

Napoleon's principal physician. Born at Dricourt (Ardennes), he was first of all put to studying law, but then switched to medicine, despite the poverty of a long apprenticeship. Eventually, in Paris, he was appointed physician at La Charité Hospital. And in 1787 he was promoted to the chair of medicine at the Collège de France. He had become an expert (for the time) on diseases of the heart and chest, which brought him to the attention of the First Consul, who befriended him and retained him in a professional capacity for the duration of his rule.

He visited Napoleon every morning and was held in great esteem, although he had to put up with the not-infrequent jibes that much medicine was 'highly paid quackery'. Sometimes though he got his own back. After Napoleon had declared his interest in anatomy and expressed the wish to know more about the human stomach (his own weak spot), one day Corvisart showed him a stomach, brought along in his pocket-handkerchief. The Emperor took one look at the glutinous mess, then rushed from the room to be violently sick! He did not bring up the subject of anatomy again; but he accepted the doctor's suggestion to use liquorice lozenges as an aid to digestion; also to add water to the Chambertin he drank.

Josephine too used to seek Corvisart's advice. In her later years she became something of a hypochondriac, and at one point the good doctor, obviously a psychologist as well, cured her of a series of alleged headaches by giving her bread pellets wrapped in silver paper.

Napoleon created him a baron in 1805 and a member of the *Institut* in 1811. After 1815 he retired from practice to write a number of books and to lecture.

DAVID, Jacques Louis (1748 – 1825)

Napoleon's favourite contemporary painter – and a man who in turn came to idolise his patron, celebrating many of the great events of the Empire in his work, most notably the coronation ceremony of 1804, now in the Louvre. He was regarded as the foremost painter of his day by a majority of his fellow-artists including Mme Vigée Lebrun, the sculptor Canova and even Prud'hon (1758 – 1823) whose studies of *Psyche* and marvellous drawing of Andromache embracing Astyanax are considered among the best works of the period. David painted 'big', and in a grandiose manner – although with much attention to detail and often vivid colour contrasts. But there is a neo-classical austerity about these works as well: and as such they typify the visual arts of the Consulate and Empire and were to dominate French painting until the incoming romanticism of Ingres and later Delacroix.

Originally a pupil of Boucher, David won the Prix de Rome in 1771 and stayed abroad over the next few years. When he returned to Paris in 1783 he was in total revolt against the softness and innocence of French art under the later Bourbons. His *Oath of the Horatii* of 1784 is hard, dramatic and clearly the work of a new force in painting. Likewise his *Death of Socrates* (1787), another 'never give in, death before dishonour' work. During his period outside France he had become a fanatical Revolutionary, an admirer of Republican Rome, which neither his acceptance into the Academy nor the purchase of his *Brutus* by Louis XVI did anything to moderate. Upon the outbreak of the Revolution he was there ready and eager to become its official illustrator...

He voted for the death of the King, brutally sketched Marie Antoinette on her way to the guillotine, designed the new ceremonials and then sat as a member of the capital's Committee of General Safety at which he said 'Let us grind plenty of red'. However, he then fell into disfavour himself and spent seven months in prison. Rehabilitated under the Directory, he became a member of the *Institut* and painted the *Sabine Women* (first shown in 1799).

Both time and Napoleon himself, combined to tame and modify him; as well as converting him to the idea of France becoming an Empire. He is much admired for his portraits of Napoleon and those of Sériziat, Madame Récamier and the stabbed Marat in his bath, a quill still stuck between his fingers. But the larger canvases continue to be the real attention-grabbers: the *Coronation of Napoleon* and the *Distribution of the Eagles*. When Napoleon saw the former, depicting the moment when he crowns Josephine, he exclaimed: 'Well done, David! You have guessed what I had in mind and shown me as a French knight!'

As one of the most prominent of the former regicides he fled from the returning Bourbons, settling down in Brussels to a somewhat drab-grey later life – although the Belgians did vote him a suitably empiric funeral.

DELAVIGNE, Casimir (1793 – 1843)

A favourite young poet and playwright of Napoleon's, Delavigne was born at Le Havre, and taken to Paris at age 10 where he fell very much under the Emperor's spell. He wrote a long poem celebrating the birth of the King of Rome which pleased Napoleon no end, and the Emperor intervened personally to exempt Delavigne from conscription because of his delicate health.

From this point on he won wide fame under the *régime*, mostly with poems about national events; and even after 1815, did not automatically fall from favour. Louis Philippe became one of his admirers and in 1833 he had tremendous success with his play *Les Enfants d'Edouard* concerning the killing of the little English princes in the Tower of London, (inspired by the painting by Paul Delaroche). He spent his final years living in Lyon.

DENINA, Carlo Giovanni Maria (1731 – 1813)

Napoleon's chief librarian; and a gifted historian. Born at Piedmont, and educated at Saluzzo and Turin, in 1753 was appointed Professor of the Humanities at Pignerol; where he incurred the displeasure of the Jesuits and was forced to resign. He then became Professor of Rhetoric at Turin University and wrote a magnum opus: *Delle Revoluzione d'Italia* (1769-72). He again brought upon himself the animosity of the Jesuits, this time not only losing his job but also being banished from Italy; after which he went to Berlin and worked for Frederick the Great, publishing his 'life and times' of the Prussian king.

In 1804 Napoleon invited him to Paris as his personal librarian. He continued to be hounded by the religious authorities but never lost the Emperor's protection. Among his later works were *Storia dell' Italia Occidentale* (6 vols. Turin 1809-10) and *Tableau de la Haute Italie et des Alpes qui l'Entourent*.

DENON, Dominique Vivant (1775 – 1830)

Artist and engraver who accompanied Napoleon on the Egyptian expedition and afterwards remained high in his favour.

On the voyage he did much sketching of Malta, the Greek coastlines and the island of Crete; and in Egypt itself, whilst considering Julius Caesar, and Antony and Cleopatra, is credited with the sternly Republican remark: 'It was here the empire of glory gave way to the empire of voluptuousness'!

Napoleon sent him to examine and make new drawings of the antiquities of Upper Egypt, including the Temple of Edfu where the locals had started building their houses on the roof. But he complained that Desaix's corps didn't allow him enough time. He had to do his drawings mostly while on horseback. Of Ptolemy's temple at Dendora he wrote: 'The Greeks invented nothing!'

Back in France he was appointed Director of the Louvre – and on occasion got a mild ticking off from the Emperor for opening up late and keeping the public waiting. Later he was rebuked again for adding a chariot with a statue of Napoleon to the four bronze horses from Venice which topped the Arc du Carrousel. 'Get them off there immediately,' the Emperor snapped. 'The arch is intended to glorify the army, not me!'

However, there was no question of his being replaced and his tenure of the office of director resulted in a considerable enlargement of the Louvre's scope as a museum and art gallery.

DUPLESSIS-BERTAUX, Jean (1747 – 1815)

An artist who was also considered the finest and most technically advanced engraver of his day and in this capacity much favoured by Napoleon. His reputation rests largely on two portfolios: the enormous *Napoleon à La Grande Armée* containing 146 prints, nearly all by Bertaux; and *Tableaux Historique* (Paris, 1806): 25 battle scenes after the original paintings by Carle Vermet.

FONTANES, Louis de (1757 – 1821)

Political writer and poet; also something of an informal adviser to Napoleon on cultural affairs.

Today his poetry is largely forgotten, but under the Empire his pamphlets and articles carried much weight – the kind of weight he liked to throw about, for he could be singularly severe in his judgements. As for instance when Napoleon thought of displaying to the public for their comments a model of a new wing proposed for the Louvre by Fontaine and Percer. His adviser was withering in his scorn. 'Why should one bother about popular taste?' he demanded to know. 'It is certainly not to be trusted!'

In political matters, on the other hand, he was shrewd and generally pragmatic. Thus we learn of his counselling Chateaubriand on his proposed speech after being elected to the Academie Française. It was (and still is) a tradition within the Academy that the first speech should be one of praise for the member whose passing has created a vacant seat. But in 1811 the deceased member was Joseph Marie Chénier, a regicide, while Chateaubriand had become a royalist again in his sympathies. 'Mention Chénier at the beginning – then get on with the business of praising Napoleon. At least you can do that sincerely,' Fontanes told him bluntly. This was sound advice which the new member chose to ignore – as a result of which his speech didn't get read.

Fontanes belonged to the *Institut* and all the best clubs and eventually became a peer of the realm, which he continued to be after the second Restoration. In this last capacity he was one of the small band of peers who voted for the deportation rather than the execution of Marshal Ney.

GEOFFROY SAINT-HILAIRE, Étienne (1772 – 1844)

Naturalist. Born at Etampes, he first of all (evidently to please his father) took a degree in law. But already he was attending the lectures of Fourcroy and Daubenton: doctors with a strong leaning towards natural science. Fired by the possibilities, he now refused to consider any other way of life.

He was still only twenty-six when he accompanied, with eagerness, the expedition to Egypt. By this time he had helped enlarge the zoo in the Jardin des Plantes and co-authored with Georges Cuvier a massive book about orang-utans.

From now on zoology would remain his obsession. Whilst working at the new Institute in Cairo he had made a number of important studies; and returning to Paris in 1802 he settled down to putting his freshly acquired knowledge to good use. He published works on the Nile crocodile, the ostrich, the polypterus (previously unknown in Europe, but a Nile fish with common features to some mammals) and on the mummified ibises he'd collected from the Tombs of Thebes. He agreed with Jean Baptiste Lamarck's theory of evolution and so must be considered another of the forerunners to Darwin.

Elected to the Academy of Sciences in 1807, he was also the recipient of the Legion of Honour – as well as accompanying the Grand Army down through Portugal – collecting specimens and sometimes helping himself from museums.

Unhappily the work of his final years was made difficult by his increasing blindness.

GENLIS, Stéphanie Felicité du Crest de Sainte-Albin, Countess (1746 – 1830)

An odd choice, purely from a literary standpoint, for Napoleon to befriend. However, he seems to have liked her personally and he gave her a safe haven in France again after her earlier flight from Robespierre and the Committee of Public Safety.

Her background was more aristocratic than rich, coming from a Burgundian family of the Autun area. As a child she had been put into a funded convent, but by 1770, largely self-educated and after a marriage to Charles Brûlart de Genlis, a colonel in the Grenadiers, she became lady-in-waiting to the Duchess of Chartres and the mistress of the Duke of Orléans, the appalling 'Philippe Egalité'. The latter made her governess to his children, the eldest of whom was the future King Louis Philippe. She wrote a number of books for children and about their education, espoused the cause of the Revolution but then as a Girondin was forced to flee to Switzerland. She moved to Berlin, was expelled by King Frederick William of Prussia, as 'a dangerous influence' and then settled in Hamburg.

Napoleon invited her back to France after 18/19 Brumaire. He was extremely flattering about her work; perhaps because it was greatly admired by Madame Campan. He also gave her some rent-free rooms near the Arsenal and a pension of 6000 francs.

She now, under the Consulate and the Empire, wrote most of her best and most popular books, including the *Mademoiselle de Clermont* (1802). Meanwhile Napoleon consulted her on matters of *étiquette*, although not, in view of her previous life, about morals...

Her pension was taken away under the restored Bourbons, but she lived just long enough to see her pupil Louis Philippe enthroned as 'King of the French', the first monarch of the country to wear a bowler-hat and carry a furled umbrella.

GÉRARD, François Pascal Simon, Baron (1770 – 1837)

Historical and portrait painter; in the latter capacity much favoured by Napoleon and Josephine.

Born in Rome of servants at the French embassy, he later studied in Paris under David. He was also a Revolutionary, becoming a member of the Tribunate.

His painting of *Count Belisarius Begging* (bought by Louis Bonaparte) caused a sensation at the Salon of 1795. In 1805 he was commissioned to do paintings of Napoleon as Emperor and of the Battle of Austerlitz. This led to his painting all of the Imperial family, Marshal Ney (now in Les Invalides) *et al*.

Through Talleyrand he was forgiven his former Revolutionary principles and became a court-painter to the Bourbons and to Louis Philippe, who retained him to decorate the Panthéon.

Sometimes he worked in collaboration. There are large canvasses he executed with Guérin and Steuben in the Louvre and at Versailles.

GERICAULT, Jean Louis André Théodore (1791 – 1824)

An historical and (especially) horse painter; also a gifted sculptor.

Born in Rouen, the son of a lawyer, he attended the same school as Delacroix, but often played truant to hang around circuses and stables, studying horses. Carle Vernet advised him to give up painting. However, he persevered and then achieved a breakthrough when his portrait of Lieutenant Dieudonné of the *Guides de l'Empereur* (now in the Louvre) won the gold medal at the Salon of 1812. Further success came with his *Charging Hussar* and *Exercise à Feu* in 1814. He enlisted in the King's Musketeers at the Restoration and then in 1815 went to Italy, not returning until 1818 when he painted the controversial *Raft of the Medusa*: today his most famous work other than those involving horses.

Ironically his principal obsession was the cause of his death. While out riding in London he was thrown from his horse and broke his neck.

GROS, Jean Antoine, Baron (1771 – 1835)

Painter. Born at Toulouse and studied under David, although he was later to react against his teacher's work: 'Spartan painting is a contradiction in terms!'

He owed his popularity originally to the patronage of Josephine. He was a good-looking young man, slightly effeminate, but with dark, flashing eyes. It was largely due to his wife's influence that Napoleon took him on the Italian campaign of 1896 – only to find he was too busy to sit for a portrait. In the end he did: but on Josephine's knees each day after lunch, while he drank his coffee. Making the most of these short sittings Gros went on to paint the most famous battle picture of the Italian war: Napoleon bareheaded holding France's flag and risking his life on the bridge at Arcola.

After this the painter's reputation was assured, and he was to remain under Napoleon's patronage throughout the Consulate and Empire. His *Plague-stricken at Jaffa* was the triumph of the *salon* of 1804 and, hung with a symbolic laurel and palm leaves, was purchased by the state for the enormous sum of 16,000 francs. He used more colour and movement than David; and in his subsequent battle paintings, most notably Aboukir and Eylau, he was meticulously exact as to the number of men involved as well as representing the emotion and power of those occasions.

Under the restored Bourbons he largely devoted himself to working on the ceiling of the Salle des Colonnes in the Louvre. With the fall of Napoleon much of the spirit and excitement had departed from the French army; and from daily life.

Gros made one last desperate attempt to stem the tide of the new Romanticism. At the Salon of 1835 he exhibited a painting which he felt expressed all that was most characteristic and best about the First Empire style. It was booed and jeered by the young Romantics and by the fashion-conscious of the day. Following this the painter drowned himself in the Seine.

HANY, Réne Just, Abbé (1743 – 1822)

France's leading minerlogist. Born at St.-Just. In 1803 Napoleon ordered him to write a special *Traité de Physique* and made available to him all the samples and discoveries from the Egyptian expedition. In 1815, upon his return from Elba he decorated Hany with the Legion of Honour for his services to science.

INGRES, Jean Auguste Dominique (1780 – 1867)

Arguably the best French painter of his time, coming between the public popularity of David and the final, mature emergence of Delacroix. His finest work was to be achieved after the Empire, but he owed his start to Napoleon. The latter was always very keen to help young men with talent and commissioned a portrait from Ingres when the painter was virtually unknown. Delighted with the result, he then commissioned a work illustrating scenes from his favourite Ossianic poems. Upon completion the painting was placed in Napoleon's bedroom at the Palace of Mombello and an outstanding artistic career was underway.

Eventually, under the Restoration and the Orléanist monarchy, Ingres became the accepted leader of the new Romantic movement. But he paid tribute to his original mentor with the huge *l'Apothéose de Napoleon I*.

ISABEY, Jean Baptiste (1767 – 1859)

Court painter, famous miniaturist and lithographer. Originally a pupil of David's, he first came to the notice of Napoleon and Josephine when he was the drawing-master at Madame Campan's. (He subsequently fell out with the formidable Madame at Michel Ney's marriage ceremony. He had decorated the church and lit the evening's reception. But his manner seemed to imply that he and not the newlyweds had become the real 'star' of the occasion.)

Much patronised by the Emperor and Empress – although once ticked off by the former for painting him with a stoop. He designed most of the coronation costumes and later supervised the *fêtes* at St.-Cloud and the Tuileries. Later he painted Napoleon's visits to factories in Rouen and at Jouy (now at Versailles).

But his chief claim to fame remains his miniatures: a remarkable group based upon Napoleonic celebrities which is today a principal treasure of the Wallace Collection in London.

After 1814 Talleyrand took him to Vienna to paint the Congress (the resulting canvas is at Windsor Castle) and he was retained as a court painter by Louis XVIII, Charles X and Louis Philippe.

LESUEUR, Jean François (1760 – 1837)

Composer – and Napoleon's principal preference of the contemporary French school.

Born at Abbeville and received a thorough training in church music at the cathedral of Sées (Normandy). He then settled in Paris and came under the influence of Sachini, who advised him to write for the stage. Also around this time (the mid-1780s) he was appointed the musical director at Notre Dame where he caused controversy by his use of novel and dramatic effects within the context of religious writing. He even preceded one sacred work with the equivalent of an overture. (Obviously Sachini had spotted his true vocation!)

When he turned to opera on a regular basis the enormous success of his *La Caverne* in 1793 led to his becoming an inspector at the new Conservatoire. However, he lost the position due to a quarrel with the director who accepted an opera by Catel instead of Lesueur's, *La Mort d'Adam*. As a result, for a time he suffered great economic hardship until Napoleon appointed him *maître de chappelle* in succession to the ailing Paisiello. This was really the plum musical sinecure in France and Lesueur went on to conslidate his position with the five-act opera *Ossian, ou Les Bardes* in 1804. Based upon Ossian's Celtic poems it was almost bound to appeal to Napoleon, who decorated him with the Legion of Honour and also presented him with a gold snuff-box inscribed: *L'Empereur des Français à l'Auteur des Bardes*.

In the same year the composer wrote a special Te Deum and a mass for the coronation. He wrote other successful operas, notably one with Louis l'Oiseau de Persuis (1769 – 1819): *Le Triomphe de Trajan*. In 1813 he became a member of the *Institut* (Académie des Beaux-Arts) and after the second Restoration, composer to the chapel of Louis XVIII. But the greater importance of his final years was as a teacher. Reappointed to the Conservatoire, no less than twelve of his pupils gained the Prix de Rome: Bourgeois, Ermel, Paris, Guiraud, Berlioz, Prévost, Ambroise Thomas, Elwart, Boulanger, Besozzi, Boiselot (who married one of his daughters) and Gounod...

The mere mention of Berlioz reminds me that Lesueur liked his orchestras big too.

The terrible pity, I think, is that Napoleon didn't live to hear the mature music of Berlioz; because I can't think of any other composer whose works describe *la gloire* and the sheer grandeur of the First Empire better. Within a remarkable range of emotion, fire, melodic beauty and brilliantly advanced orchestration he charts the rise and fall of France's fortunes over the beginning of the 19th century with unconscious but uncanny accuracy. And especially in the 'Requiem', opus 5 of 1837 with its vast forces: 100 strings, double woodwind, a massive choir, four brass bands and eight sets of timpani. It was an appropriate work to play at Les Invalides in 1840 when Napoleon's remains were brought back from St.-Helena. As the normally modest composer remarked to Liszt: 'If ever there was a requiem meant for such a ceremony, I swear it is this one!'

MÉHUL, Étienne Nicholas (1763 – 1817)

I don't find him one of the most inspiring composers, although his opera, *Joseph* is fairly caracteristic of French music of the period. His music has sincerity and at times a natural passion, but hardly the melodic strength ánd consummate authority of Cherubini.

The son of a cook, he trained as an organist with the monks at Val Dieu. Later he gave keyboard lessons in Paris while working his way into the more influential operatic circles.

As a light opera composer he became prolific. *Timoléon* (with a libretto by Joseph Marie Chénier), *Ariodant, Bion, Joseph, Persée et Andromède* and *Le Retour d'Ulysse* are probably his best-known works in this field. Already a member of the *Institut* (from 1795) Napoleon created him Chevalier of the Legion of Honour in 1802. He then wrote a *chant lyrique* to be sung at the unveiling of a statue of Napoleon at the Institute.

However, he also put one over on the Emperor for promoting Italian composers at the expense of their French contemporaries. He composed the opera *L'Irato* entirely in the Italian style, sat beside the country's head of state at the first performance and said nothing when the latter pronounced: 'Italian music has no equal!' At the end, when his name was read out as composer, Napoleon turned to him and smiled. 'By all means try to trick me again,' he said . . .

MEISSONIER, Jean Louis Ernest (1815 – 1891)

Painter. Born too late to belong to Napoleon's real *élite*; or to meet the Emperor in person – a fact which he greatly regretted – neverthless he became imbued with Bonapartist feelings to an extent which his more distinguished and talented fellow-artists Ingres and Delacroix found surprising. He went to a lot of trouble to get to know and question those Bonapartist officers who still held positions under Louis Philippe, and – since the French felt a new kind of pride in Napoleon's achievements – he began to sell his paintings for high prices.

He was a good draughtsman and skilled in his composition and use of paint. Of many works devoted to the subject, easily the most famous is that of the Emperor crossing snowy ground on his white charger. The sky is overcast and Napoleon is accompanied by a body of 'grumblers' of the Imperial Guard. Meissonier had consulted the lithographer Raffet (1804 – 60) on what conditions were truly like in Russia. Then, to sense something of the cold in person he is reported to have spent the night on top of his own snow-covered house, climbing down in the morning and with thawing-out fingers painting parts of his blue-and-white frozen face (seen in a shaving mirror) into the overall complexion of the Emperor.

MONGE, Gaspard, Count (1746 – 1818)

Mathematician (specialising in geometry) and founder of the École Polytèchnique.

Of all the French scientists of the period he remained the closest to Napoleon as a human being. In fact, so keen was the then General Bonaparte to have him join the Egyptian expedition that he went and knocked on his front door personally. (Only to be nearly turned away by a maidservant because, with his youthful good looks, she mistook him for a pupil!)

The son of a knife grinder, Monge was a person of simple habits but a great teacher nevertheless. In Egypt Napoleon made him President of the new *Institut* in Cairo – with himself as Vice-President. Several soldiers complained of the time their commander spent with his 'Pekinese dogs' as they referred to the scientists and artists. However, the general was not to be deflected from this second side of the expedition's overall purpose.

Monge was a practical man as well as a teacher. He'd invented a fire engine and under the Revolution had assisted the government by melting down church bells to make cannon. In Egypt he went on many excursions with Napoleon and on one occasion climbed the Great Pyramid at Giza with him.

At the Siege of Acre he nearly died due to dysentery. Napoleon had him moved to his own tent where he could care for him more easily.

Back in France and in power he created Monge a senator, then later a count.

PAISIELLO, Giovanni (1740 – 1816)

The Italian composer who Napoleon on several occasions referred to as his favourite. Admittedly this was usually when he was on bad terms with Cherubini, but his appreciation for the simplicity and grace of Paisiello's music does appear to have been quite genuine. He described him as a Correggio among composers and once said he could listen to the aria *Già il sol* from his pastorale *Nina* every night of his life...

Born at Taranto, the son of a veterinary surgeon. As a child it was said he possessed one of the finest singing voices of his time – which led him to study operatic composition at Naples and later a court appointment to the Empress Catherine in St.-Petersburg.

Back in Italy, and coming to the personal attention of Napoleon, in 1797 he was commissioned to write a funeral march after the death of General

Hoche. Then in 1801 the First Consul summoned him to Paris as musical director of his private chapel. At first he was pleased to accept; but he had to contend with much jealousy and backbiting from his French contemporaries. Also his health began to suffer in the northerly capital. The lukewarm reception given to his opera *Proserpine* finally decided him. Despite Napoleon's attempts to keep him on he returned to Naples, where he accepted commissions from both Joseph Bonaparte and the Murats.

In all he wrote over a hundred operas, but *Proserpine* was the only one with a libretto in French.

RÉCAMIER, Jeanne Françoise Juliette – 'Julie' – Adelaide (1777 – 1849)

She posed as a member of the *élite* while it suited her purposes, but as time went on this façade crumbled away and eventually Napoleon banished her.

Nevertheless, she was important to the arts: because from the beginning of the Consulate until even as late as the July monarchy her *salon* was the literary and often the political focus of Paris. Only an invitation to the Tuileries was valued more.

Born at Lyon, her maiden name was Bernard. She was married at fifteen to the baker Jacques Récamier, forty years her senior and once installed in Paris her beauty, wit and, of course, wealth, gained her an immense social standing. Under the Directory she befriended Josephine (which then also meant Paul Barras) and set about building her *salon* into the arbiter of contemporary taste. Her bedroom, for instance, furnished with mahogany, bronze swans carrying wreaths of flowers above the bed, classical lamps and nude statuary was regarded as the last word in interior decoration.

But politically she was a royalist (no doubt due to the influence of Chateaubriand). Napoleon she came to regard as a *parvenu* and also she snubbed Josephine, refusing to become her lady-in-waiting. Meanwhile at her *salon* the disaffected gathered – Bernadotte and others – to poke fund at the new-style monarchy. However, only until the Emperor's order against her: when royalists and intellectuals alike realised their jokes at the expense of the Empire were no longer to be tolerated. After this they began to marry their sons and daughters into the Napoleonic *noblesse*.

Madame Récamier was only banished from the capital. She revisited Lyon, then travelled to Rome, to Naples (where she plotted with the Murats) and she stayed for a considerable period with the likewise banished Germaine de Staël at Coppet. By this time though her lifestyle was a good deal diminished, since her husband had speculated and lost a large part of his fortune in 1805 – when the Bank of France refused to come to his aid. Upon the first abdication she moved into the convent of Abbaye-aux- Bois, where she held mini-*salons*. Then, after 1815 it was back into the centre of Paris and a social whirl patronised by the Bourbons. Her gentle, languid beauty (painted at its best by Baron Gérard) had formerly enthralled Lucien Bonaparte and even the surly, ambitious General Moreau. Now, unim-

240

paired, it made Chateaubriand jealous, Benjamin Constant awestruck, the Duke of Wellington overly attentive, Prosper de Barante (who she was genuinely fond of) prostrate and such European nobility as Prince Augustus of Russia and Adrien and Matthieu Montmorency, her humble flatterers.

RÉMUSAT, Auguste Laurent de (1762 – 1823)

The superintendant of plays at Napoleon's theatres in the Tuileries and at St.-Cloud. (Although it must be explained that in this position he carried far less weight with the Consul and Emperor than the playwright Lemercier; also that he had no influence upon the public theatre of France.)

Born at Toulouse and into a family of minor nobility, prior to 1789 he was *avocat-général* at the Cour des Comptes; and again to the *aides* in Aix-en-Provence. When the sovereign courts were abolished he was sent to Paris by the Cour des Comptes to lobby the new government and generally look after their interests. He remained in the capital throughout the period of the Convention and in 1796, with the Terror over, he married Claire de Vergennes: better-known after her death as 'Madame de Rémusat', authoress of the celebrated *Mémoires* and *Correspondence*.

By the time of the Consulate they had been left dreadfully poor. However, fate, in the person of Josephine, took pity on them. She made Claire de Rémusat a lady-in-waiting and coaxed Napoleon into giving the husband a prefect's job. Later he was promoted to chamberlain and finally to the theatre position.

He evidently pleased Napoleon with what he did (the selection of plays, their staging, etc,) – but considerably annoyed him when the Rémusats became too friendly with Talleyrand. 'I am very sorry, but Rémusat will have to go', snapped Napoleon. 'He is not devoted to me as I understand devotion!' After this outburst though he relented and the superintendent stayed – to his master's cost.

Without doubt Rémusat was in Talleyrand's pocket by the first abdication crisis. And when Savary ordered the Vice-Grand Elector to leave Paris (thus ensuring he couldn't treat with the Allies on an official basis), it was arranged that Rémusat, on volunteer duty with the National Guard, should turn him back at the capital's gates – on the flimsy excuse that he had no passport to leave. Talleyrand made a show of being upset then returned to prepare his house for the Tzar to stay with him...

Under the Second Restoration Rémusat became prefect for the Haute Garonne and afterwards the Nord.

RÉMUSAT, Claire Elizabeth Jeanne Gravier (1780 – 1821)

The much-admired memoirist.

Both her grandfather, a former ambassador to Sweden, and her father, the 'Master of Requests' at court prior to the Revolution died under the guillotine just a few days before the fall of Robespierre. She was sixteen when she married Auguste de Rémusat.

Despite the many favours bestowed upon both her husband and herself by Napoleon, the *Mémoires* (published by her grandson in 1879/80) are not particularly kind to the First Consul/Emperor. In her letters to her husband, written between 1804 and 1813 (amidst signs that the Empire was collapsing), everything she has to say about their benefactor is good, almost glowing. But then (probably due to the influence of Talleyrand) the Rémusats switched their allegiance to the Bourbons and this is reflected in the memoirs. For example, Talleyrand's undoubted involvement in the kidnapping and execution of the Duke of Enghien is played down and Napoleon made to take the full responsibility. 'If all those fools were to kill me,' she reports him as saying, 'they would not get their own way. They would only put back the angry Jacobins!' Also she writes that 'he became harsh, violent and pitiless to his wife'. In fact he was never violent with Josephine and even after their divorce she remained the most important woman in his life.

SPONTINI, Gasparo Luigi Pacifico (1774 – 1851)

Another of Napoleon's favourite composers – and again particularly prolific in the operatic field.

Born at Maicolati, the son of peasants, he studied in Naples and travelled to Paris in 1803, immediately attracting attention with his impressive cantata: *L'Eccelsa Eara*. But it was his opera *Milton* of the following year, with a dedication accepted by Josephine, which made him a fashionable figure among the *élite*. Napoleon paid him to write a further cantata celebrating the victory of Austerlitz – and suggested an opera based on the life of Cortez, which when produced brought on stage no less than fourteen horses!

Today he is best known for *La Vestale*, an opera based on the idea of a love affair between a Roman officer and a Vestal virgin. The virgin, due to her new-found *inamorata*, lets the sacred flame in the temple go out and is condemned to death. But the officer rescues her and then marries her in front of his troops...

Spontini dedicated the work to Eliza Bonaparte, and, of course, the work is imbued with high praise for the army. Despite this, its fine music and a libretto by the popular Étienne Jouy, the Academy of Music formally rejected the work. However, Josephine intervened, Napoleon ordered its production and the success with the public carried it on through two hundred performances.

STAËL, Anne Louise Germaine, Baroness de (1766 – 1817)

She is such a good friend that she would throw all her acquaintances in the water just for the pleasure of fishing them out again!
– Talleyrand

The writer – some literary critics believe of genius – who aspired to belong to the *élite*, (and, in fact, hoped to dominate it); but who, upon being rejected, then became Napoleon's implacable enemy.

Born in Paris of Swiss descent, she was the daughter of the financier and government minister Jacques Necker and Suzanne Curchod. Her literary abilities were revealed from an early age, although she did not begin to publish until 1786: *Sophie* a novel, followed in 1790 by the play *Jeanne Grey*. Also in 1786 she married the Baron of Staël-Holstein, an attaché at the Swedish legation. Marie Antoinette is said to have used her influence with King Gustavus III of Sweden to get the baron appointed permanently to the Paris embassy; otherwise though it was a marriage of convenience. He benefitted from Necker's fortune – she, as an ambassadress of a foreign power, used her position to establish an important *salon* ... and later to gain her immunity from the Terror.

Not particularly attractive to look at, nevertheless she still managed to 'sleep around'. Talleyrand fathered her first child and then for several years she had the equally unattractive Benjamin Constant as her lover. Before this she had fallen for the dazzling General Bonaparte and in her intense way believed she would come to rule France by his side.

Under the Directory she wrote to him during his first Italian campaign. She addressed him as both 'Scipio and Tancred, who unites the simple virtues of the one to the brilliant feats of the other'. Napoleon was amused, but didn't bother to reply. Undeterred, when he returned to Paris she tried to invade the privacy of his bathroom ('Genius has no sex') only to be turned away. Finally, she ran him to earth at Talleyrand's. Ignoring his love for Josephine, she demanded to know 'What kind of woman do you admire most?'

'The one who runs her house best', he countered.

From this point on she determined to persecute him by word of mouth and even moreso with her pen. 'I cannot remain indifferent to such a man!' she told her friends. She persuaded her father to publish a booklet attacking the new constitution. Napoleon as First Consul, recognising her hand behind it, banished her from Paris, but not from France. He continued to be partially amused by her goings on. As he later remarked to Las Cases: 'She carried on hostilities with one hand and supplication with the other!' Meanwhile she informed her devoted Constant: 'He fears me. That is my joy, my pride and my terror ...'

She retreated to Coppet, the Neckers' estate at Lake Geneva and apart from intermittent attacks upon the object of her former passion devoted herself to the writing she is now famous for: *Delphine* (the novel which portrays Talleyrand as a woman), *Corinne*, and her extensive book about Germany. Eventually, having broken with Constant, in 1811 she secretly married a Swiss officer named Rocca, twenty-three years her junior. But this did not lessen her feelings against the Emperor. As he said, wearily: 'Coppet is an arsenal whence munitions of war are sent out all over Europe.'

As a stylist she can be both brilliant and witty; but her books are marred by some very woolly thinking. Politically she can't make up her mind whether to be a republican or a monarchist. And she makes the ludicrous suggestion that France should turn Protestant (simply because she was one herself). Admittedly her home at Coppet became the focus for half the intelligentsia of Europe. However, Byron at last, while listening to her denounce 'the tyrant of Paris', remembered her at an earlier date in London and his words are perhaps a suitable epitaph: 'She harangued, she lectured, she preached English politics to the first of our English Whig politicians the day after she arrived in England. And she preached politics no less to our Tory politicians the following day. Even the King himself was not exempt from her flow of eloquence.'

Napoleon obviously preferred to be!

TALMA, François Joseph (1763 – 1826)

Napoleon's favourite actor and close friend; probably also the best French tragic theatrical interpreter of his generation.

The two had met as young unknowns and when both were extremely short of money. But they shared Revolutionary ideas. Napoleon was a great devotee of Voltaire, and eventually Talma landed the main part in Voltaire's *Mahomet* and his career took off. He is alleged on many occasions to have got his young officer friend free passes and a grateful Napoleon saw the play time and time again, never tiring of Talma's performance.

When finally he came to power he made sure that Talma was the best publicised and most patronised actor in the Paris theatre; he gave him a handsome annuity from the national treasury and in 1808 took him off to meet the Tzar Alexander at Erfurt. Talma duly performed (a recitation) and the Tzar was equally captivated by his abilities.

He was a frequent dinner guest at the Tuileries and never lost favour. During the Hundred Days he was playing *Hector*, which Napoleon found particularly apt. Chateaubriand had once remarked that Talma must have given Napoleon lessons in how to act the Emperor. Napoleon took this as a compliment. 'It shows I must at least have played my part well,' he says.

Theatre

The Consulate and First Empire were a good period for French theatre. If anything the high standard of acting (Talma, Mesdames Lamballe and Molé-Raymond and Mlle George) was betrayed by poor playwrights. Napoleon himself preferred the classics; or Voltaire. He had the good taste to ignore the flattering hacks: Sevrin, whose play about 18/19 Brumaire was staged at the Théâtre Favart only three days after the event, and Léger,

Chazet and Gouffé whose so-called 'dramas' about St.-Cloud and the elevation of the First Consul were put on at the Troubadours.

The best writers of the period, Chateaubriand, Constant and the younger Stendhal, all seem to have been interested in the written, rather than the spoken word. Of the successful playwrights of the time (Aignan, Andrieux, Brifaut, Ducis, Harleville, Legouvé, Lemercier and Raynouard), not one has left a work which would be considered for production today.

Lemercier (Népomuchène) alone merits our attention in connection with Napoleon's *élite*. A verse dramatist with a withered arm and a longstanding dislike of Chateaubriand, he was also a member of the Tribunate and spoke out there against the First Consul becoming Emperor. Even so, Napoleon continued to patronise him – as well as suggesting he wrote a contemporary tragedy. 'Sire, I am waiting,' Lemercier replied. This was just before the expedition to Russia.

Lemercier was important to the régime in one other respect. He was the man Napoleon regularly consulted on matters of theatrical censorship.

(THE) VERNETS, Carle (1758 – 1835), Horace (1789 – 1863), Jules (1792 – 1843)

All popular painters under the Empire.

Carle, born in Bordeaux, was himself the son of a famous marine painter. He was taken to Rome as a child and then enrolled at the French Academy. He received a number of commissions under Louis XVI and therefore his family came under immediate suspicion when the Revolution broke out. His sister was guillotined and he himself had to do a 'midnight-flit' from his apartment in the Louvre. However, under the Consulate and Empire his fortunes were restored. Origially something of an artistic all-rounder (buildings, caricatures, lithography), he now began to concentrate on history and battles. He became second only to Géricault in painting horses; and Napoleon loved his representations of ordinary soldiers: the Guard cavalrymen, Mameluks, Cossacks, the Polish Light Horse, 'gendarmes' *et al*. Plus the larger canvasses: *Austerlitz, Napoleon at Madrid*, and the *Battle of Marengo*. He was also a superb watercolourist. His series based on the uniforms of the Grand Army is at present hung in the Defence Ministry in Paris.

Horace. Actually born in the Louvre, he grew up to be even more of a Bonapartist than his father; and for a time under the Empire he served in the National Guard. He entered his first battle-painting at the *salon* of 1810 and in 1812 won first prize for his portrait of Prince Jerome. A prolific artist, he often worked on a very large scale: *Les Adieux de Fontainebleau, Napoleon Signant son Abdication* and *Napoleon à Charleroi*.

He was in great disfavour with the restored Bourbons when he published the immensely popular *Incroyable et Merveilleuses*, satirising the returning

Ultras' old-fashioned clothes, and the generally sloppy appearance of the Allied troops occupying Paris. Not surprisingly his *Barrière de Clichy*, showing the defence of the capital in 1814, was rejected by the *salon* of 1822 for political reasons. After this he largely devoted himself to portfolios of less-controversial engravings and lithographs (frequently in collaboration with Eugène Lami). However, in 1828 he became Director of the French Academy in Rome and, during the anti-Bourbon revolution of 1830, more or less France's ambassador there.

He returned to Paris in 1835 (replaced in Rome by Ingres) and spent most of his remaining years involved in another enthusiasm: book illustration. Napoleon III created him an official painter to his court.

Jules. Thought to be a cousin of the other Vernets. A portrait-painter and miniaturist, he exhibited at the *salon* from 1812 through to 1842, winning first prize at the *salon* of '34. He was also a prolific painter of the main celebrities of the Empire and its aftermath, though I would say a less-gifted miniaturist than Isabey.

=9=

The Household

Never forget that our servants are also human beings!
– Napoleon

BASTIDE

Napoleon's melancholy tailor.

The melancholy is probably best expressed by the fact that the Consul/Emperor spent so little on his clothes – except for those few truly grand occasions when the responsibility for ceremonial robes and uniforms would normally go to Isabey or another leading artist and Bastide was lucky if he got a financial share in their make-up. Otherwise Napoleon liked comfortable clothes – and ones that lasted for a long time, with Bastide being expected to repair and keep them in good condition.

Nor would his master spend money on hats. He preferred the same shabby old black hat, lined with white satin and when off-duty kept it in an equally battered-looking leather chest. However, it did become a most famous part of his profile.

BAUSSET, Louis François de

Prefect of the Imperial Palace. The overall administrator at the Tuileries, senior to both Bénézech and the chamberlains.

The Emperor once remarked that if *he* had to run France then someone else had to make a good job of running the place where he lived and worked. He needed everything around him to be calm and quiet and kept to the strictest timetables. Bausset was responsible for most of the appointments to domestic places at the Tuileries; but he chose well and knew even better when to delegate, especially to the hard-working Bénézech. He made sure that Napoleon was never disturbed by noise as he worked. Also that his personal security was never left to chance.

He later published his *Mémoires Anecdotiques sur l'Interior du Palais et sur Quelques Événements de l'Empire*, 1805-14. Apart from his praise for his former master, one realises how well the palace functioned with a comparatively small staff: an example to bureaucrats and domestics both before and since.

Bausset's most onerous task used to come during Napoleon's lunch-break, when he had to read to him what was in the press that day. This was always a touchy subject, particularly if copies of the London papers arrived. Rather than risk an outburst of temper he would carefully substitute the title: 'Emperor' for where the English journalists had written:'Boney'. Sometimes though, Napoleon would snatch the paper from him – and even with his lack of English could recognise the jeering nickname.

BEAUMONT

Chamberlain. Beaumont was normally on duty at the Tuileries to usher in those who had appointments or were summoned to an interview with the Emperor. He would also make the introductions at social and diplomatic receptions and advised those with invitations on what to wear and how to behave in Napoleon's presence. He was disliked by some who attended because of his excessive fussiness, while others, like Marshal Ney, flatly refused to wear the over-decorative attire of a courtier.

BÉNÉZECH, Pierre

Superintendant of the Tuileries. He was in charge of most of the day-to-day detail of making the place function: as distinct from the protocol and the ceremonial side of things which were the concern of the chamberlains. His duties included everything from ensuring there was always hot water for Napoleon's daily baths, to buying flowers and shrubs for the gardens. He even had to supervise building repairs and maintenance; although not rebuilding.

He was highly efficient. Under the Empire the court was considered one of the cleanest and best-run in Europe. He also kept very good accounts (always important to Napoleon) and made it clear that any servant found pilfering faced instant dismissal.

Napoleon thought him unusually harsh in forbidding the workmen to wander about the gardens in their dirty overalls, but Roederer sided with Bénézech on this occasion. 'Working clothes are for working, not for strolling,' he said.

BERNIER, Étienne

Priest. Napoleon was not a deeply religious man but he believed deeply in the restoration of the Catholic faith to France. Bernier was a doctor of theology who had fought on the side of the Chouans in the Vendée against the Revolutionary government. Nevertheless when he arrived at the Tuileries in 1800 (to witness the signing of peace with the Vendéeans) the First

Consul welcomed him and listened attentively to his arguments. He developed a great liking for the stout cleric and kept him on as an unofficial confessor/adviser. More importantly though he made full use of him during the negotiations which led to the Concordat with Pope Pius VII.

Afterwards, apart from Cardinal Fesch, and more than Cardinal Maury (the Archbishop of Paris) and Jean Portalis (the Councillor of State with special responsibilities for religious affairs), Bernier had more influence than anyone with Napoleon over the restructuring of the Catholic hierarchy in France. Within this restructuring he himself was chosen as Bishop of Orléans.

CÉSAR

Coachman. Also a notorious drinker; over which Napoleon displayed a remarkable tolerance. This was just as well, since in the assassination attempt at the Rue St.-Nicaise it was probably César's drunken-driving which saved the First Consul's life.

It was Christmas Eve, 1800 and the night when Georges Cadoudal's agents had planned to blow up Napoleon and his family on their way to the opera house. They had filled an enormous wine-cask, on a cart drawn by a Rosinante-like mare, with explosives: gunpowder and sharp stones. It was placed on the Consul's established route and the fuse inserted. A pathetic, unknowing 14-year-old girl had been given a handful of sous to hold the reins.

At the Tuileries, meanwhile, Napoleon had announced that he was too tired to go to the performance that night. But Josephine persuaded him it would do him good. The work was the *première* in France of Haydn's, *The Creation*. So Napoleon put his coat on and got into the carriage. Josephine, Hortense and Caroline would be travelling with the Consul's principal ADC Jean Rapp in the carriage behind, but because Josephine had been fussing over a new shawl from Constantinople their departure was three minutes behind Napoleon's.

In the Rue St.-Niçaise, as soon as the escort of mounted grenadiers were passing, the conspirators lit the fuse. At the sight of the mare and cart nearly blocking the road any normal coachman would have slowed down to edge by. Not so César. Well into his cups, he whipped up the horses and fairly tore through the gap. They were into the Rue de la Loi when the bomb went off. The explosion was so great that half the Rue St.-Niçaise was ripped apart. Several grenadiers were unseated when their horses bolted. Nine people died, including, of course, the innocent girl; twenty-six others were injured. Napoleon was unhurt: merely concerned for those who were. In the following coach Josephine fainted, Hortense suffered a cut hand and Caroline, heavily pregnant, also fainted. (Her child was later born an epileptic.) The inebriated César was the hero of the hour.

On another occasion though, Napoleon scared the living daylights out of

César: *when the coachman was sober*. If anything the First Consul was more dangerous driving a carriage-and-four than he was as a solo rider. But he took it into his head to take over the reins from César while they were out in the park. Josephine and also Cambacérès were with him. The horses had been presented to him by the people of Antwerp and were young and mettlesome. They immediately set off at a gallop.

'They're getting out of control,' César shouted, horrified. 'For God's sake, keep to the left!' And Cambacérès, even paler than usual, cried: 'Stop, stop or you'll smash us all up!'

In fact the horses were out of control and Napoleon could do nothing to control them. They were dashing along at an incredible pace and heading for a pair of iron gates, when, fortunately, one of the wheels struck a milestone...The carriage was turned on its side, but at least it brought the horses to a stop. The First Consul was thrown upon his face and knocked out. Josephine and Cambacérès escaped with bruises. César, also thrown, got up shaking and clutching his back.

Napoleon, when he came round, treated the matter as a joke. He had his bruises treated with eau-de-cologne and enjoyed himself hugely at Cambacérès fright. At the same time he admitted he'd never felt so close to death before. And then pointing to the still-trembling coachman he said: 'One must render unto Caesar the things that are Caesar's! Let him keep his whip. Everyone to their own trade.'

CONSTANT, Benjamin

Valet. Not to be confused with the novelist of that name, although his own *Mémoires* are a lively and often humorous account of Napoleon and the *élite* in private. They are factual rather than critical and from them a very clear picture emerges of the Consul/Emperor on a day-to-day basis. Constant was also greatly liked by Josephine and generally went with his master on campaign.

A Belgian, he had served Prince Eugène before Napoleon and then never had a day's leave until the establishment of the Empire. He gives us a detailed description of the First Consul's lifestyle at the Tuileries. His master occupied only eight rooms of the palace, while Josephine had her own bedroom and dressing room on the ground floor. After rising at six, and bathing and shaving, Napoleon's working hours were long and hard. We discover that he paused occasionally to take snuff, which he didn't inhale, or to suck pieces of liquorice. Also that he was as loathe to waste time on eating as he was to spend money on clothes. His shoes had to last two years, his linen six, and Constant was forever brushing down his breeches and uniforms to make them look more presentable.

Again we are told that he was both friendly and considerate towards his servants. He liked nothing better than to see even the most menial tasks performed with speed and efficiency. Moreover he required an atmosphere of harmony around him while working. When happy he hummed to himself; when in a bad temper he poked the fire vigorously or kicked the logs, which then made him angrier still because he burned his shoes! He was very quick-tempered, but this seldom lasted for long.

Most of all though he was a man in a hurry – who, even when he went to the theatre, rarely stayed for more than one act.

As befits a valet, there is a good deal in these memoirs about dress, and about other European dignitaries. The Consul's uniform, he tells us, was a red coat without facings and with gold-braid. He refused to wear a cravat, preferring a black stock.

The German princes and princesses never cease to amuse. There is Louis of Bavaria, who on a visit to Paris falls asleep at the opera, and the King of Würtemberg, the fattest man Constant had ever seen. He notes how Josephine tried hard not to laugh at their wives' enormous powdered wigs and the panniers which filled out their dresses. She whispers to him how odd it would look if they leaned on one side.

Napoleon's own *élite* is also closely observed. We learn of Jerome Bonaparte's falling in love with an actress at Breslau – who promptly marries one of his servants. And of Duroc's loudly abusing Constant in Spain – only to be ticked off himself by the Emperor for doing so.

There are travel stories from all over Europe (some of the inns were atrocious; the rooms dirty, the servants lazy, the meat done to a cinder). And there is a most sympathetic portrayal of Josephine at the time of the divorce. This was, Constant insists, a truly painful sacrifice by her husband.

Following the first abdication the valet was accused of embezzling 100,000 francs which he claims he buried on Napoleon's own orders. So upset was he by this charge that he refused to go to Elba. But he still attaches no blame to Napoleon in his book.

DUBOIS

Dentist. He received an annual retainer from Napoleon of 6000 francs but his position at the Tuileries was really a sinecure, since Napoleon's strong white teeth rarely required attention. The First Consul/Emperor cleaned his teeth twice every morning, first with a special paste prepared by Dubois, then with finely powdered coral. Finally he scraped his tongue and then rinsed out his mouth with a solution of water and brandy.

DUNAN

The gifted and imaginative *chéf de cuisine* at the Tuileries. Also a man whose culinary talents often brought him into conflict with his employer.

Napoleon liked a simple diet. He liked lentils, haricots blancs, underdone meat flavoured with garlic and also chickens: especially Chicken Marengo, garnished with eggs, tomatoes and langoustines. He drank Burgundy, usually Chambertin diluted with water and he expected the meal, including coffee, to be served and consumed in twenty minutes.

In contrast Dunan, formerly chef in the household of the Duke of Bourbon, regarded his inventions and preparations as a fine art.

He expected meals to be serious and unhurried affairs, accompanied by rich sauces plus a lavish variety of desserts. 'You're making me overeat,' Napoleon complained. 'In future no more than two dishes!'

On another occasion he requested *crépinettes* of pork, a kind of strong sausage. Dunan considered them vulgar and served up *crépinettes* of partridge instead. Napoleon, in a huff, sent for a straightforward roast chicken. Dunan threatened to give notice. Eventually though tempers cooled on both sides. Dunan moderated his sauces and Napoleon diplomatically ate a little less if he thought the dish too elaborate.

In any case the chef always kept his real ill-tempers for Méot, his arch-rival and opposite number with King Joseph Bonaparte. For Méot, although an outstanding cook, was also a terrible braggart. He headed his notepaper: 'Controller of His Majesty's Mouth' and always tested his roasts with a ceremonial dress-sword. Needless to say, he had few friends in his own profession.

DUPLAN

Hairdresser and manicurist. He first gained an official position as Josephine's hairdresser. Napoleon, throughout the Consulate, continued to grow his hair long – although his wife persuaded him that regular washing was better for it than powdering. As Emperor, because his hair was thinning he took to having it trimmed once a week by Duplan, and combed forward – hence his nickname within the Imperial Guard of *Le Tondu* or 'the shorn one'.

He was also very particular about his hands. He didn't like gloves unless it was truly cold but he liked his nails pared down and clean. For this reason alone, after being on campaign Duplan was soon sent for to do a proper manicure.

JARDIN, pére

Napoleon's equerry. His master accepted that he was the best, if not the kindest trainer of horses in France – although he once complained (to Roederer): 'Because he's so good, I never have a horse to ride...with anyone else I would have sixty!'

The truth is, Jardin *had* to be good. Unlike Murat, Ney, Lasalle and others among his senior appointments – all properly trained as well as natural horsemen – Napoleon was an appalling rider. The ex-artilleryman's spindly legs (and later, plump thighs), never did grip his mounts with real firmness. He would roll around the saddle at anything above a processional trot. Even the devoted Constant remarked upon the Emperor's 'less than graceful seat'. Even so, he liked to ride for exercise. Also there were the many occasions when he needed reliable horses in battle. Consequently every precaution was taken to ensure that those selected for him were thoroughly broken in.

Jardin would hardly have gained the approval of our modern equestrian clubs. Horses intended for Napoleon's personal use underwent a very tough training. They were taught to bear pain without surprise: struck over the head and ears repeatedly with whips. Pistols, even maroon rockets, were let off near them; drums beaten and flags waved in their eyes; and finally heavy objects, sometimes live sheep and pigs, hurled under their hooves. However, it worked. Not one of Jardin's trained steeds ever let the Emperor down: except when required to do so!

Constant also notes: 'The equerry's achievement was all the greater because His Majesty always made a point of buying Arabs.'

Handsome yes, but temperamental.

ROUSTAM-RAZA

Napoleon's personal bodyguard. An enormous Mameluk, who never presented himself in anything but traditional dress: plumed turban with a badge of the Islamic crescent moon, embroidered jacket, baggy trousers and a jewel-handled sabre – plus a fearsome black moustache.

Originally given to Napoleon by the Sheik of Cairo, he was seldom afterwards very far from his master's side: even at the Tuileries, holding the First Consul/Emperor's mirror while he shaved. He also helped Napoleon on with his boots and slept across the doorway of the Imperial bedroom each night like a devoted dog.

He accompanied Napoleon on all the big campaigns, including Russia (where he found the cold appalling), and in the subsequent battles for France fought with great bravery at Brienne and at St.-Dizier, where he took 'great delight' in sabring a number of Cossacks.

However, following the first abdication he refused to serve on Elba. He didn't like what he'd heard about the mosquito-infested island. For this reason at the start of the Hundred Days he was ordered to Vincennes. But he survived to be present at the bringing back of the Emperor's remains from St.-Helena.

SÉGUR, Louis Philippe de

Master of Ceremonies for the big public occasions; and notably for the 1804 coronation in Notre Dame. His advice was largely taken by Napoleon but not over the question of imperial emblems. 'The Gallic cockerel belongs in the farmyard,' he told Ségur, 'while the lion is man's enemy!'

Instead he chose an eagle and the bee as his emblems.

An hereditary count, scion of a noble family of the *Ancien Régime*, Ségur had originally served as an emissary of Louis XVI's to the American colonists in their independence struggles. He was also the father of Philippe Paul de Ségur, the Napoleonic soldier and author.

THIARD, Auxonne Théodore

Chamberlain – but only until 1807 when he found himself in disagreement with the Emperor and left his service. However, he had kept a diary while at the Tuileries and eventually wrote his *Souvenirs Diplomatiques et Militaires, 1804 à 1806.* Despite their earlier quarrel the book is very favourable towards Napoleon.

TOURNON – SIMIANE, Camille de

Another chamberlain, replaced under the Empire by Beaumont. Napoleon made up his mind that Tournon's diplomatic and administrative abilities ought to be exploited more fully and posted him as a special envoy to Rome; later he made him the prefect at Bordeaux.

He preferred not to serve the Bourbons and devoted the last years of his life to writing two books about Rome, published in 1831.

=10=

Coda: In Exile

The sensation excited in the little, interesting Colony of St.-Helena on the arrival of this extraordinary Guest, may be more easily imagined than described. Curiosity, astonishment and interest combined to rouse the inhabitants from their habitual tranquillity, into a state of busy activity and inquisitive solicitude.

– William Warden

Letters written on board His Majesty's ship *Northumberland* and at Saint Helena in which the conduct and conversations of Napoleon Buonaparte and his Suite, during the voyage, and the first months of his residence in that island, are faithfully described and related.

On St.-Helena Napoleon was surrounded by both enemies and friends.

Foremost of the enemies was the suspicious and unsympathetic Irishman Sir Hudson Lowe, the island's governor. He restricted the ex-Emperor's physical exercise (riding), tampered with his mail, obtained the dismissal of the friendly doctor, Barry O'Meara and generally frustrated what would have seemed, (coming from any normal prisoner), very simple and reasonable requests. He also effectively cut the household expenditure at Longwood from £20,000 a year to £12,000. Napoleon was forced to sell off most of his silver-plate and at one point threatened to go and beg for his supper at the English officers' mess!

Lowe's meanness towards the French even included trying to hold on to a bust of the King of Rome which had arrived on the storeship *Baring*. However, he was supported in all of these actions by the British Colonial Secretary Lord Bathurst; by the resident surgeon Walter Henry; and by over two thousand troops, of whom there were never less than one hundred on sentry-duty, while others observed Longwood through telescopes. (More than once their prisoner mocked them by standing at the door naked and dripping from his bath.)

Napoleon had disembarked at St.-Helena on October 17, 1815 and at first took up residence at The Briars, a house about a mile and a half from the

255

tiny capital of Jamestown. It belonged to a British merchant by the name of Balcombe and according to Warden (his doctor on the voyage out), he got on wonderfully well with this family. 'He (Napoleon) frequently makes one of Mr Balcombe's parties,' Warden records, 'where he is neither troublesome or intrusive, but conducts himslf with the manners of a gentleman and a lively demeanour that promotes the general vivacity of the domestic circle.' Then he adds: 'I have since seen, in the English Newspapers, accounts of his playing at cards for sugar-plums, being impetuous with a child, and engaging in something like monkey-tricks; for which there is not the least foundation of any kind.'

Soon though, another enemy, the prickly and irascible Admiral Sir George Cockburn insisted upon the prisoner's removal to the more easily guarded Longwood, a house of some thirty rooms, but poorly built, musty and decayed as a result of the tropical climate, and infested by a different kind of enemy: rats. The servants often killed as many as twenty a day. Often they scuttled inbetween the diners' legs at table and one was found trying to nest in Napoleon's hat! In the five and a half years the ex-Emperor was kept at Longwood they were never entirely eliminated.

The house consisted of an entrance hall leading into a drawing-room, which in turn opened into a dining-room with passages leading to an oblong court, surrounded by offices, a surgery, the domestics' rooms and a wing with Napoleon's sitting-room, billiard-room, bathroom and bedroom. In the wing opposite were the kitchen, another small dining-room for the priest and doctor, the quarters of the Montholons and an orderly room.

As regards friends on the island, there were the already-mentioned accompanying French officers: Montholon, Bertrand, Las Cases and Gourgaud, together the wives and children of th first two named. (Albine de Montholon often flirted with the ex-Emperor, but Fanny Bertrand became his truer confidante. 'Oh Doctor,' she remarked tearfully to Warden, 'we are indeed too good for St.-Helena!') In addition there was a chaplain: the Abbé Vignali (later the bearer of Napoleon's will); the maître d'hotel, Cipriani, complete with livery and silver-buckles (he later died on the island in 1818); and an excellent cook, Jacques Chandelier, formerly chéf de cuisine to Pauline Bonaparte and who, until his stomach cancer became too painful, delighted his new master with such local desserts as fried bananas covered in a rum sauce.

Then there were such servants as Louis Étienne St.-Denis (nicknamed 'Ali') who cleaned the boots, helped in the garden and also looked after Napoleon's collection of books. But by and large the more menial tasks at Longwood were performed by recruits on the island (an opportunity for Lowe to infiltrate his spies).

Finally, there are two men at Longwood who require separate profiles, if only for the fact that they were uniquely-placed observers.

ANTOMMARCHI, Francesco (1789 – 1838)

Napoleon's ultimate doctor on St.-Helena and therefore the last member to join the *élite*: although Napoleon had mixed feelings about him and he was certainly not the most suitable of medical men. He diagnosed the ex-Emperor's cancer as hepatitis, then gastritis, and subjected him to quite the worst treatments.

Born at Morsiglia in Corsica, most of his previous experience had involved post-mortem work and anatomical specimens. He left Gravesend in the *Snipe* on July 9, 1819 and arrived at St.-Helena on September 20. Three days later Napoleon subjected the doctor to a full verbal examination. Upon discovering he knew little or nothing about chemistry he said afterwards: 'I'd give him my horse to dissect, but I wouldn't trust him with the cure of my foot!'

Antommarchi's *Derniers Moments de Napoleon* (1825), have since been described as 'mendacious', 'an exaggeration' and even 'wilfully wrong'. But they are lively and certainly give a very detailed account of the final days of illness – and of the subsequent autopsy which the doctor performed. This confirmed that his patient had died as the result of a 'very extended cancerous ulcer, occupying the upper part of the internal surfaces of the stomach'. Also, the last night of the Emperor's life rings true from the pages of these memoirs, with the wind howling outside and the dying man sunk in a coma. It was at 5.49 on May 5, 1821 when Napoleon stopped breathing. Antommarchi immediately stopped the clock and then gently closed the dead man's eyes.

According to the doctor there were, at times, friendly arguments between them on medical subjects – and jokes. Once, when he felt particularly unwell, Napoleon said: 'Doctor, I am dead! What do you think of that?' Another time he pulled his ear and announced with a laugh that he would 'hang this rascal of a Corsican from a tree outside his own house.'

Sometimes he would read to him passages from the French classics. Of the speech in *Racine* when Mithridates outlines his plan of attack against Rome the doctor recalls: 'He read it with the delicacy and truth of expression which would have done honour to a professional actor.'

Napoleon nicknamed the younger Corsican 'Dottoraccio'. On the other hand, when Antommarchi gave him tartar emetics (antimony potassium) which made him roll around the floor in agony, he then became convinced the doctor's diagnosis was wrong. Nor could the latter's prescribed diet have helped much: 'Three small quantities of broth, two eggs, a little cream and a glass of claret diluted with water'.

After a while Napoleon refused to take any more of Antommarchi's preparations. He said they only added to the pain and caused further vomiting. The human body was like a watch that could not be opened, he went on. If a jeweller attempted to probe it with clumsy tools then he often did a great deal more harm than good.

257

The diary records his concluding judgement on the subject: 'Our hour is marked, and it is not in the power of any one of us to take a portion of life which nature refuses us.'

MARCHAND, Louis (1792 – 1876)

Valet. (His mother had been nurse to the King of Rome.) Appointed to the position following the controversial accusations levelled at Constant Marchand remained with Napoleon throughout the Longwood captivity and was a principal beneficiary (after Montholon and Bertrand) in his will. Apart from this he was also remembered in the will as 'having tended me with the kindness of a friend'.

In 1823 the valet married the daughter of General Brayer of the 'Sacred Battalion' of the Imperial Guard. He returned to St.-Helena in 1840 for the exhumation of the Emperor's remains and accompanied them back to France. In 1869 Louis Napoleon made him a count of the Second Empire.

In his *Mémoires* (not published in their entirety until 1955) we have an invaluable day-by-day account of Napoleon during his exile.

He would rise at six, put on his dressing-gown and Morocco slippers, sip coffee or tea, wash, shave and then be rubbed down with eau-de-Cologne. Then – until Lowe put an end to it – he liked to go for a ride. He lunched at ten, and afterwards worked for two or three hours dictating his campaign memoirs. Following this he would bathe: for at least an hour, often an hour and a half. At four he would receive visitors; or go to the Bertrands' house and play with the children. Finally, he would read or correct his dictation until Cipriani, the *maître d'hôtel* announced dinner.

Naturally there was much boredom. The exiled Emperor had close on two thousand books with him, but complained that he felt the need of sixty thousand. Also there were numerous petty 'pinpricks' – all totally unnecessary – from the insensitive Hudson Lowe. There was one incident in particular when the governor wouldn't allow Marchand to order a new pair of shoes for Napoleon without first showing him that the old ones were worn out.

Marchand did much of the nursing of his master during the terminal illness. In his delirium, the last question he asked was: 'What is the name of my son?' Later the valet thought he murmured: 'France. The head of the army. Josephine.'

Bibliography

I did read a tremendous number of books; and several of the rarer ones I've managed to own. There is no point in listing all of them, because often I would pick up just a single fact or cross-reference. On the other hand – and by way of appreciation – I would like to recommend the following shortlist. I have found them to be particularly good on the varying facets of the Napoleonic period.

BEAR, Joan. *Caroline Murat*, (London 1972).
An underrated book. I agree with her on Murat, if not quite about Caroline.

BONNAL, General H. *La Vie Militaire du Maréchal Ney* (3 vols.), (Paris 1906 – 1914).
Unfortunately unfinished, but an important biography nevertheless.

CHANDLER, David. *The Campaigns of Napoleon*, (New York 1966).

COOPER, Duff. *Talleyrand*, (London 1932).
For coverage of Fouché as well as Talleyrand.

CRONIN, Vincent. *Napoleon*, (London 1971).
Well-researched and a sympathetic portrait of Napoleon both at home and in public.

GLOVER, Michael. *Legacy of Glory, The Bonaparte Kingdom of Spain*, (London 1971).
For King Joseph, Jourdan *et al.*

GRONOW, Howell Rees. *The Reminiscences of Captain Gronow*, ed. Nicholas Bentley, (London 1977).

KURTZ, Harold. *The Trial of Marshal Ney*, (London 1957).

LACHOUQUE, Henri. *The Anatomy of Glory*, transl. Anne S.K. Brown, (London 1961).

The definitive book on the Imperial Guard.

LAING, Margaret. *Josephine and Napoleon*, (London 1973).

LONGFORD, Elizabeth, Countess of. *Wellington, The Years of the Sword*, (London 1969).
Includes superbly-written accounts of the Peninsular War and the Waterloo campaign.

MARBOT, Général Baron Marcellin de. *Mémoires* (3 vols.), (Paris 1891).

MARRIOTT, Sir John A.R. *The Mechanism of the Modern State*, (Oxford 1927).
For Napoleon's intervention in Switzerland.

MARTINEAU, Gilbert. *Napoleon's Last Journey*, transl. F. Partridge, (London 1975).

MASSON, F. *Napoleon et sa Famille* (4 vols.), (Paris 1897 – 1900).

MASSON, F. *Josephine*, (Paris 1899).

MASSON, F. *Josephine Répudiée*, (Paris 1901).

NAPIER, William. *The War in the Peninsula*, ed. Brian Connell, (London 1973).

PARQUIN, Denis Charles. *Napoleon's Army*, (London 1969)

PERNOUD, Georges & FLASSIER, Sabine. *La Révolution*, (Paris 1959).
Eyewitness accounts.

ROSS, Michael. *Banners of the King*, (London 1975).
The rebellion in La Vendée.

RUSSELL, John. *Paris*, (London 1960).
For architecture and references to painting and sculpture. Also the best general book about the capital I've read.

SÉGUR, Count Philippe Paul de. *History of the Expedition to Russia*, (2 vols.), (London 1825).

SIX, Georges. *Dictionnaire Biographique des Généraux et Amiraux Français de la Révolution et de l'Empire*, (Paris 1934)
Another definitive volume.

THIBAUDEAU, Antoine Claire. *Le Consulat et l'Empire, 1799 – 1815,* (10 vols.), (Paris 1834 – 35).

THIERS, Adolphe. *Histoire du Consulat et de l'Empire*, (21 vols.), (Paris 1845 – 69)

VOSSLER, Lt. H.A. *With Napoleon in Russia*, transl. Walter Wallich, (London 1969).

WARDEN, William. *Letters Written on Board His Majesty's Ship, The Northumberland and at St Helena*, (London 1820).

YOUNG, Peter. *Napoleon's Marshals*, (London 1973).

The majority of other source books and memoirs are referred to within the text.